Growing Up Girl

Also by Valerie Walkerdine

Daddy's Girl: Young Girls and Popular Culture
Mass Hysteria: Critical Psychology and Media Studies (with L. Blackman)

*Also published by Palgrave

Growing Up Girl

Psychosocial Explorations of Gender and Class

Valerie Walkerdine
Helen Lucey
and
June Melody

palgrave

First published 2001 by
PALGRAVE
Houndmills, Basingstoke, Hampshire RG21 6XS
Companies and representatives throughout the world

PALGRAVE is the new global academic imprint of St. Martin's Press LLC
Scholarly and Reference Division and Palgrave Publishers Ltd (formerly
Macmillan Press Ltd).

ISBN 0–333–64783–1 hardback
ISBN 0–333–64784–X paperback

This book is printed on paper suitable for recycling and
made from fully managed and sustained forest sources.

A catalogue record for this book is available
from the British Library.

10   9   8   7   6   5   4   3   2   1
10   09 08 07 06 05 04 03 02 01

Printed in China

June dedicates this book to her family, **Richard, Anthony** and **Dominic**.

Helen dedicates this book to the memory of her father, **Denis Lucey**.

Valerie dedicates this book to **Brian** and **Margaret**, who are still standing despite having been made redundant and having to reinvent themselves more times than they may care to remember.

Contents

List of Tables

Acknowledgements

We would like to thank the girls, young women and parents who took part in this research and gave so generously of their time and thoughts. The research reported in this volume was supported by grant number R000234–680 from the Economic and Social Research Council of Great Britain. The research was carried out in the Department of Media and Communications, Goldsmiths College, University of London. Thanks are due to Anjum Yazdani, who worked with us for a short time and whose work and insights contributed to the ideas contained in this book.

Helen would like to thank all her colleagues at the School of Education, King's College, London, for their welcome and support, particularly Diane Reay, whose insights, good humour and enthusiasm have been a daily tonic. Helen would also like to thank Joanna Ryan, whose help has been invaluable.

June would like to thank the Media and Communications Department at Goldsmiths College, and also numerous colleagues for their help and support during the research, especially John Beecham, Noski Deville and Jonathan Whitehorn. She also wishes to thank Diana Bremner, Hilde Halpern and Fran Lacey.

Valerie would like to thank the University of Western Sydney, Nepean – where she is currently Foundation Professor of Critical Psychology – for providing time and support needed to complete the writing of this book.

V. W.
H. L.
J. M.

Chapter 1

Introduction

This book is about something that refuses to go away: social class in Britain. We write this book at a moment when new forms of subjectivity, organisation and community are very much on the agenda. The challenge is to understand the role that class plays in relation to gender today, when almost everything that traditionally defined class has broken down. We are no longer in an era in which progressive social change towards any kind of socialism or social democracy, backed up by trade unions or union struggles, is on the agenda. We no longer have a large manufacturing base to provide the pivot for understanding social stratification based on class divisions. Rather we are confronted with huge changes in the global labour market, changes that have caused the British economy to become dominated by the service sector, the technology and communications industries and a huge and powerful financial sector. In the new global economy, the stable Fordist model of manufacturing has given way to downsized industries that are shadows of their former selves. Many of the new manufacturing industries are not even British owned and products are assembled in different places, with capital, production processes and workers now being much more mobile.

What used to be the working class is now dispersed into the service industry, their labour based on individual contracts, piecework, home work and work in call centres, jobs for life having disappeared. The Fordist working class drew its strength and unity from the large numbers working in one location, with mass occupation of a single factory space. In the new labour market there are huge salaries to be made, but equally there is massive unemployment of men, who used to be the backbone of the working class. As the 1997 hit film *The Full Monty* made clear, men who formerly worked in factories are struggling to reinvent themselves in the light of a new economy in which some women have the economic power they have lost. Women's employment, however, is divided between those who have the educational credentials and skills to enter the professional and managerial sector and those who leave school with few or no qualifications and enter a labour market characterised by poorly paid, often part-time work, little job security and periods of unemployment. They may be the sole breadwinner in their family.

These changes have been so profound and so successful in absorbing the rhetoric of internationalism and progressivism that there appears to be very little space left for notions associated with the traditional social democratic parties. The Blair government is fully committed to globalism, and its attempts to reduce the welfare state are quite in line with monetarist practice. By and large it sees its job as the humane management of an inevitable global shift. In this context, for social democrats the end of 'welfarist dependency' and words such as autonomy, grass roots organisation and social capital provide the basis for a mode of government with some element of personal control at a time of profound but inevitable change. Expressions such as 'life-long learning' have replaced 'jobs for life' in recognition of the inherent insecurity built into the system. Such a shift demands subjects who are capable of understanding themselves as autonomous agents, producers of their present and their future, inventors of the people they are or may become (Giddens, 1991). However, such self-invention demands a particular kind of psychological subject, stand-alone people who are aware of and responsible for their own thoughts and actions. Such subjects are the psychological subjects of modernity and are made, not born, made through the psi sciences that create the appropriate subject of a neoliberal democracy (Foucault, 1979; Rose,1999; Henriques *et al.*, 1998).

Nikolas Rose (1992) argues that neoliberalism – that is, a form of liberal government that depends upon subjects who are free and rational agents of democracy, recreated in the context of globalism and economic rationalism – demands a psychological subject who is capable of 'bearing the serious burdens of liberty': 'However apparently external and implacable may be the constraints, obstacles and limitations that are encountered, each individual must render his or her life meaningful, as if it were the outcome of individual choices made in the furtherance of a biographical project of self-realization' (ibid., p. 12). If we think about the end of jobs for life and the production of a culture of uncertainty, self-invention through a discourse of limitless choice provides a way to manage the government of potentially unruly and disaffected subjects. This project requires acceptance of certain kinds of psychological discourse as a true description of oneself. Here psychological discourses and services (counselling, as in chat shows, popular psychology books with titles such as '*Women Who Love Too Much* or *Do It Now!*', women's magazines and popular newspapers) combine with people's desire to make something of their lives. So if one is out of work, one has to transform oneself into the right kind of employable subject. This transformation is taking place alongside the transformation of the social fabric of Britain – changes in the labour market, the breakdown of old established communities, feminism and new ethnicities, to name just a few. How do people cope with such complex demands? What are the social and psychological mechanisms by which they cope with the complexity of their social positioning?

As we shall see in Chapter 2, Beck (1992, p. 93) puts a positive gloss on this situation, suggesting that being the producer of 'one's own labour situation' makes people responsible 'for their own social biography', and that this in turn has positive psychological consequences. He believes that it gives ordinary people control over their own destiny and allows them a certain self-consciousness that could lead to what he describes as emancipation. We shall argue throughout this book that this is a far too idealistic reading of the situation. It subscribes to the notion that the production of us all as neoliberal subjects, as rational and autonomous psychological individuals, is both a solution and an easy process. We argue that while his analysis of what is happening economically may indeed be correct, the production of girls and women as subjects is far more complex and problematic than his analysis suggests.

It could be argued that we are witnessing the complete collapse of civil society, hence the attempt further to develop the psychological and social characteristics of the Robinson Crusoe economic man of liberalism (even if that man is now female). This subject has to be able to cope without strong community roots or ties, hence the desire to make subjects responsible for their own lives through networks of 'social capital'. Social capital is a term used by sociologists to describe the informal resources and networks that can be drawn on to aid in the production of social policies in an era of declining government support and welfare provision.

First and foremost, the issue that this book addresses is the remaking of girls and women as the modern neoliberal subject; a subject of self-invention and transformation who is capable of surviving within the new social, economic and political system. However, just as in many ways the arguments of the globalists and neoliberals are old arguments in a new guise, it will be shown in this book that class still insists upon its presence even in the midst of its remaking. The terrible and central fact is this: it is social class that massively divides girls and young women in terms of their educational attainment and life trajectories. Middle-class young women succeed spectacularly at school and enter the new labour market equipped with a degree from a well-established university, just as they have been doing for some time. Conversely, none of the working-class young woman in our in-depth qualitative study made it to a well-established university by a straightforward route. Indeed we suspect that the situation was even worse than it had been in the 1960s and 1970s, despite the expansion of higher education. Via a hard and painful route a small minority of them got to university and hence to professional careers, but most did not succeed at school and entered the poorly paid labour market we spoke of above.

It is class, that anachronistic concept of modernity, that more than anything explains the divide between young women entering the labour market today. The authors of this book, all of whom grew up in the working class at various times in postwar Britain, struggled to make sense of this and to understand what it might have to tell us about girlhood and womanhood, as well as about Britain today. We found a Britain as bitterly divided as it had been in our childhood and youth. We found the same divisions of wealth and poverty, but set in a completely different historical moment, with its own, very different social and cultural conditions. Without wanting to adopt an old left position, it is clear that in new millennium Britain class is just as important as it ever was. The gains of the 1960s and 1970s have been shown to be ephemeral and it is wishful thinking, self-interested or otherwise, to pretend that class has disappeared, either as a tool of analysis or as a concrete fact.

How, then, is female subjectivity produced in and for this new moment? We shall address this complex question in the chapters that follow. In attempting to understand the specific production of young women we explore the complex social, cultural and psychological dynamics of young womanhood today and the path taken in producing the social divisions that confronted and challenged us in the research we recount here. (The young women discussed in this book were part of a research project on transition to womanhood in Britain.) The point for us is that class has not gone away, and the challenge is to understand the new forms it takes.

'Tomorrow's women'

The introduction to the British think-tank Demos's publication *Tomorrow's Women* (Wilkinson *et al.*, 1997, p. 8) states:

> As male jobs disappear, women's importance in society is set to rise, as is their confidence. Forty percent of women believe that women are naturally superior to men. Women will soon make up a majority of the workforce and Britain is becoming increasingly shaped by feminine values. Values such as empathy, care, community and environmentalism, are now central to British society...Work has become more important for women, and nearly all groups of women have become relatively less committed to the family over the last ten years.

An earlier publication by the same organisation (Wilkinson, 1994) argued that women's entry into the labour market was set to rise hugely in the professions, management and business, while male participation in the workforce would shrink dramatically.

While Demos describes this situation in a rather easy and celebratory manner, it is nonetheless referring to a huge change in the global labour market. That is, in all industrialised and post-industrial nations the rise of the service and communications sectors has meant a huge rise in women's employment, some of it part-time and poorly paid (for example in telesales, telebanking and other services), while traditional, male employment in manufacturing especially working-class employment, has declined dramatically.

We want to take some time to explore what Demos was talking about in *Tomorrow's Women* because it is indicative of a tendency to describe women as personality types, which fits in with the idea that the neoliberal subject is a psychological subject with a set of life-choices. If we examine the discourse used to describe women's participation in the labour market we find a series of typologies that invite readers to identify themselves as one of five 'types': 'Networking Naomi', 'New Age Angela', 'Mannish Mel', 'Back to Basics Barbara' and 'Frustrated Fran'. These personality types conform to advertising categories (types of consumer identity), in common with the move from production to consumption and reflecting trends in 1980s market research. The first four types of women exemplify the differing modes of entry into the professional and business labour market and are for women with qualifications. The fifth, Frustrated Fran, can be characterised as traditionally working class, although class is never mentioned as such.

The Frustrated Frans are relatively young – under 35 – and in social groups C1, C2 and D. Many are single parents. Their jobs are typically unskilled, part-time and on fixed-term contracts, and they give little in the way of fulfilment or reward.

> According to Synergy's survey, a solid 15 percent of all women feel they are getting a raw deal out of life and we estimate that some 33 percent of all women share many of Fran's frustrations. Among this group, many are mothers with young children who feel hemmed in by the lack of state support, the absence of affordable childcare and the unhelpful attitudes of their male partners...Fran feels cut out of the action, and lacks confidence in herself. Thirty one percent of all women in Synergy's survey say they suffer from poor self-esteem, and 27 percent say they feel resigned rather than optimistic. Rather than being supported by her 'sisters' she finds herself increasingly marginalised by the successes of Mannish Mel who also has the education, support and determination to succeed. By 2010 some of the resulting anger could be ready to explode. Already demonstrating a mix of pessimism, escapism and rage, Fran is as likely to turn on women as men, with the girl gangs of the 1990s possible harbingers of things to come (ibid., pp. 142–3).

Even the celebratory Demos presents the 'female future' as highly polarised, and in this new labour market feminism is seen as producing sharp divisions amongst women. It is the C1s, C2s and Ds, the traditional working-class women, who are frustrated with their lot, who work, but in poorly paid jobs, with no protection and no benefits, or manage as single parents on welfare. But the reduction of women to these neatly packaged personality types covers over huge social divisions between women in the labour market. These social divisions are rarely spoken of but are absolutely central to an understanding of what happened to the young women in the research discussed in this book.

It is a deep irony that at the very moment when many commentators argue that class is a concept of modernity that has no place in the postmodern global world of work, in which working-class men are doing the least work (in the traditional sense of working-class manual work), that class as an indicator of social difference should continue to be such a reliable predictor of the different life paths and chances of the young women who took part in our research. Put simply, the gap between the employment opportunities for girls from families categorised as middle or working class during the 1970s was as huge during the 1990s as anything we might have expected two, three or four decades earlier. Yet the context of that difference had completely changed from the previous decades, because the world of work had changed with the decline of manufacturing and the rise of the communications and service sectors, along with job security and everything that went with it. Demos optimistically characterises this new world of work as a place of new feminisation, a female future in which female values and female participation are in the ascendant. But this downplays the enormous importance of the divisions between the types of women that Demos characterises. The Frustrated Frans in Wilkinson *et al.*'s study are by and large, in our research at least, girls who were born into working-class families in the 1970s. But to characterise them as simply frustrated and angry is to miss the complexity of the plot, a story far more involved than Demos would have us believe. So the distinction between those young women who are set to enter the professions and business, the difference between Fran and all the other categories, is the difference between those who grew up working class and those who are middle class. It is almost as stark as that. Almost. We will problematise that simple dichotomy and the notion of feminisation. But something else troubles Demos's starry predictions, that is the future may not be as rosy for young women set to enter the professions as Demos suggests. For Demos these are mere descriptions, not discourses through which new feminine subject positions are produced and regulated. However there are those who argue that the feminisation thesis presented by Demos and others blurs another change that is happening Britain. That is, women are being allowed to enter the professional and managerial labour market at precisely the time when the status of professions in particular is changing. Adonis and Pollard (1997, p. 67) argue that

> the thirty years since the mid-1960s have seen the rise of the Super Class – a new elite of top professionals and managers, at once meritocratic yet exclusive, very highly paid yet powerfully convinced of the justice of its rewards, and increasingly divorced from the rest of society by wealth, education, values, residence and lifestyle. It is a seminal development in modern Britain, as critical as the rise of organised labour a century ago, and rivalled in contemporary significance only by the denigration of the manual working class.

They assert that professionals now have far less status and are paid far less than the new elite in the financial and multinational sectors. Woman are thus being allowed to enter the professions at precisely the time when these professions are being devalued and high-flying men are going elsewhere. It is this new, largely male, super-class that eighteen years of Tory rule allowed to flourish and which continues under the politics of the new style 'third way', in which an autonomous, self-invented subject must be produced to cope with the terrifying uncertainties of the new labour market.

This period, then, is one of massive transformation of the social fabric of Britain, a transformation in which patterns of inequality are no less stark, just differently organised. Hence, the terror of those working in the public sector about loss of security, status and salary, the loss by most people of any sense of job security, the uncertainties facing young people with low or no qualifications. All this at a time when Britain is witnessing no absence of wealth, especially in the south-east. Indeed the media are full of stories of executives on million pound bonuses enjoying spending sprees.

Such momentous changes have certainly not destroyed inequality but they have changed it, so that the old certainty of community support in traditional working-class areas has been badly dented. In this scenario, constantly remaking oneself is a necessity for all, irrespective of social location. The loss of 'jobs for life' has affected all sectors of the working population. And in the realm of consumption, late capitalism in the West operates saturation marketing techniques, that attempt to create a demand for marginal goods and services. These marketing techniques feed an ego desperate for self-invention and convinced of the need for personal transformation as a means to keep at bay loss of status and poverty in this changing world.

A huge number of self-help books and television chat shows (from Oprah to Parkinson to Letterman) tell us how to present our selfhood for public scrutiny, mirrored by the work accomplished in the social work office, school or law court, for example. At the turn of the century, this is a culmination of what was a scientific project at its beginning. Ordinary people are not made in the image of the autonomous psychological subject (Henriques *et al.* 1998) – they are to become it.

What does it mean, then, that the self-invention demanded of workers in the new flexible economy should include the adoption of characteristics predominantly constituted as 'feminine'? As we know only too well, it was the feminine (along with the mad, the childlike and the primitive, for example) that was outlawed by post-Enlightenment rationality, especially in the public sphere. What does it mean, too, that the working-class labour movement of old, constituted largely of men, understood political struggle as an intensely masculine endeavour in which emasculation or feminisation was what everyone was so afraid of – an impotent movement, a soft and passive and docile workforce? What does it mean both materially and metaphorically that that workforce is predominantly female – not only for a politics and practice of work but also for an understanding of class?

Adonis and Pollard's 'super class' may be mostly men on very high salaries, but as Adkins (2001, pp. 8, 83) argues, the rest of the workforce is deemed to take on those characteristics ascribed to femininity, even if they are men:

> those who are concerned with feminisation do not assume – as was the case in the early discussions of feminisation – that femininity pertains only to women. Hence it is not assumed that the aesthetics of femininity concerns only women workers. Rather the issue to be explored is the ways in which in a range of jobs both women and men are increasingly performing the aesthetics of femininity. And in these ways those who are concerned with such processes aim to shed light on the de-segregation of jobs, the movement of men into women's jobs and women into workplace positions which have traditionally been associated with men, as well as on the ways in which work and workplace identities are currently constituted.

Cohen and Ainley (2000) echo this point when they say that 'the sexual division of labour is no longer anchored in the material differences in the work process or to the musculatures of the labouring body. In this context, the persistence of the distinction between so-called "men's and women's work" is now open to question along with the whole social construction of gender.'

It is the necessity for self-transformation that Blackman (1999) argues was characterised by Princess Diana – a psychological subject *par excellence* who constantly had to remake herself. It is women, of course, who have faced reinvention so obviously. The transition from mother and housewife in a long-term monogamous marriage to a working woman often bringing up children alone is a large one. If we also add that women have long been invited constantly to remake themselves as the (changing) object of male desire, then it becomes clear that women have long had to face the recognition that the unitary subject is a fraud and that constant and perpetual self-invention is necessary. Now, it is men, and particularly working-and lower-middle-class men who now have to face the necessity of constant self-invention and to produce for themselves a marketable (feminised) image, perhaps for the first time. Self-invention is a painful necessity for ordinary people and a way of coping with today's uncertainties, when it is no longer possible to know who, what or where you are or are supposed to be. This remaking is a psychological project and it is for this reason that we use the term 'psychosocial' to describe our work. We do not think that class and gender relations can be fruitfully explored without understanding the production of women and men as subjects.

How, then, did our group of young women come to approach the invention of themselves at the end of the twentieth century and what does that tell us about the transformation of work, class and gender at the start of the twenty-first century?

Gill was 21 and at Oxford. She had done very well at school, getting top marks in all her public examinations, although she had been very anxious about not being good enough. She was clever and socially confident, and set to enter a profession. She wanted to find a partner and start a family once her career was well established. Anna was also 21. She had left school at 16 with good qualifications in public examinations, but had not carried on with her education because she was pregnant. Her daughter, Katie, had been born when she was 16 and single. She later worked as a manageress of a fast food restaurant but thinking of returning to education, and of one day owning her own home.

These two young women were very different, separated by class, education, aspiration and motherhood. Yet they were both part of a changing social and cultural scenario. We want to discuss these changes and the way in which they relate to the lives of young women growing up in Britain today. Although our examples are British, they reflect a global trend. While the infractions of the class system in Britain may indeed be specific, no country is escaping the changes discussed here. It is therefore crucial to document what happens to young people and try to understand the profound processes of social and cultural change that confront us. This book seeks to begin to do that by looking at aspects of what it has meant to grow up female and British over the last 21 years.

Boom and bust

During his term of office the former Conservative prime minister, John Major, announced that Britain was now a classless society. The irony of this statement was not obvious to some in the boom economy of the 1980s, a boom experienced by many countries across the

Western world. However as boom turned to bust in the 1990s the claim began to appear sicker and more hollow, but things were changing. It was more common now to talk of an underclass (Field, 1989) because so many previously working-class families had no work. In addition to this, critics spoke of 'the feminisation of the economy' (Wilkinson, 1994) to explain the changes in the job market. The period from the oil crisis, civil rights protests, second wave feminism, mass strikes and the Winter of Discontent of the early 1970s, through Thatcherite individualism and get-rich-quick greed, the end of the Cold War and the transformation of Eastern Europe, rise of the Pacific Rim, the decline of the Marxist Left and the rise of eco politics of the 1980s to the feminisation and global labour market of the 1990s, are the changes through which a group of young women we worked with have lived their lives. How has growing up a girl been produced and transformed within that period? How do the changes in the lives of girls and their families relate to those social, cultural and economic changes that accompanied the much-hyped rise of 'girl-power'?

It is that interweaving we want to explore in this volume. Just how are girls' subjectivities created in the social spaces that open up for them in specific historical circumstances and social and cultural locations? To understand this, we worked with three groups of young women. The first group of 30 girls were born in 1972/3 and were first seen when they were four years old. They were the sample for a study conducted by Barbara Tizard and Martin Hughes (1984), which investigated young children learning at home and at school, using audio recordings of the girls at home with their mothers and at nursery school. The sample comprised 15 working-class girls,[1] and whose parents were not educated beyond school leaving age and whose fathers worked in a variety of unskilled and semiskilled manual occupations (for example window cleaner or driver, occupations defined as working class by the Registrar General's classification of occupations) and whose mothers either did not work or worked part-time. Fourteen of them were white and one was mixed-race. The data collected by Tizard and Hughes was reanalysed by two of us (Walkerdine and Lucey, 1989) to examine some of the specifically classed aspects of mothering and gender socialisation. We also saw these girls and their families when the girls were 10, when we looked in detail at their educational trajectories (Walkerdine, 1989, 1998). The girls were 21 when we contacted them again in 1993.

The second group comprised eight girls, all from the same infant school, who formed the basis of three studies: two on girls at home and at school (Walkerdine, 1989, 1998) and the other on young girls

and popular culture (Walkerdine, 1998, work carried out in collaboration with June Melody). These girls, born in 1978, were six at the time
of the first study and 16 when we contacted them again in 1993. They
were a mixed class and ethnicity group, containing white working-class
and middle-class girls, a black working-class girl, an Asian middle-class
girl and an ethnically mixed girl whose parents came from Britain and
Malta. Because we felt that any study of growing up female in Britain
needed to have a wider representation of ethnicities, we also recruited
two African-Caribbean, one mixed-race and three Asian 21 year olds,
also of varying social class. Their childhood histories had to be gleaned
from our contact with them at 21, rather than throughout the process
of their growing up.[2] It is on our work with these young women and
their families that we base our analysis of growing up girl.

It is important to note that work of this kind is qualitative rather
than quantitative. That is, it takes a relatively small group of subjects, in
this case young women, and studies them in-depth. This is in contrast
to studies that encompass many people but study them only super-
ficially. While we cannot say that our small group is representative of
all young women in Britain, the patterns that emerged from the study
are certainly suggestive of what is happening in Britain today. We used
two principle research methods: the in-depth interview and the video
diary. We interviewed all the young women twice, at least a year apart
using a semistructured interview format. The interviews typically lasted
between one and three hours. We also interviewed the parents,
although in their case only once. In addition to this, we felt it important
to give the young women an opportunity to create their own narrative
of their lives and saw this as an alternative to an intrusive ethnography.
We do not discuss the video diaries in this volume because they are the
subject of another book, *Girls on Film: new visible fictions of femininity.* (Pini
and Walkerdine, forthcoming). In terms of the interviews, we took
extensive fieldnotes in which we described our own thoughts about
and reactions to the interactions that had taken place. We describe this
in detail in Chapter 4.

Femininity and class

It has often seemed as though feminism has been more able to cope
with differences of race and ethnicity, which challenges the universalism of the category 'woman', than with class differences. Indeed class
has recently presented a huge stumbling block for contemporary
politics in the West. However in the last few years, while the left has

mourned the demise of the working class, an increasing number of academic women from working-class backgrounds have started to write about class, but in quite different ways (for example, Steedman, 1986; Kuhn, 1995; Skeggs, 1996, 1997a; Walkerdine, 1991; Walkerdine and Lucey, 1989; Tokarczyk and Fay, 1995). Like some American writers before them (Sennett and Cobb's *Hidden Injuries of Class* and Lillian Rubin's *Worlds of Pain*), they write about subjectivity: that is, what it is like to live the specificities of classed location at a particular time and in a particular place. Some of this work has an autobiographical turn. All of it challenges the writing about class as a writing about Others by academics who can only gaze at that class from an incredulous distance. This work discusses the issue that class is lived as an identity designation and not simply as an economic relation to the means of production. We know that under certain economic conditions of capitalism, class was formed as a major tool of social regulation: 'classification' was the means by which governments, certainly from the nineteenth century onwards, made sense of their difficult-to-govern urban populations, as well as to differentiate the emerging bourgeoisie, from the aristocracy. Radical politics used such designations to link political transformation through revolution with a recognition of class belonging, involving a psychological project requiring a transformation of perception or consciousness (Walkerdine, 1996, 1997). 'The working class' became the repository of fantasies of Otherness and promises of transformation, which for so long failed to be delivered, until disappointment bred destruction and the cry that there was no longer any 'real' working class (Gorz, 1982).

This issue of the 'real' is a difficult one. The idea of a real working class implies something that exists materially below the modes of its representation. But actually Marx argued that the working class was made through the struggle of the proletariat to recognise itself as a class, which necessitated a recognition and consciousness of its historic and revolutionary mission. Therefore, the working class did not automatically exist in any straightforward sense: it was not simply produced by its relation to the means and ownership of production. In this sense we can begin to understand that the working class is not an unproblematic designation of a real group of people whom we might struggle to describe adequately. Rather the working class is a group of people who exist historically and culturally, and their designation is heavily contested. This is not the same as saying that the materiality of their oppression and exploitation is non-existent, but that that materiality is made to signify in and through the discursive practices in which it is produced. These are sites which are replete with fiction and fantasy (Foucault, 1979; Walkerdine, 1996).

Judith Butler (1990) makes a related point in connection with the political use of concepts of identity, namely that identity politics depends upon a concept of a secure identity, behind which groups rally. She remarks that 'to the extent that we understand identity-claims as rallying points for political mobilisation, they appear to hold out the promise of unity, solidarity, universality'. As a corollary then, one might understand the resentment and rancour against identity as signs of the dissension and dissatisfaction that follow the failure of that promise to deliver – such identity claims are 'phantasmatic sites, impossible sites, and hence as alternately compelling and disappointing' (ibid., p. 188). These quotes typify the belief in the identity of the working class and the opposite sentiment that the working class no longer exists, and demonstrates what is invested in the use of that term. In an era in which there is so much assertion that the working class no longer exists, it is hardly surprising that there is mobilisation behind the term to assert its validity, including work in which the authors of this book have been involved. This is not to say, therefore, that the term is useless but to understand it as a discursively produced category and therefore as a site of struggle and contestation. When we use the term, and its corollary 'middle class', to designate the young women in our study, we need constantly to remind ourselves of the constitution of these categories and continually to rethink their importance and usefulness in the discussions that follow.

Because what Butler calls the 'cycle of compulsion and disappointment' has been visited upon those designated working class, and because the left in Britain have so rarely found the working class they wanted to see, a number of issues about 'class' have been ignored. Work has concentrated on revolutionary possibilities or the absence of them, including the reactionary nature of white working-class men, as against the hope for resistance in their subcultures, so a huge number of topics have simply not been investigated, in particular the lives of girls and women, except with respect to motherhood (Walkerdine and Lucey, 1989) and lived subjectivity more generally. In other words, how do working-class people manage their daily lives, how do they cope, what are the practices through which their subjectivity is produced? In addition to this, in much social science research middle-class subjects are taken to be the norm and hence there is little serious analysis of the production of middle-class subjectivity. We seek to address this with respect to the lives of the young women in this volume. There are, in Foucault's terms, huge gaps and silences in the discourses of class and these need to be interrogated in order to understand what has not been articulated and how classed subjects have been constituted. What place, then, do the old and new apparatuses of 'class'-ification have in the making of the young woman as subject?

In attempting to understand and address these questions we need to approach classed identity precisely in the way set out by Judith Butler, that is, as both a phantasmatic category and yet one that has considerable power to explain the social, cultural and material differences between the young women discussed in this book. This means that the intersection of the social, cultural and psychic in understanding subjectivity is vital to our endeavour. It is for this reason that we have used the term 'psychosocial' in the subtitle of our book. In particular we shall explore the place of unconscious and conscious processes in the making of the social. In that we are following in the footsteps of a considerable amount of earlier work (for example Henriques *et al.*, 1998; Frosh 1999; Hollway and Jefferson, 2000).

While we do discuss recent sociological work on class in Chapter 2, it is also important to utilise insights from post-structuralism (for example Henriques *et al.*, 1998; Rose, 1999), and also to go beyond them. In particular we want to address the ways in which the practices of self-invention for young women work in a way that is at once psychological, social and cultural. Just as Cohen and Ainley (2000, p. 89) argue that 'youth research has to find a way forward beyond economism and culturalism, to create a third space between a narrow empirical focus on transitions and a quasi-anthropological concern with exotic instances of youthful deviance and difference', so work on class and gender has to find that third space. It is towards that new kind of work that this volume gestures. We argue that an understanding of how young women and their families live subjectivity is crucial to understanding how class and gender operate in the present. While the sociological Foucauldianism of Rose and others is highly important for this work, it is not enough by itself. It is the situated and specifically local character of how people live and transform their lives that is important. The new cultural geography has attempted to get to grips with some of that local specificity of space and place. It is the deep embededness of the production of subjectivity in the social and cultural that we are exploring here. The social, cultural and psychological are so strongly entwined with each other that a disciplinary teasing apart does violence to the actual mechanisms. We shall explore this in detail by means of a number of case studies in the chapters that follow.

Post-industrial societies and the regulation of femininity

Girls from professional families are doing very well at school and boys from families from lower occupational groups are doing badly. This is often presented as girls' good performance versus boys' poor performance, but this is far from the case. Boys from professional families, generally speaking, are not allowed to fail (Lucey and Walkerdine, 1999), while girls from lower-income families are not doing very well at all. What has changed, therefore, is the gendered composition of middle-class educational success. Because there is far more emphasis on girls' academic attainment than in previous generations, the success of these girls constitutes a serious threat to the academic hegemony of boys from professional families. The fact that this is now socially sanctioned and supported to some extent (*viz* the large number of women MPs in Britain, Gill's List in the USA and similar developments in other countries), means that we need to understand how professional feminine subjects are constituted to take this new place in the social order. We shall examine this in Chapter 8.

So how is classed femininity and masculinity produced and regulated at the moment? Not only has the manufacturing base declined, but also the trade union practices though which classed masculinity was articulated for many years have been eroded by anti-union legislation. If those traditional practices, as one of the sites through which classed subjects have been constituted, have declined, then in what ways do subjects who previously understood themselves as working class now understand their class location? In the 1980s cultural studies focused on patterns of consumption in relation to judgements of identity, arguing that class was dead (Nava, 1997), so the shifts and changes in these practices of production and consumption, poverty and wealth, boom and bust should lead us to expect some uncertainty about class membership. Indeed politicians such as Margaret Thatcher in Britain and Ronald Reagan in the US specifically developed strategies that promised a transformation of class. In Britain these were the right to buy council houses, the flotation of public utilities on the stock market, stressing that anyone could own shares, and so forth. To understand these practices and their effectivity, one has to examine not only material changes but also patterns of fantasy and defence, hope and longing – in other words what people longed to be and what they guarded against being.

These issues of fantasy and defence, unconscious processes, are central to our approach to our topic. It is therefore important to understand the 'resentment and rancour against identity' upon which these political strategies were based and to compare and contrast it with the 'necessity for self-invention' to which the new workers are subjected.

In a country such as Britain, haunted by the terrible privileges of class, the attempt to produce a different identity for working-class people must have involved a huge pull. While the middle-class left was demanding the retention of a working class that was the 'phantasmatic site' of revolutionary consciousness, the right was pulling these subjects in the opposite direction. It could be argued that the left's fantasy of the working class represented the reverse of their own upbringing. Much counterculture in the 1960s depended upon the rejection by middle-class young people of their 'bourgeois' practices. This meant that any arrangement that was not bourgeois was actually coded as working class. So, for example, living in communes, not adopting petty bourgeois morality, not doing the washing up were understood as signs of class opposition and class allegiance. In addition to this, working-class men and women became dangerously sexually attractive as Others for these young people. In these myriad ways, the left constructed an attractive fantasy of what it meant to be working class that bore little relation to the modes of regulation through which, at that time, working-class people were subjected. This meant that, consequently, working-class subjects rarely conformed to the fantasies projected onto them. It is not difficult to understand that such subjects became the target of the left's huge disappointment, in their failure to live up to their own dreams for the transformation of their lives. What Thatcher in Britain (Reagan in the US and now Howard in Australia) offered, by contrast, was a different set of dreams, dreams in which they would no longer be poor and exploited, the butt of middle-class prejudice. If the strategies of social regulation held up working-class people as pathological to the middle-class normal (see Blackman, 1996) then it is not surprising that being associated with extremes, whether of deviance or political position, was not a favoured site of working-class fantasy.

Contents

We shall attempt to draw out the points made in this Introduction in the chapters that follow. Chapter 2 explores issues of class in more detail, examining in particular the ways in which the transformations in class and classed identities impacted upon the families in this study. We examine how certain families fared in the boom and bust of the 1980s and 1990s, a time of huge economic and political change in which council houses were bought and sold, for example. We think about how the young women and their families in our research understood their own class location and whether it was an issue that mattered to them at all.

Chapter 3 deals with women and work, looking in particular at how the changes in the labour market have impacted upon the lives of young women and their career and occupational landscapes. Chapter 4 looks at the use of psychoanalysis in exploring the importance of emotions in our research. We argue that emotional issues are central to an understanding of subjectivity, and here we get to grips with aspects of the method we used in our interviews and give specific examples to illustrate the complex character of the psychosocial.

Chapter 5 examines previous research and debates on class and educational success, placing this study in the light of that previous work. We begin by revisiting the arguments we made when some of the girls were four and the kinds of issue raised in order to understand what happened to them as they moved through education. We go on to examine the patterns of educational success and failure among the young women in this study, and think about how these might be understood.

Chapter 6 discusses the few young women in the study who grew up working class and who did well at school. Chapter 7 puts that perform-ance into context by exploring the making of the bourgeois rational subject as feminine. In particular, we examine the ways in which the body and mind of both groups of girls are regulated and the way that this both links and opposes intellectuality and femininity, though quite differently for the different groups. Chapter 8 takes this issue further by placing it in the context of teenage motherhood, examining in particular the young women in the study who became mothers. We are also concerned also to explore the way in which upward mobility through education and femininity through motherhood intersect in complex ways for some of the working-class young women. Chapter 9 discusses the impact of this work in respect of understanding the changes in the labour market and the future of femininity.

It is with this in mind that we turn to an understanding of the transformations of class and gender relations over the last 21 years, looking particularly at what has happened for the families in our study, in terms of both their circumstances and the way in which they see themselves. We shall be asking how, in the light of the transformations in the practices through which class and gender were produced, these young women and their families negotiated the slippery path of self-invention in the context of the left's rancour against the failure of the fictional identity of the protorevolutionary worker on the one hand and the Thatcherite invitation to them to reinvent themselves as consuming individuals on the other.

While new discursive, economic and social organisations intervene – in the form of the new individualism, globalism and the transformed labour market – old practices of subjectivity continue to exist and yet are transformed materially and discursively. Class is still written across the bodies and minds of young women, but it produces signs whose name can only ever be whispered and which can more easily be read as evidence of personal failure and pathology than social inequality and oppression. It is this conjunction and its consequences that has such profound implications for the lives of all in Britain today.

Notes

1. In Tizard and Hughes (1984) study, class was defined by a combination of the Registrar General's classification of occupations and the length and level of education. So, for example, the working-class group tended to have fathers in manual work and both mother and father had a minimum amount of education, while the middle-class group consisted of parents who had gone through higher education, and at least the father, and usually the mother, were in professional occupations. It was a condition of the study that no mothers worked more than part-time at that stage.

2. Three of these girls dropped out of the study, leaving one middle-class Asian girl, one working-class Afro-Caribbean girl and one working-class mixed-race girl. We had a particular problem recruiting Asian young women but were greatly helped in this part of the work by Anjum Yazdani. Most of those who did express interest in taking part in the research had great misgivings about doing a video diary. At the social level this seemed to be related to family and community codes on honour and loyalty. Video diaries are an expression of individualism that does not lie easily with membership of a family and community group. Importantly, the loss of anonymity the video diaries entailed also threatened individual exposure.

Chapter 2

Social Class Revisited

Gender, class and labour in new Britain

It was perhaps the hit film *The Full Monty*, released in 1997, that first captured the popular mood about something that had been happening for some time in Britain and elsewhere: the erosion of the manufacturing base of the country since the 1980s, transforming the industrial core from a heartland to a wasteland.

Manufacturing was supplanted by financial services, which, along with the communications and service sectors, became the mainstay of the British economy. Traditional male working-class jobs dried up and, as the film shows so graphically, many working-class men struggled to find new types of work while coping with the rise of women's employment and economic power, though of course many women were still employed in low-paid, part-time work.

Another media product, a BBC serial called *The Missing Postman*, illustrates well the gendered reactions to the huge and terrifying changes that were taking place. The postman in the title has been made redundant, but he refuses to give up his work and cycles around the country personally delivering his last sack of letters. In the process he becomes a *cause célèbre* and a fugitive. On his travels he meets many men who have also lost their jobs and are now working in the service sector. It is they who most count him as a hero, the man who refuses to give up. The devastating losses suffered by these men have left them with no sense of how to cope or where to move on to. As they struggle to comprehend the savageness of the changes that confront them, many are also overwhelmed by the accomplishment with which their wives cope with these changes and positively face the prospect of self-transformation. Meanwhile the postman's wife 'comes to life' after her husband's disappearance. She demolishes the interior of her home and redesigns it with such panache that the media crews sent to interview the postman after his return concentrate instead on her dramatic interiors. She is remade as an interior decorator with a lucrative living at the very moment he is broken by defeat. His only way out is to leave again, this time on an adventure to Italy to deliver one more letter.

Just as for the missing postman's wife, self-invention by women in the new labour market presents opportunities that are not open to men. Like the missing postman, many men can see only loss ahead of them and cannot face what feels like a loss of manhood and feminisation, or what Cohen and Ainley (2000, p. 83) call the loss of 'musculatures of the labouring body'. The possibilities offered by feminisation are not viewed as positive, but of course for many women, whatever their class location, the opening up of areas of the labour market formerly denied them is exciting and offers many possibilities, even though it also brings the double burden of work and family.

In this book we shall explore how young women and their families set out to remake themselves inside the practices of self-invention and self-regulation available to them in contemporary Britain. In particular, we want to establish how this moment of transition and transformation is one of loss and uncertainty as well as hope and excitement. The young women from professional families have to cope with not only the loss of security that the new economy brings, and therefore uncertainty about the reproduction of the middle class, but also their remaking as a new female professional elite at a time of a labour market shift that puts high-flying men elsewhere and devalues the status of the professions.

Young women from erstwhile working-class families have to face the realm of work throughout their adult lives, unlike any other generation before them. They face a 'girl power' that tells them they can be what they want in a labour market that cruelly sets limits on any ambition, together with an education system that classifies them as fit for certain kinds of work depending on their academic capabilities. In the context of Rose's (1991) psychological subject who is capable of bearing the serious burdens of liberty, this will often be understood as a psychological failure, which produces its own wishes, anxieties and defences. In addition to this, their families face the prospect of a stakeholder democracy with the fantasy that they too might join the middle class, the property- and share-owning class that Thatcherism made possible through the sale of council houses and the privatisation of public utilities such as electricity, gas, rail and telecommunications. Thus the biggest self-invention of all lies in the possibility of the working class remaking itself as middle class, a possibility that has been ambiguously signalled from at least the 1950s (Gorz, 1982). How, then, is that self-invention approached in our study?

The reinvention of the working class

We want to point out the way in which the Conservative policy on the sale of council houses in the 1980s paved the way for the working class to reinvent itself and masquerade as middle class, a masquerade that in fact has never worked entirely. What has happened over the past 21 years to the families who took part in our study? No family has been left untouched by the changes we have described. But this is not a treatise about the pros and cons of different sociological approaches to class. Nor is it our aim to present a new stratification scheme based on these changes in order to 'fix' individuals (women or men) in an easily identifiable structural or subjective location, though we will engage with debates on the empirical investigation of social class. Nor will we present arguments about 'collectivities' and 'class action'. What we shall attempt to do is examine and understand the ways in which social class, despite the enormous changes in the Western world, remained a powerful force in the lives of the subjects of this study and that its salience lay not only in where the young women and their families had ended up by the time of this study, but also in the processes through which they came to be there (Roberts, 1993). We wish to look at how people locate and understand their own histories in the light of these changes.

For some theorists and political pundits, the challenge of articulating the massive societal changes of the last 20 years in terms of class appears too great and it is simpler to give up on the idea that class as a concept has any useful place in the work of sociology and politics (Holton and Turner, 1989; Pahl, 1989). But can there really be a turning away from the living of oppression and exploitation, as if it were only ever an intellectual concept, existing in the minds of academics and the left as elegant and linear theories of history? We shall examine the argument that 'class doesn't matter any more' in the light of the dramatic changes in the economic and social structures of post-industrial countries and what the subjects of our study had to say about class.

The families we worked with told us that there were extreme class polarisations around a number of life experiences – all of which point to the existence of a system of stratification that is undergoing a profound transformation but is strongly resistant to eradication.

There is no denying that class is etched deeply into our culture and our psyches. There are of course other aspects to stratification across the developed world, with age, geographical, cultural and religious differences all acting as the basis of discrimination. However social class, alongside gender and race, remains one of the most powerful factors in the shaping of our lives and dealing our 'life chances': how we are born, what illnesses we have and our chances of overcoming them, where we live and, of course, the work we do, which has been the backbone of stratification schemes since the 1950s (Marshall *et al.*, 1988; Halsey *et al.*, 1980; Eder, 1993; CPAG, 1997). In Chapter 5 we explore how class shaped the educational lives of the girls, and in Chapters 6 and 7 how this in turn affected their transitions to a more independent young adulthood.

Laying the ground work

Within sociological debates, the theoretical ground on how changes in the postwar economy have affected class relations has, until very recently, been carved up between two dominant perspectives: neo-Marxist and neo-Weberian. While Marx recognised that there were divisions within the working class, he envisaged that common experience of the exploitation that lay at the heart of the capitalist class structure would remove these divisions. In Weber's model however, the complex workings of the market and the expansion of bureaucratic organisations would produce many more divisions among and between the propertied and the propertyless classes. Rather than the deepening antagonism that Marx asserted would inevitably occur between the two main classes – the bourgeoisie and the proletariat – Weber posited a plurality of class groupings and the existence of diverse forms of conflict between all these social groups.

However the rise of postmodernism posed a serious challenge to 'grand narratives' such as Marxism, which were viewed as unable to theorise the diversity and plurality of social experience (Mercer, 1990; Crook *et al.*, 1992). Neo-Weberian models that already contained the notion of 'fragmentation' have fared rather better in the deconstructive onslaught of postmodern and post-structuralist enquiry, although some have taken the idea of fragmentation further, arguing that classes have been subject not merely to change but also to disintegration (Beck, 1992). In particular Beck maintains that individualism in later modernity is different from the rise of the bourgeoisie because it is the product of the labour market and 'manifests itself in the proffering and application of a variety of work skills' (ibid., p. 93). 'The educated person', he claims, 'becomes the producer of his or her own labor situation, and, in this way, of his or her social biography' (ibid., p. 93). This idea very much echoes the position of Nikolas Rose (1991) on the serious burdens of liberty that we explored in the Introduction. But in fact Beck puts quite a different and much more optimistic spin on it than Rose. He suggests that the loosening of the bonds of class sociality makes possibile the production of proper individuals who can take their place in a differently defined polity.

For Beck, 'There is a *hidden contradiction between the mobility demands of the labor market and social bonds.* As Georg Simmel argued in the case of money, this means loosening local and constructing non-local networks. By becoming independent from traditional ties, people's lives take on an independent quality which, for the first time, makes possible the experience of personal destiny' (Beck, 1992, p. 94). He wants to 'unite individuals and groups as self-conscious subjects in their own personal, social and political affairs' (ibid., p. 101). He asks whether in fact this will lead to social emancipation or political apathy. For Beck, then, self-invention is a way to move beyond a stultifying traditionalism, and in this respect it shares much with bourgeois individualism. It is only by recognising themselves as individuals that people can become the autonomous subjects through which progressive social change can be accomplished. Beck's account is also hyper-rational. There appears to be no difficulty about the act of transformation, no deep sense of loss about the end of tradition.

In this book we argue that this particular narrative of the present political conjuncture fails to engage with the complexity of self-invention and the difficult position of women, and it reads class only as an economic category while we understand it as deeply implicated in the production of subjectivity, as written on the body and mind. Indeed Beck recognises that upward mobility is implicated in the move towards self-invention, but calls that expectation of upward mobility through education an illusion because 'education is little more than a protection against downward mobility' (ibid., p. 94). This is profoundly important for our argument. As we shall see, the middle-class desperation for excellence can be read as a desperate attempt to maintain a class position, that is, to guard against downward mobility. Conversely the dreams of working-class girls to 'become someone' can equally be understood as illusory. How, though, is class to be ignored and self-invention produced if the erstwhile working classes in Beck's account cannot actually remake themselves as middle class through occupational mobility? This structural contradiction lies at the heart of some of the problems that, as we shall see, faced many of the young women in this study. The concept of fragmentation has been used in other areas of stratification theory, in relation both to gender and to race, and with it a concern to explore the ways in which different aspects of inequality interrelate (Anthias and Yuval-Davis, 1992).

Broadly speaking, in the intellectual and political climate of the late twentieth and early twenty-first centuries, with its emphasis on diversity and differentiation, most traditional class analysis (with some neo-Marxist exceptions, for instance Abercrombie and Urry, 1983; Scott, 1991) has been conducted within a neo-Weberian framework. However there have been some notable exceptions, particularly in relation to gender, race and ethnicity. Feminist sociologists, for instance those drawing on the work of Pierre Bourdieu, have challenged traditional mobility studies that used quantitative indices as their empirical base, and have highlighted the ways in which the formation of gendered subjectivities cannot be made sense of without an understanding of the complexities of class positioning and articulation (Savage *et al.*, 1992; Butler and Savage, 1995; Skeggs, 1996; Hey, 1997a; Reay, 1998a; Devine and Savage, 2000). Traditional approaches to the study of race and ethnicity have tended to focus on conflict between white and black groups, but often in a way that has sidelined or even ignored class and gender positioning (Cashmore and Troyna, 1983; Miles, 1989). Reynolds (2000) points out that in discussions of class and race there is an assumption not only that all black people are working class, but also that black people have no interest in social class identity, 'as race provides the defining characteristic in shaping their subjectivity' (ibid., p. 82).

But what Bradley (1996, p. 143) calls the 'new sociology of ethnicities', which is heavily influenced by postmodern and post-structuralist accounts and focuses on identities, cultural practices and racist discourses , has been able to incorporate class as one of the social processes through which racial and ethnic difference is produced and reproduced (Gilroy, 1987, 1993; Donald and Rattansi, 1992; Tizard and Phoenix, 1993). The notion of 'hybridity', developed by Homi Bhabha (1990), adds another dimension to the theories of fragmentation and helps us to explore the dynamic formation of contemporary ethnic identities in a post-colonial world.

Bradley (1996), in an excellent summary of recent work on class, points to the deep contradictions that exist in the sociological literature. In particular the opposition between the concept of postmodern multiple identities and modern class identities is played off against the ever-present stark class inequalities in Britain in respect of salaries, health, teenage pregnancy, educational achievement, housing and crime (ibid., p. 45). It is precisely this opposition that this study hopes to bridge. These inequalities were starkly played out for the young women and their families in our research, and yet they were still having to remake themselves as new subjects, subjects beyond class, as though class were absent and did not matter. It is these contradictions and their social and psychological implications that we explore here. As Bradley says, 'class is everywhere and it is nowhere' (ibid., p. 45). She suggests that it has no definite physical signs or markers, which makes it hard to observe, but we argue that everyone, whatever their class position, detects the minutiae of class-difference signs and uses the information delivered by these signs in the making of difference every day of their lives. It takes place regardless of the fluidity of boundaries or transformations in economics. It is subtle and complex, but deadly, and gives us a way to explore class that goes beyond the economic and sociological disputes.

Indeed Bradley draws up some strategies for the future study of inequalities, which recognise and attempt to go beyond the present disputes about class (ibid., pp. 203–4). The first strategy is to accept Lyotard's idea that local narrative should replace grand narratives, and to reject general theories of inequality, looking instead at the study of particular manifestations of inequality in specific contexts, tracing their history and the discourses implicated. Her second strategy is to accept the first but to recognise that the local manifestations of inequality 'exist within the framework of powerful and controlling unitary tendencies, notably that of the globalisation of capital'. Thirdly, the literature suggests that previous modernist theories were flawed because of their 'failure to appreciate the way that different dynamics of inequality intersect'. Societies, stresses Bradley, are both fragmented and polarised (ibid., p. 210).

While much of the theoretical work utilised by the authors of this book falls within Bradley's first strategy, it is the deep intransigence of class inequality that demands we adopt a position more akin to her second strategy, while attempting to acknowledge her third strategy. As we shall see, inequality is lived locally by the families in this research, but the globalisation of capital places particular demands on the constitution of subjects that cross those local boundaries.

Throughout the traditional sociological discussions of social class there has been an assumption that the links between structure, consciousness and action must be the basis upon which both empirical and theoretical work should proceed (Goldthorpe and Marshall, 1992). Such debates have assumed that what is interesting about working-class people is the production of a change in consciousness that will somehow activate their potential as a protorevolutionary group. In fact little attention has been paid, even within the newer approaches discussed above, to the social and psychic practices through which ordinary people live, survive and cope. This, as we have explained in the Introduction and elsewhere (Walkerdine, 1997), is because the political imperative has been to find the masses wanting in various ways, as not resisting enough for the left, or too pathological for liberal social democracy. This has had the effect of completely occluding any debate on or understanding of the practices of living, the process of subjectification and the formation of subjectivities. To engage with this issue we shall address the practices through which the families in our study were formed, together with an understanding of the emotional and unconscious aspects of their location.

Locating Erica and Sharon: two working-class girls

We shall now explore the lives of two families touched by the trans-formations of the 1980s. Erica Green was a white working-class girl who first took part in the study when she was six. Ten years later we found that the family had moved from their council house in London to north-east England, where they had family connections. Mrs Green gave Helen Lucey instructions on how to find the house: 'You can't miss us, the sign is on the gate'. The sign certainly was on the gate, a gate that opened onto a wide gravel drive that swung across a vast lawn and garden. At the end of the drive, on one side these was a paddock and a stable with a horse in it, and on the other an imposing and attractive detached house that had been renovated and extended. In the drive were two large new, cars with personalised number plates. This was not the modest upward mobility the team had imagined.

Over the next few days, as Helen spent time interviewing the family and recording Erica at work,[1] all the members of the family were keen to show Helen around and, with immense pride, tell her about the fruits of their success: the small business that was doing so well, Erica's horse, the cars (including the one which awaited Erica when she passed her driving test), the beautiful views from their expensively furnished house, the landscaped garden, the new kitchen. They had 'made it' and wanted this to be known and recorded.

So what was the Greens' story, and what does it have to do with the changing story of class in Britain? In 1984, when Erica was six, Mr Green was a skilled craftsman working for a small firm, and Mrs Green worked part-time as a dinner lady. They were managing financially, but were by no means wealthy. Then came the breaks. As council tenants the Greens had bought their Georgian terraced house under the Right to Buy Act of 1979. At that time the gentrification of specific locales in the borough (typically areas containing unmodernised properties at far lower prices than in more established or more extensively gentrified middle-class areas) was in full swing (Butler and Savage, 1995; May, 1996). During the early 1980s Mr and Mrs Green painstakingly set about a complete interior restoration of the house. Working on a small budget, they did most of the work themselves, with Mrs Green researching period decor and design with the help of books from the library. Mrs Green's mother also had a house in the area (though much more modest) but had moved back to northern England a few years earlier. They had been dreaming of moving out of London for some time, but just as the Greens' house was finished, two things happened: Mr Green hit a health crisis and house prices hit an unthinkable high. In 1986 they decided it was time to sell both houses and join Mrs Green's mother in the north. With the sizeable profit from the sale of the houses they were able to buy a franchise of the business where Mr Green was floor manager and go it alone.

Sharon Cole was another white working-class girl who took part in the study when she was six. Her father worked for the local council as a security guard and was a member of the Labour Party; her mother worked as a lavatory attendant and was a shop steward in her union. They lived on a large council estate (about half a mile from the Greens), which was gaining a reputation for crime: Mrs Cole had been mugged once and their flat had been burgled six times. Like the Greens they were worried about their children's future in a poor inner-city borough. As Mr Cole put it:

> In that year, yeah. I think we were a bit worried about how the children were going to be brought up because Sharon herself was only six, seven at the time, the boy Richard was only ten and we decided then that if they kept living in that environment of so much violence, and it was easier to steal than to work, which happens – you can't blame the kids, it's actually true, it's the government that causes it, you know what I mean. And what we decided then, was that it would be better to move.

As with the Green family, this decision to move coincided with a crisis with Mr Cole's health and he was medically retired from his job. Unlike the Greens, the Coles had no property on which to capitalise: they had not been tempted to buy their flat on a run-down council estate. However, with their savings and Mr Cole's early retirement payment they too managed to escape London and bought an ex-council house in a suburban Thames estuary town. Mrs Cole ran a small catering business. Mr Cole showed Helen the extension he was building onto the kitchen, explaining how he was going to do this and that job and what it would look like when it was finished. Both parents stressed how 'safe' and 'quiet' the area was, how the schools were so much better. They too felt that they had made real improvements in their lives and those of their children. The move out of London and into their own house was a move up and one of which they, like the Greens, were proud.

In 1995 Roy Hattersley, then a senior member of the opposition Labour Party, argued that it was futile to mourn the end of full-blooded socialism and claim that the Labour Party was abandoning working-class values as the working class had already abandoned them themselves (Hattersley, 1995). Hattersley nostalgically referred to the 'solidarity' and 'community' amongst miners and shipbuilders in order bitterly to counterpose this nostalgic view to 'the age of the almost universal middle class – individualistic, self-confident, suburban in attitude and aspiration if not in income and lifestyle'. What did his comments have to do with the Coles, the Greens or the other working-class families in our study, nearly all of whom had achieved some measure of social and/or economic mobility in the past 20 years? Did this necessarily mean the end of the class story for them and their children? Both the Coles' and The Greens' stories, as well as the stories of many other working-class families in our study, spoke directly to the sentiments expressed in Hattersley's article. But his swiping at working-class people through a sentimental contrasting of past and present left the working-class families in this study nowhere to go; they were reproachfully marooned on 'individualistic', 'aspiring' and 'suburban' islands. In that sense their reinvention of themselves as 'suburban' signalled precisely that 'free individual' that Rose (1991) and Henriques *et al.* (1998) speak of. What these authors say is inevitable, Marxist sociologists take as a signal of 'the end of the working class' (Gorz, 1983).

It was a particularly accusing version of the discourse of classlessness and one which, because it lay the demise of the working classes firmly at their own feet, effectively removed any legitimate complaints they may have had about the political party that was supposed to represent them. Furthermore this kind of analysis of change has nothing to offer our understanding of how the economic, political and personal processes and events of these families took them (in all of those spheres) to where we found them, or of how they defined themselves.

Social class has all but disappeared from mainstream feminist analysis, though it is significant that contemporary feminist work that has retained the concept of class as an important social division is almost entirely carried out by academics who themselves have come from working-class backgrounds (see Mahony and Zmroczek, 1997). Is this because, as not only Mr Green but also many of the young women and their parents reflected in their comments on class position, social class is so hard to define? Or is it because mainstream academics cannot bear to describe the oppression that constitutes those divisions and are therefore happier to go along with the idea that social class is irrelevant, or that classes simply do not exist anymore (Pile and Thrift, 1995)? Or is it, as Skeggs asks of feminist writers, that for those who now get to write and represent feminist and cultural theory, class is not experienced or felt as immediately as gender? (Skeggs, 1997a, p. 6). And when we talk about class, what do we mean? The class structure? Identity? Consciousness? Action?

When asked which social class he thought he belonged to, Mr Green asked 'where do you draw the line?' To this we could add another question: what do you draw the line with? There are a variety of conceptions that contribute to the enormous lack of clarity that characterises contemporary debates on stratification. However social classes have been generally conceived of as objective entities that can be empirically investigated. To this end the occupational structure has enduringly been seen as providing a framework within which the 'class structure' can be mapped (Rose and O'Reilly, 1997). A common feature of all approaches that aim to measure the class structure via the structure of employment is that many of the measures they use, for example the Registrar General's classification scheme, are descriptive schemes devised for social policy purposes rather than as a contribution to debates on theoretical class analysis. Crompton (1993) asserts that one major source of the many confusions that have arisen (and continue to arise) in the various strands of class analysis, is the divergence between those who have focused on empirical investigation of the class structure and those who have conflated consciousness and structure into facets of the same phenomenon.

There is a very real sense, of course, in which 'occupation' is hopelessly inadequate in capturing the nuances of class relations in either a Marxist or a Weberian sense because it can only refer to social relations at work, the technical division of labour. Connell (1977) argues that some of the survey research on class 'emasculates' (an interesting choice of word to say the least) the concept of class itself: it makes a claim to empirical understanding, but produces only a 'bloodless' knowledge (ibid., p. 33), which reduces the lived experience of class to an abstraction for the purpose of statistical treatment. In response to this unhappy situation, sociologists in the 1970s and 1980s (Wright, 1980, 1985; Goldthorpe, 1983) began to develop schemes that, in contrast to gradational status or common-sense schemes, claimed to reflect the structure of actual class relations. These 'relational' schemes were constructed on the assumption that underlying class processes and relations are reproduced within the employment structure.

It is particularly important to note here that it is in the debates on postmodernity that the importance of consumption has been signalled, of a move away from a stress on production and its links with classes and social communities as categories of modernity. The increasing focus on consumption has become one of the factors contributing to debates on the end of class. The argument has emerged that employment itself is becoming less significant and that people's identities are being increasingly expressed and manifested through consumption (Offe, 1985), and that it is consumption rather than production that is becoming more relevant for the analysis of stratification systems. The importance of class and locality have broken down and young people in particular have looked to consumer goods as means of self-fulfilment and identity (Seabrook, 1978). In recent years, commercial organisations began to focus heavily on ways of locating and targeting existing and potential customers, and it became necessary to devise classification systems that could accurately measure the relationship between structural factors such as location, job, income and, increasingly important, lifestyle, of which aspects of consumption were taken to be indications.[2] These kinds of scheme, originally devised for the commercial market, were taken up by political parties in an attempt to group and then predict the voting behaviour of sectors of the population (Worcester, 1991). These were the schemes, in fact, that were used in the Demos study discussed in the Introduction (Wilkinson *et al.*, 1997).

The new interest in performativity (for example see Butler, 1997) has meant that identities are often described as shifting and mobile, not fixed or class-related, and as being produced within an arena of consumption. Hence younger people are often understood as being subject to more mobile categories of identity than their parents' generation, in spite of the constraints of class, gender or race. However, as we shall see, such work ignores the issue of the regulation of identities or subjectivities, which severely limits the apparent freedom to become 'who everyone wants to be', which is such a feature of late capitalism. Diane Reay (1998b) goes further when she argues that there is an intrinsic deceit in such postmodern accounts which, though concerned to map the changes in media, style and consumerism in general, show a stubborn unwillingness empirically to address the issue of who can and cannot afford to consume. The ability to enter into and maintain consumption practices is, after all, closely linked to and to a large extent dependent on an individual's class location in the first place. Rosemary Crompton, in her review of debates on consumption and class analysis, shows that despite the very real changes in the structure and pattern of paid work, class schemes deriving from the job structure still provide a useful indicator of life chances and opportunities, and that these class schemes have not yet been superseded by consumption-based indicators (Crompton, 1996, p. 125).

Sociology's constant striving to come up with a class scheme that can locate all individuals (whether structurally or subjectively as in Goldthorpe's scheme) speaks of the overriding desire to produce a kind of 'uncontaminated' measure of social class. Secondly, the quest for one free from corruption is theoretically and practically bound up with the fixation on 'class action'. Even in debates relating to class and consumption, the theoretical drive of the possibility of resistance amongst the workers persists and pervades (Lash and Urry, 1994; Thompson and Ackroyd, 1995).

But the goalposts were moved in the 1980s: an historical blend of global recession, mass unemployment, including the collapse of the youth labour market, the breaking apart of traditional manual industries and with them their communities, new technologies, persistent anti-union legislation, and the promotion of meritocratic philosophies (in education and at work) meant that traditional conceptions of class also began to break up. How then can we understand the girls' and their parents' self-location in the 1990s. The Greens had indeed achieved a material transformation, but did this constitute a transformation of class and therefore of class consciousness? The Coles, like the majority of the working-class parents in this study (67 per cent), had become home owners. Few of the the parents worked in what could be described as traditional manual jobs, they had holidays abroad and a number of them had two cars. Crucially, they hoped for more. Does this mean they had become middle class? And what does 'middle class' mean nowadays?

All too often class theorists have, through their imagined objective and scientific relationship to the subject of class, envisaged themselves as being outside or beyond the class system. With this distant objectivity comes a superior wisdom, which overrides any knowledge that the subjects of their study may possess. Indeed the subjects' knowledge (should they, for instance, identify themselves as middle class when they are objectively located within the working class) can be disregarded altogether as a 'false' knowledge or 'consciousness' of class actualities in favour of the 'true consciousness' of some Marxists (Ainley, 1993). But the ways in which people express their opinions and feelings about class (and that includes the refusal or resistance to engage with such a notion) is crucial to the status of class as a theoretical and political tool and to our understanding of class as it is lived today.

The water is muddy enough, but it gets muddier when we talk about the subjective aspects of class. For naturally enough, people's perceptions of class vary according to age, gender, nationality, ethnicity and so on. Age is especially significant as each generation constructs and disentangles the different social practices into which it was born in a new way, though this does not mean that socialisation processes are irrelevant. However, neither can we assume that social consciousness is simply reproduced in an unaltered way. The world into which young women enter adulthood is vastly different from the one in which their parents lived as 21 year olds, so how can they possibly experience and therefore understand class in exactly the same way as their parents?

Emotional landscapes of class

We asked all of the young women in our study and their parents what social class they thought they belonged to. The young women were also asked if they thought they would remain in the social class they were in now. Most of the girls, working and middle class, defined themselves accurately in relation to the class scheme that had originally been used to stratify the sample. All of the girls and their parents were able to give some basis on which to define their own and others' class locations. However some interesting differences emerged. The most commonly cited indicators of class location for the working-class sample were home ownership, money (which was linked to job and home ownership) and education. Only two of the young women made reference to 'traditional' working-class jobs when talking about class, citing 'miner' as a typically working-class occupation. Jacky said:

> I'm not too sure what working class is and that, but it's like working class is like, in the mines, or like working in an office or something, so... I suppose they're working class and middle class because they've got good values and that sort of thing.

It is interesting to note that miners were the most publicised labour group in 1980s Britain, the very group defeated by the Thatcher government to signal the death-knell of trade unionism. It was this group that Jacky remembered, although she would have been 10 at the time of the 1984 miners' strike.

Having something of your own: house ownership and working-class subjectivity

It was common for the working-class parents and their daughters to make direct connections between home ownership and perceived class location. Geographical location fuses powerfully with type of housing tenure to produce a 'geography of exclusion' (Massey, 1995), in and through which understandings of space and place provide a sorting mechanism, sifting out the type of people we are and the type we are not. Sharon Cole identified herself as middle class because 'this isn't a council house, this is our own house and that's it really'.

For Satinder, a British Asian 16 year old whose family moved from the inner city to the suburbs of London, locality and size of house (rather than tenure) were just as important in the family's project of social mobility.

Satinder: I think when we were in Hackney we were working class... I don't know where the line lies.

JM: Well what changed for you to start seeing yourself as middle class?

Satinder: I suppose having a bigger house. Yeah, I suppose it was probably that.

What is invisible in her account of class mobility is how, not only in Britain, but also across Europe, the US and Australia, the processes of residential differentiation and, crucially, the imagery of 'racial segregation' have played key roles in the social reproduction of race categories and the organisation of objective and subjective space (Smith, 1989, 1993; Back *et al.*, 1998). Although the area in which the 16 year olds grew up was and remains a multicultural one, differentiations in terms of social class, race and ethnicity remained highly visible on the spatial landscape. White professionals such as Hannah's parents were able to move into the area without loss of class location (May, 1996). They were part of the process of the area's gentrification, a process that Cross and Keith (1993) suggest was the story of 'pioneers' who 'fearlessly enter decaying parts of the city in order to 'revitalise them'. However, while the cultural diversity of the locality was celebrated by the new 'cultural classes' (May, 1996), black, Asian and ethnic families living in the same area were implicated quite differently in its designation as a 'site of social deprivation' (SEU, 1998). For families like Satinder's (as well as for many of the white working-class families) moving out of the inner city and into the suburbs was one way of attempting to escape the stigmatising effects of the 'urban imaginary', which threatened to fix them as part of the 'underclass'.

Sharon Cole pointed to the step upward that the family had taken by moving out of the inner city:

> I'd say we're middle class now we've moved here. And other things like, I don't know, it's a lot cleaner round here and quieter at night. My aunty still lives there and to be honest, I don't really want to go to her place to visit like, I don't want to go back there.

The family may have indeed felt different because they had moved to an area that they experienced as safer and more pleasant, but that did not mean that they failed to recognise their difference from professionals living in the same area. What did it mean that they no longer felt able to call themselves working class just because they had moved out of danger? A former council house in a quieter neighbourhood outside London was enough to make them feel different, but was it enough to make others see them as middle class? The painful process of self-transformation may appear to have been easily accomplished in the home-owning, share-owning democracy, but it is just as difficult as it ever was. In some ways more so, because now anything is supposed to be possible. In the new 'third way' there appear to be no split and fragmented subjects, caught in the interstices of self-regulation and invention.

Perhaps it is not surprising that the middle-class families did not concentrate on houses or money, after all they already had these things and although they may have experienced financial anxiety, the ownership of property was, for most of them,[3] a fact of their family histories. In 1974/75 when the 21 year old girls were four, all but one of the middle-class families were owner-occupiers – 13 owned houses and 1 owned a flat. All of the middle class families had private gardens. Of the working-class families, 6 lived in council accommodation without gardens, the rest in terraced houses with small back yards or gardens. Only 3 of the working class families were owner-occupiers at that time. In 1993 six of the middle-class families owned second homes in Britain or abroad. For middle-class families, to own one's home does not signify a transformation in structural and identity terms in the way it does for working-class people, nor is it viewed in the same way.

In 1979, when the Conservative government put in place legislation allowing council tenants to buy their homes at discounted prices (legislation that had in fact been instigated by the previous Labour administration), there was an outcry from sections of the left, who accused the working classes (in a similar vein to Hattersley's words cited earlier) of abandoning traditional community values in favour of a misplaced and individualistic desire for personal gain. Again, this accusation spoke of 'false consciousness' and the ease with which working-class people allowed themselves to be shamelessly manipulated by capital. But the Coles' and Greens' stories spoke of a quite different experience and motivation. Neither family were naive in their decisions, one to sell their council house and achieve the kind of upward mobility that certainly would have been impossible without the profit from it, the other to move out of their flat on a badly run-down estate to buy a cheap house outside London. Mr Cole was an active member of the Labour Party for many years; his socialist credentials were valid, and yet he and his wife chose to become home-owners. Mr Cole succinctly placed his own decision to become an owner-occupier within a broader political context. What he articulated so sharply was a matrix of emotional and structural processes that constituted a personal and political moment:

> What she [Thatcher] actually done was give the so-called poor the chance to own – and everybody wants to own their own house, I don't care who you are. The people who says 'Oh I'd rather be in rented accommodation' are talking porky pies. They want their own bricks and mortar. And what it boils down to, she give it to them. And then she put the screw on and said 'Now you've got your mortgage you can't afford to do nothing. You

can't afford to strike, you can't afford not to work.' And that was it, so she had you.

Krieger (1986, p. 84) emphasises the crucial role that housing and the 'sale of the century' (Ainley, 1993) right-to-buy policies played in local and national elections, arguing that the already fragmented working class were 'disillusioned' and 'worn out by the failures of social democracy'. What is far less articulated in this account is the power of such legislation to tap into deeply embedded 'structures of feeling' about class location, or emotional responses that permeate the collective rather than being solely located in the individual (Williams, 1961). The Right to Buy Act was most potent in offering a way, for some the only way they would ever get, of achieving any kind of measure of social mobility or social respectability. In the 1990s the emphasis on social exclusion brought geographical location starkly to the fore. In particular the large local authority estates such as that which the Cole family moved away from became the focus of intensely stigmatising discourses in the media (Toynbee, 1998; Phillips, 1998; Hugill, 1998) as well as the object of interventionist strategies of regulation (Cohen *et al.*, 1996; Social Exclusion Unit, 1998). If, as Thrift and others assert, 'Places form a reservoir of meanings which people can draw upon to tell stories about and thereby define themselves' (Thrift, 1997, p. 160), no wonder so many working-class families grabbed with both hands the chance to move out of places that were discursively constructed through notions of deviance, deficit and failure (Reay and Lucey, 2000) in an attempt to tell a different story about themselves. In this sense, then, location and place have a central role to play in understanding class in the present. In particular, as work from the tradition of cultural geography demonstrates, class is something that is located spatially. It is in the neighbourhood and the house, and, as we shall see in the next section, it is marked on the body.

Class codings of taste and style

While neo-Marxist and neo-Weberian theorists continue to engage with the categories and quantifiers of social class, Pierre Bourdieu (1984) has contributed to a shift of focus on contemporary theorising of class to include a complex analysis of the interrelationship between class and culture. Within this model the distribution of different kinds of 'capital' (economic, cultural, social and symbolic) locate (and have the potential to move) the owner through social space. The markers of the possession of these different kinds of capital are both abstract and material, encompassing taste, education, lifestyle, accent and cuisine (see Skeggs, 1997b). Importantly for our analysis, Bourdieu defines social class not only in relation to the arena of production, but also to the more general, though more complex conceptual space of social relations.

The middle-class sample did not mention home ownership and far fewer spoke about money as a defining factor in class location. Instead they prioritised education as central to the determination of class position, and this in turn was likely to surface in comments that brought up and utilised the notion of 'privilege' and 'opportunity'. Importantly, this was also true of the working-class girls who were heading for or were already at university. Other studies (Frazer, 1988; Holland, 1993; Phoenix and Tizard, 1996) have found that middle-class youngsters have more of a grasp of the complexity of social stratification. It seemed to be the case in our study that the middle-class girls and their parents were able to articulate far more clearly the nature of what Bourdieu (1984) would term 'cultural capital' in relation to class position. As Hannah, a white middle-class 16 year old, said:

> I suppose I think of it as being a kind of ethos.... It's about something much bigger than the profession of your parents yeah. And it's also about taste and about dress and about interests. You can spot it a mile off even though it's not to do with money.

Bourdieu's theorisation of social class highlights the sensitivity of our cultural antennae to the qualitative, subjective, micro-distinctions through which social class location is expressed and understood. By displacing linear representations of class in favour of a theory of social space in which power is distributed in the form of different types of capital, the borders and boundaries of social class are opened up, made more fluid. Hannah's own social location can be understood within this framework. Her parents, both from traditional middle-class families, had opted for communal living as a young couple in the 1970s. Their shared house was only a walk away from the Greens', in the same, run-down part of London, and Hannah went to the same primary school as Erica, Sharon, Satinder, Zoe, Rebecca and Eleanor. Although her parents were graduates, the family were not financially well-off when Hannah was growing up; they had made political and lifestyle decisions that eschewed more traditional routes into profes-sional occupations. However, while they were not wealthy in material terms they possessed considerable cultural and social capital, all of which served to protect the erosion of their social position. Hannah grew up in an area deemed economically and socially deprived, she went to the local, predominantly working-class primary school. But the distinctions between her class position and that of girls like Erica and Sharon were at the same time both subtle and hugely significant. At six years old she was the only child in her class who did not have a television at home; while Rebecca played at 'talent shows' where she and her friends performed pop chart songs to each other, Hannah was learning to play the violin and battling with the discipline of a daily practice regime.

Because Bourdieu views the knowledge of taste and style as a possession, as a kind of capital, while his analysis can pick up the articulacy of Hannah's remark it misses something much more subtle and much more painful. If Hannah could 'spot it a mile off', it would be ridiculous to assume that the targets of her pejorative evaluations would not also be able to spot it in themselves and others, even if they could not theorise it in the way that Hannah's upbringing had taught her to do for many years (see Chapter 5). But in this analysis class is in everything about the person, from the location of their home, to their dress, their body, their accent. These are not simply matters of capital that one does or does not possess. They are ways in which a kind of subject is produced, regulated, lived. Otherness is in the myriad large and small signs through which people recognise themselves and categorise both themselves and those from whom they seek difference, distance.

Indeed that recognition and the fragile move from pejorative to acceptable classification and judgement is exactly what Sharon Cole described when she called herself middle class because she had moved away from a dangerous council estate. It is what Erica Green talked about when she described the highs and lows of her move to the north of England. Underneath the bright veneer of the success story of upward mobility conveyed by the house and the lifestyle, lurked the possibility that some signs of middle-class status (the house, the horse and so forth) were contradicted by others (dress, style, accent, behaviour, intelligence, for example). Such a move, then, may have produced envy in others but it may not have produced Erica's ambition 'to be respected in Hampwick'. This extraordinary ambition for a 17 year old speaks volumes about the way in which she clearly recognised the signs of class location. They were not capital that she either possessed or failed to possess, but rather complex psychosocial signifiers that located her as a subject within a number of practices. These fictional discourses, marked even on her body and mind, inscribed her and inscribed the nuances of class, but more than this, they produced patterns of hope and longing, pain and defence. They were lived deeply, emotionally, consciously and unconsciously, as we shall discuss in Chapter 4.

Mr and Mrs Green's insistence that things were different in the north: that people took you for what you were and did not judge you on what you owned, or your job – they were as happy socialising with 'lords and ladies' as with the bus driver – could be taken as a sign of a complex defence against a fear that in fact they were not really fitting in. Indeed this reading is supported by Erica's feelings about class and her identification as middle-class. Erica said that she could be a 'bit of a snob' at times and mentioned disliking and 'looking down on' some people because they lived in council houses. What an extraordinary statement! Erica had come absolutely to identify with the Other. She was the one who only a few years before had lived in a council house. It was because she knew only too well what that meant that she could now take the position of the middle-class subject and the Other her previous self. This statement revealed the huge amount of shame she felt about that previous self. It also tells us something of how this shame must be defended against. In becoming upwardly mobile she had to attempt to erase every possible mark of what she used to be. She had to become more snobbish than those who had been born middle class, who could afford to say that class didn't matter to them. Her very pain and shame helped to tie her to the very thing she longed to get away from. And more than this, she believed at some level that she did not deserve what she now had, that she was still the stupid little working-class girl:

> I've lost a lot of friends since I started to work. Because all they're saying is, you know, I'm getting like a leg up in the business. And, er, they're getting nowhere you know.

Indeed we found that the working-class girls' and their parents' talk on social class generally and their own class location in particular was infused with a desire to distance themselves from the painful position of being 'one of them'. 'They' were the 'scruffs', the rough working class, the 'underclass', the poor, the homeless or the hopeless.

The Registrar General's system of classification located Mr Green as skilled manual working class in 1983, though at the time he and his wife defined themselves as middle class. In 1993, despite their economic success they were far more cautious about defining themselves in this way.

Father: Well everyone likes to say they're middle class, but I mean I work for a living so … it's a difficult one. We don't look at class to be honest.

Mother: Working class …
Father: … well we've got a bit better than that …
Mother: … a bit more than the average working …
Father: … yeah. I mean if you work for a living, you're working. I mean you're working class. But obviously there's different levels of working class people.
Mother: Not middle class.
Father: I've known people to say they're middle class and they've got nowt. So where do you draw the line. I don't know.

This extract reveals something of the manoeuvring that is often involved in discussions of class and tells us something extremely important about the emotional consequences of social mobility for working-class people. Mrs Green wanted to assert her working-class identity while Mr Green also wanted their success to be recognised in economic and in cultural class terms. The idea that they had achieved economic success and security as well as familial happiness was one that all of the family wanted to present and promote to the outside world. And yet those same achievements courted danger, in the form of other working-class people's envy. This envy, together with the conflation of class with accent (Hey, 1997b) threatened to dislodge part of the foundations on which the family had constructed their sense of 'belonging' to the area, which was heavily dependent on Mrs Green having been born and brought up there. If they were not careful they could be accused by the kinds of working-class people that they themselves used to be, as 'above themselves' or 'posh southerners' – either designation would signal difference and exclusion. Throughout the book we will be developing the argument that success of almost any kind for working-class people is a highly contradictory affair. For working-class people, aspirations, wanting more and wanting to show it off can easily mean being implicated in a process of treachery (Reay, 1996).

The painful recognition of Otherness as marked on the body was displayed by many of the young-working class women, a feeling that they were less, lacking, a lack that had to be carefully hidden in some circles and revealed in others, a complex hide and seek game that amply demonstrated both that the working-class subjects knew exactly how they were positioned and that they knew fragmentation for what it was. That is, a complex game in which it appeared possible to be one thing in one circumstance, another in another, a masquerade or passing. For Christine, a white working-class girl whose parents had consistently emphasised the value of education and who was heading towards university, her studious manner and hard work in an inner-city comprehensive school was understood as class difference by the other working-class pupils:

> Well um, 'cos they [mum and dad] always say they're working class anyway and just, we haven't got a lot of money. We're not really, kind of, poor or anything, 'cos it seems as though working class people are considered as poor. But I see myself as working class but it's like, at the [school] when I first went there, I was like, well that's one of the reasons I was treated so badly, 'cos a lot of the people thought I was middle class. And they just thought 'oh, what's she doing here'. . . . because they kind of, at the time they didn't like the idea of me being, they thought I was middle class, and a lot of people still think I am middle class.

While Christine described herself as not poor, her family were certainly far from financially comfortable: her father was a semiskilled manual worker who regularly suffered acute bouts of chronic illness, they lived in a council house, did not possess a car and did not go on holidays. The standards by which she judged poverty were quite other from those used by more wealthy families who went to great lengths not to become anything like as poor as Christine's family. Nor did Christine escape the contradictions of class when she went to college. Christine was becoming more aware that her 'image' as middle class was founded on a public presentation of herself as 'respectable'. However this respectability was extremely fragile and open to compromise by the fact that she and her family lived on a council estate. She had just begun a relationship with her first boyfriend, who came from a professional middle-class family. She described the first time he gave her a lift home:

> I just thought, um, he probably doesn't realise, um, where I live or – cos to me it's not a problem, um, but I think to other people it can. Cos he dropped me off and he was quite shocked that I lived on a council estate. And, um, just expected me to live somewhere else I think.

The sometimes baffling complexity (to outsiders and insiders alike) of the British class system is and has always been intricately coded around 'taste' and 'style', with strong distinctions being made by the middle classes between 'old' and 'new' money. Amanda, a middle-class 21 year old who attended a highly exclusive and established boarding school, summed it up when she said:

> I suppose especially now after the 80s and stuff there are a lot of people who've made it big in business and stuff in a way that there might not have been before. ... I mean I went to school with a few people like that who like, whose parents have made it really big and they were definitely more into having like a white piano or something than, you know what I mean, 'cos and having quite a showy sort of house and things.

The Green family had undoubtedly made an economic transformation from working class, but the mooning gnomes in their garden, their personalised number plates and their choice of furniture might well have been seen as 'vulgar' by the middle-class families in this study. Erica desperately wished to see herself as 'above' her working-class contemporaries and she had every chance, through her parents' business, to become economically well-off. But the path she was on at the time of the interviews certainly meant that she would not follow the kind of route deemed essential to educate and groom middle-class girls on their path to 'well-rounded', seemingly confident, well-travelled maturity. Neither she nor her parents were part of the 'chattering classes' or 'dinner-party society', and their working-class origins betrayed them at many turns. No easy or painless self-invention there. The economic mobility the Greens had achieved and many other working-class families hoped for was so much more fragile than the educational mobility of both the parents and the girls from working-class families, though both of these routes to upward mobility were fraught with the most painful emotional defences, as we shall explore in Chapter 7.

Being 'in the middle'

There were a number of contradictory self-classifications, especially in the working-class group, who were more likely than the middle-class subjects to define themselves as something other than working class and describe themselves as middle class (27 per cent). Roberts (1993) found that for many subjects, middle class was seen not as being different from working class but as being in the middle, being ordinary, neither rich nor poor. Phoenix and Tizard (1996, p. 434) also found that the young people in their sample classified as working class were 'less likely than those assigned to the middle classes to name the class to which they were assigned as the one to which they belonged'. But being 'in the middle' escapes both the roughness that Erica Green looked down on and being termed a 'snob'. In the age of self-regulation and self-invention it is a pretty safe place to be.

Working-class people who identify themselves with the bourgeoisie have traditionally been a problem for the left, particularly those for whom Marxist thought was their starting point. Marx conceptualised the bourgeoisie as somehow lying 'between' the working and ruling classes in terms of class consciousness, and therefore untrustworthy and vacillating in their allegiances (Ainley, 1993). We could say, therefore, that the implications for some Marxist theorists of large numbers of what have been traditionally viewed and classified as the working class, becoming subjectively and objectively middle class through a combination of structural necessity or fortune, desire and will, are politically disastrous. Social mobility and the swelling of the middle classes from the ranks of the post-industrial, white-collar, working classes represents an end to the possibility of the masses achieving true 'consciousness' of its real destiny. Falsely trapped in the mantle of middle-classness, these workers instead wedge themselves and become wedged 'between' consciousness and action.

We would suggest that defining oneself as 'in the middle' speaks of a different kind of 'action' and 'transformation' for working-class people. Beverley Skeggs (1997a) asks whether or not a subject's own identification with class categories is relevant to subjectivity, given that 'dis-identification' from being seen as working class seemed to be the motor driving the subjectivity of the working-class women who took part in her study. But as Skeggs says, 'to dis-identify we need to know from what the dis-identifications are being made. Recognitions have to be made, resisted, challenged for (dis-)identification to occur' (ibid., p.123):

> Well I can at least say I'm working class now I've got a job. I don't know what I was when I was on the dole. Under, at the bottom I suppose. I used to hate it if I had a problem with my giro or anything, I mean some of them down there talk to you like you're nothing (Eleanor, 16, white working class).

Through these comments come the painful feelings about ascription of class belonging. For Eleanor, the 'underclass' represented her total negation as a subject – she was 'nothing', while Sharon would have liked her new location to count as evidence of a changed class location. In this analysis, self-invention can be understood as a tricky process, fraught with the nuances through which class location is read off the bodies, the behaviours, the speech, the dress, the housing of the young women and their families. What can the trumpeted self-invention be, then, other than a masquerade fraught with the terrors of being the object of so many social projections?

As mentioned earlier, it has been feminist academics from working-class backgrounds who have sought empirically to investigate and theorise subjectivities of class and gender. Social class never was confined to the occupational structure (even if its theorisation was) and it is the cultural analysis conducted by these feminist writers that has shed most light on the lived experiences of working-class women and men (Steedman, 1986; Walkerdine, 1990, 1997; Hey, 1997b; Reay, 1998a;). For instance Skeggs' (1996, 1997a) powerful analysis of 'respectability' as both a marker and a burden of class is particularly useful in relation to what the young women in our study and their families articulated about their subjective locations. She argues that respectability has been a key concept in the formation of classed subjectivity since the nineteenth century, and that while it is most important and explicitly articulated by those who lack it or are found wanting, it is just as central to the subjectivity of the middle classes as they have historically defined themselves against those who do not possess it .

The comments of the working-class girls and their families in this study were shot through with a desire for a respectability that lies in the contradictory and often elusive space of 'the middle'. Importantly, this safe middle, ground not only relies on the actual, discursive or symbolic existence of the pathological poor, but also on its equally feared opposite, the rich. So 'they' can just as powerfully be 'posh', 'stuck-up', rich, envied for their privilege. Importantly, this envy is psychically defended against and experienced as contempt (as we discussed in relation to our own envy of the middle-class families in *Democracy in the Kitchen*, Walkerdine and Lucey, 1989). Whoever 'they' are, their otherness is what must be avoided – whether the otherness of poverty or privilege:

> Middle class, I'd say – well, working class to my mind is someone that goes round talking like that. Middle class, they've got a bit more respect for everything, and upper class are just idiots, because they've got no brains and they've got brilliant jobs (Jenny, 21, white working class).

I don't think I'd be upper class. 'Cos they've got loads of money and that, and um, some of them are right snobs and all that, so I wouldn't like to be like that. I'd like to have their money but not to be like some of their attitudes and that (Jacky, 21, white working class).

I'd put myself in the middle class I think. I think there is an upper class now and between the upper class and the lower class there's a big gap isn't there? But I'd put myself in the middle class.... Don't get me wrong, I'm a working person and I work for the family and everybody else, you know, so they've got different things indoors, but I work for them. I think – I'm no snob, don't get me wrong, but I suppose I'm middle class yes, but I mix with everybody, so I suppose I'm somewhere in the middle. I get on with life and enjoy life to the best you can. I'm no snob, but I suppose as you say, middle class (Anna's father, white working class).

We would argue strongly that it is far too simplistic to see those working-class subjects who identified themselves as middle class as somehow under a hopelessly false illusion. However, neither do their self-classifications speak of 'collectivism' and community. It is not the language of Marxism, traditional socialism, the trade union movement or the old style Labour Party. If we consider the practices of regulation, which depend so heavily on the use of normalisation and pathologisation, together with Conservative and other political injunctions against extremism, it is not surprising that being in the middle – not rich, not poor, not Other or extreme – feels like a safe place to be compared with the terrors of other possible positions.

Refusing class(ification)

An equal number of working-class and middle-class girls and parents at first resisted the question about their class location and expressed frustration at the divisiveness of the concept of class. They felt that it was wrong to categorise people, to 'put them into boxes', and felt that individuals should be taken on their own merit rather than judged as being in one class or another. In these comments there was a strong desire to wish class away, but at the same time, there was an uncomfortable awareness of social inequality and difference:

I don't really put myself into a class. ...I think it's all stupid, this class business. I mean it's all um...material things, isn't it? It's all your...it's whether you've got money really. Whether you've got a big car, a nice car, a big house and luxury this, luxury that. I mean, what is that? I mean, it's just stupid...you shouldn't look on somebody as a class, I mean you

> should look at them for what they are, not class (Zoe, 16, white working class).

> I don't know. I don't really think nothing about class really. I think having class is . . . like what class you're in is a bit stupid really. I mean a person's a person. I don't really pay much attention to like working class, upper class, lower class. (Patsy, 21, white working class).

> Yeah, it's the kind of thing that you really wish that people weren't aware of, but it is still there (Amanda, 21, white middle class).

> I feel I don't properly belong to any class, I also think there shouldn't be such things anyway. I think the idea of a classless society is what we should be aiming at (Amanda's father, white middle class).

What came up powerfully in this study was the desperate desire of all the working-class subjects to make their lives 'okay'. We would argue that this desire was central to their identification of themselves as middle class. They were not mistaken in imagining that the middle classes had 'enough' materially, or at least more than they had. No wonder they wished, on some but not all levels, to take themselves out of a class that, in Britain, has always had to struggle economically. All the working-class parents and many of the working-class girls spoke of a fantasised future in which they would have 'enough' materially and emotionally. The kind of success the Green and Cole families felt they had achieved was precisely articulated around this concept of 'enough'. What also came up in relation to the working-class girls was that while many saw themselves as working class at the moment, that was not where they wanted to be forever. Much was invested in a hopeful future in which dreams of mobility and release from paid employment featured powerfully:

> I'm working class at the moment. [But] not for ever . . . you know, but I'm working class at the moment. No I want to be rich [laughs]. No um – no I don't want to be working class for ever. Holding down a nine to five job. That's not what I want to do. That's why – you know, I'm not going to do that for ever (Sarena, 21, black working class).

Indeed, who in the fiction of choice as a life project of self-actualisation (Rose, 1991) would actually *want* to hold down a nine to five job for ever? This is not the picture of 'making it' that is held out as a possible dream.

For the working-class parents, many of these desires were focussed on their children; a 'respectable' and therefore 'safe' location for them to grow up in and the provision of a financially secure future for them. The 1980s boom (coming as it did out of a deep recession) promised huge financial profits. Five of the working-class parents in this study did indeed try the entrepreneurial road during that decade, but only one of them achieved the kind of success that the Thatcherite dream promised. Mr and Mrs Green, with foresight, good timing and a heavy helping of luck, managed to ride the 1980s house price boom, escaping from London with a huge profit to set up their own successful business. For the others, financial loss and the slow running-down of their small business was the norm. Katy's family moved from London to the Midlands during the mid 1980s and bought a small shop. But the business began to fail almost immediately:

> We kept going into different things, thinking that would fetch people in, but then you'd find somebody else would open a shop selling just that, you know, a few weeks later. We tried all sorts (Katy's mother).

Alternatively, for the Coles and for Nicky's family the dream of work without a boss was only achieved by dodging the social security system and becoming part of a black market economy of 'cash in hand' work and running car-boot and market stalls.

Maintaining standards, and indeed the outward expression of those standards, was a persistent theme in Erica's and her parents' interviews. Indeed Erica's ambition was to be 'respected in Hampwick', and the display of success was clearly important to the family. We do not deny that they had much to congratulate themselves about, but there was a persistent refusal by Mr and Mrs Green to engage with any subject that would send even the tiniest of ripples across this otherwise still pond. We are not saying that indications of strife or discord in the subjects' lives was a condition for their taking part in the research, rather that the need to present and unremittingly maintain a picture of 'happy perfection' is an important part of understanding the immense physical, material and centrally, psychic work that class mobility requires. Erica was the only one in the family to reveal any disturbances in the water, but to understand this we need to look back to when she was six years old.

Erica was considered a poor achiever when she was six; she was tearful and helpless in the classroom and found it very difficult to leave her mother. When the family moved to northern England she was experiencing difficulty in maths and literacy, which her parents blamed on her London primary school. She made some progress at the high-achieving local secondary school near her village, but even though her family were proud of her GCSE achievements, it was clear that school-work remained a struggle for her and her academic performance was poor in relation to the average in her school; her grades were not good enough for her to continue on to A level and she was considering a vocational course such as hairdressing or social care. At that point her parents suggested she join the family business. By the time of the second interview, when Erica was 17, they had made her a partner in the business. We suggest that for her parents this was another golden wand that their economic success had allowed them to wave.

Nearly all of the working-class parents spoke about the worry they had about their daughters' working futures. Underlying these comments for some (especially fathers) was a sense of impotence at not being able to protect them from unemployment, poor wages or dead-end jobs. Therefore the Greens' ability to provide a means of training and a future as a partner in a successful business to a daughter who was poorly equipped for academic or employment success was, we suggest, the kind of thing that most working-class parents could only dream of. There was a curious gender-twist in this narrative in that Erica had set out on an occupational path that represents so much of what had been 'lost' in terms of traditional working-class masculinity: as an apprentice in a skilled-manual 'craft'.

But how did it feel to have achieved this dream? Once the dream had come true, did it have to be guarded fiercely? Erica's parents, like most from working-class backgrounds, desperately wished to protect their child from what they had had to do. They wanted her life to be much easier than theirs, with less work and more reward. But the dependence they produced in Erica was closely connected to their own need for protection. We heard from other working-class parents, especially fathers, that everything they had done had been for the children. For example Christine's parents put what little money they had into their children, leaving nothing for themselves – they did not own a car, smoke, drink or go out for pleasure by themselves. Instead, one of their weekly routines when Christine was six years old was to buy an educational book and go on an 'educational visit' (Walkerdine, 1997). They saw themselves as going out into the world and battling (like Mr Cole) for their sons and daughters. Does their view of their daughters as vulnerable and in need of protection tell us something important about the kinds of unconscious defence they had used to guard against the terrible vulnerability they had felt in their own lives? The desire of the poor parents for their children to have lives that were better than theirs was very strong, so strong that in many cases the parents psychically denied and wounded themselves in order to offer something better to their children. What was the effect of this on social and psychic relations within the family? For example did Christine simultaneously feel that she had to withstand the jibes of her schoolmates about being middle class while feeling a terrible guilt about letting her parents down because they had given up so very much for her? What was the effect of this on the way she understood her present and her future?

Does Erica's parents' reiteration of their acceptance by the community (even though they were 'southerners') suggest a defence against the fear that they were not in fact wholeheartedly accepted? It was Erica's comments that most often revealed the soft underbelly of the family's success story that her parents were, understandably, unwilling to expose: that while 'all this' had been significantly helped along by a 'lucky' combination of political and personal events, it had been upheld by obsessive hard work, particularly by a father who found it difficult to switch off from the business. At 17 Erica spoke of the sometimes unbearable pressure of responsibility at work, the number of hours she had to put in, how she feared that her youth would go and she would 'end up like Dad'.

Conclusion

Many Marxist and neo-Marxist sociologists operate with a notion of 'consciousness' and thus the 'conscious' aspects of identity, and they only allow in a notion of the unconscious to signal a failure to achieve revolutionary consciousness. No wonder they tie themselves up in knots, for this is what is consistently omitted from traditional analyses of class. It is implicit that the working class must make a psychic transformation in order to become a class in and of itself. But somehow these very complex psychic processes, which are seen as essential to the birth and development of such a class, are at the same time ignored, or engaged with only on the most superficial level. Indeed those aspects of Freudo-Marxism and the Frankfurt school that do engage with such phenomena, along with Lacanian-inspired Althusserian work, tend to concentrate on the infantile qualities of working-class subjectivity. There is a dearth of work that engages with the conscious and unconscious defences necessary to cope with the exigencies of daily life (Walkerdine, 1997).

In other psychological discourses the working class is viewed as psychologically simplistic (Argyle, 1996) and barely capable of transformation. Any transformations that do take place in the working class are in danger of being seen as evidence of threatening pathologies that must be vigilantly regulated, suppressed or 'cured' (Blackman, 1996). For the radical left, then, only one psychic transformation is possible and acceptable for the working class – one that allows them to put aside false consciousness and get on with the work of revolution. This is the only active shift that can take place. Lack of such a shift can only signify passivity, false ideology and false consciousness. Should they fail to make this particular transformation then the psyche can no longer exist in the equation, as if there are no other transformations that could be relevant to the structural and emotional lives of working-class people.

We argue that in the 1980s people did not want to reject the welfare state, rather they simply wanted a share of the good life that the welfare state had promised but failed to deliver. They wanted decent houses that actually felt like homes. They wanted their spirits buoyed. 'Social democracy in its shabbiness and torpor failed to replace pride in ownership with pride in community' (Krieger, 1986, p. 86). Mr Cole described himself mockingly as a 'violent midget' and a 'fighter' (Walkerdine, 1997). He had strong political and moral beliefs that he strove to act upon, as a member of the Labour Party and as an individual. His identification as someone who fought for his rights at times brought him into direct conflict with the institutions he had contact with (Walkerdine 1991, 1997). He was certainly neither passive nor duped, and he had a sharp if at times idiosyncratic analysis of the effects of Tory policies and the changing nature of social and economic relations in Britain:

> You got four houses at the bottom, massive big houses. Do you know we was a council tenant in one of those owned by the council? Do you know why we moved out? Because the roads were dangerous and the wife was scared that they'd [the children] run out into the road. So we had to be moved from there to the Exeter Estate.... How much are they worth? Quarter of a million? Must be. I kick her every night when I think about it.

Some feel that the 'zeitgeist' of the 1980s was the ideology of enterprise, as created by the Conservatives, with enterprise presented as the solution to modernisation and the intractable crisis of capitalism. Services that, post-war, had been owned and provided by the state were sold off to private companies, along with bus companies, the rail ways and the power and water utilities. Other public services were retained by the state as semi-independent agencies to be run at a profit (as with health and social services). The consumers of those services are now 'customers', redefined as 'citizens' with individual 'rights' enshrined in the contractual relations of 'charters'.

Market discourses that assert universal freedom of choice are used in defence of discourses of classlessness and serve to obscure the ways in which social advantage is maintained through the free market (Reay, 1998b, p. 261). Far from displacing the logic of class, as some would argue (Pakulski and Waters, 1996), the markets themselves shape and are shaped by social relations of class. The citizens of governmental charters do not participate collectively as informed citizens in a demo-cratic process that decides which goods and services should be pro-vided. Ainley (1993) argues that they merely choose as 'passive consumers' between the different commodities the market offers them. If you cannot afford any of the market options then you must fall back on what the run-down, overstretched welfare system can offer.

The evangelical call to individualism begun by the Thatcher govern-ment in the 1980s has been proudly taken up by New Labour in their Third Way. They are as keen as any true-blue Tory to insist on the rights and responsibilities of the individual in a free market, and have continued to put in place structures designed gradually to remove alternatives for ordinary people. The exclusionary aspects of classless-ness have impacted profoundly on working-class people, who are no longer entitled to harbour a sense of unfairness because under late capitalism every aspect of their lives, from finances to children's schooling to health, has been repackaged and re-presented as the sole responsibility of the individual and become part of their heady path to autonomous bourgeois subjectivity in Third Way Britain (Reay, 1998b).

Mr Cole's comments above highlight some of the main difficulties in trying to speak about class, and especially the working class at the turn of the century. The confusion and frustration in the many attempts to do so is palpable and runs through many public spheres, including sociological theory, political theory and the rhetoric of both right and left. Much less considered or theorised in those public debates and disciplines, but central to this book, is the way in which social class, in all its confusions and contradictions, had played a significant part in the formation of the subjectivities of the young women and the families who took part in this study.[4] Our argument is that class cannot be understood simply through any of the available sociological modes of explanation. The production of subjects from all classes and the way in which they live their subjectification centrally involves a constant invitation to consume, to invent, to choose and yet even in the midst of their choice and their consumption class is performed, written all over their every choice. From house to dress, from accent to appearance, Eliza Dolittle is as present in the early twenty-first century as she was in the nineteenth. And more than this, the living out of these marks of difference is filled with desire, longing, anxiety, pain, defence. Class is at once profoundly social and profoundly emotional, and lived in its specificity in particular cultural and geographical locations.

Notes

1. Our aim was to videorecord all of the 16 year olds at school or college. Those who were in employment and whose employers agreed were filmed at work.
2. For instance, 'Mosaic' is the brand name of a system of classification based on house type. In this scheme, postal codes are cross-referenced with information from the electoral role, census information and county court judgments to make 52 'types' in 12 'lifestyle' groupings. The JICNARS scale was (and maybe still is) the most widely used classification system in marketing and is based on socioeconomic segmentation (*Observer Life Magazine*, 1997).
3. Apart from the middle-class parents from working-class families, who need to be understood as a separate category, see Chapters 5 and 7.
4. Throughout the rest of the book, because of the difficulties we have discussed in this chapter, we shall continue to refer to the young women and their families by the class designations given to them in the 1970s and 1980s.

Chapter 3

Worlds of Work

> No. I don't know actually [when I'll have children]. It would be nice to have them soon because I don't want to be too old when I have them, but looking into the future, I can't see that they'd happen within the next five or six years at least, because simply with the demands of the job, I mean. Because the next two years after I qualify I'll be working, like, 150 hours every week kind of thing. You can't have kids then.
>
> (middle-class 21 year old)

Women have always been a problem when it comes to class analysis (Crompton, 1993). Now more than ever, the increasing participation of women in the workforce shows up the weaknesses in occupational class schemes that were devised in relation to a model of predominantly male employment and often took the occupation of husbands and fathers over and above that of the women in the household as defining class location. As such the idea that social class is an overwhelmingly masculine category has shown a particularly vigorous tenacity. In recent years, however, feminist critics have powerfully challenged this privileging of the labour market as the main site in which individuals come to understand themselves as classed subjects (Hey, 1997b). As we saw in the previous chapter, young women and their families come to recognise themselves and others as classed through a myriad of signs, which are certainly far from restricted to the workplace. As we argued in *Democracy in the Kitchen* (Walkerdine and Lucey, 1989), the work of mothering is also deeply class specific and plays a major role in producing children as classed subjects, again in a way that is not at all restricted to employment (see Chapters 5, 6 and 7). In addition they ignore the changes in the labour market and the issues raised in the Introduction.

There is a need to explore the significance of work for the production of the subjectivities of young women, their mothers and their fathers at this particular moment. Competing discourses in the 1980s and 1990s on the importance (or un-importance) of paid work and the changing nature of work had major implications not only for debates about all women, but also for working-class and middle-class men. It is not surprising that, during this period, there was media coverage of the perceived ill-effects suffered by children of professional women working full-time, and also high-profile stories about professional women who gave up work to be with their young children. It is, of course, instructive that there were no similar stories about men as fathers. Juggling the demands of work and family has never been easy, and now that women are playing a major part in the labour force there are both more tensions for them and very difficult feelings for men, who may experience this as women taking work from them.

During the 1960s and 1970s, sociology worked with models of predictability in relation to the school–work transition. The postmodern theorists of the 1980s and 1990s shifted this notion towards a transitional model that emphasises the way in which individuals negotiate risk and uncertainty – what Evans and Furlong (1997) refer to as a navigation model. In this volume we move away from that model, which assumes a pregiven psychological subject (Henriques *et al.*, 1998), towards one that understands the new and changed exigencies of the constitution of subjectivity in the present. It is in this context, as we have stressed, that the necessity for self-invention produces new discursive spaces for young women to enter as subjects, spaces that might be fraught with difficulties and contradictions, as we shall stress throughout the book. In this context, we might also think about the arguments put forward by cultural theorists that new forms of subjectivity are hybridised (Bhabha, 1990; Hall, 1992; Gilroy, 1993), that is, that the instability of identity is characterised by people who are no longer simply working class or black subjects, for example, but are class and ethnic hybrids. This idea is particularly important for understanding some working-class girls and girls from the middle class who are first-generation middle class (see Chapters 6, 7 and 8).

In the context of changing work practices, it has also been argued that there is a hybridisation and reversal of work-place gender identities (see Adkins, 1995, for a review). Adkins argues that the gendered body has been established as mobile, fluid and indeterminate. That is not in any simple sense a feminisation of the workplace that simply equates more feminine with more women. Rather, hybrid practices that demand a feminised corporeality for men to enter service work, for example, and a complex set of transformations whereby those women who enter male professional and business domains must be faced with the impossibility of crossing over successfully onto the side of the masculine. In other words she suggests that it is easier for men to inhabit feminine corporeality and performativity than it is for women to do the opposite. She cites a study by McDowell (1997), who explored women's performance on the trading floor of the stock exchange:

> While McDowell stresses that certain masculinised performances by women may potentially be disruptive of gender – for instance, perform-ances of emphatic gestures and facial grimaces by women on trading floors are understood to challenge conventional images of feminine passivity – many of the professional women stressed difficulties in per-forming masculinity at work. Some, for example, were found to adopt a feminised version of the male uniform and others to perform as honorary men, but such performances are shown to be doomed to failure, counter-productive and to often backfire. Indeed for many of the women mas-querading as a man was impossible. One of the respondents commented, for example, that it is difficult, even demeaning to try to be one of the boys, and another you can't go out and get ratted as one of the boys in the pub; it just won't work. Indeed these professional women stressed that such performances often had negative workplace consequences with, for instance, colleagues and clients finding these masculine performances inappropriate and out of place at work (Adkins, 2001, pp. 26–7).

In fact McDowell's research brings up issues that mirror incidents that happened at school to some of the girls in our research (Walkerdine, 1998). In the mathematics classroom girls were constantly berated by teachers and, within discourses about mathematical performance, for not displaying the same kind of mathematical understanding and flair as boys. Yet girls who did indeed perform like boys in the classroom did not have an easy time and were always the target of pejorative evaluations. A pushy and argumentative girl was not understood in the same way as a pushy and argumentative boy. One such girl was described as a 'madam' by her teacher. Here, then, the pejorative connotations are also sexualised. As we shall see, therefore, the world of work that these young women are set to enter may be 'feminised' but that does not mean that it is not fraught with contra-dictions, which still make it difficult for young women unproblematic-ally to enter it.

Conversely, of course, the issue of men performing femininity is also replete with its own fictions and fantasies, not least about the loss of manhood and working-class status. In an earlier phase of the research, Sharon Cole's father went to great lengths to say that he did not like the musical *Annie*, which the family was watching on video, because it was too 'feminine'. He seemed afraid of losing his status as a working-class man who struggled out in the real world for his family (Walkerdine, 1997). However, as the analysis undertaken at that time also demonstrates, media representations of the working class as feminine (in the form of a little girl like orphan Annie, for example) served to downplay their possibility as a threat. This is particularly important when thinking about the defeat and disintegration of the labour movement in Britain.

The move into paid employment has gained importance since the early 1980s as a powerful signifier of adult status for young women, as it previously was for young men, even while the means and routes through which it can be achieved remain profoundly differentiated according to class, gender and race. At 16 and 21 years, one of the biggest divisions between the girls and young women in this study was between those who were still in full-time education and those who were not involved in any kind of formal study but were in or available for paid employment. There are, then, a number of questions we wish to address in this chapter. What impact had the changes in the structuring of waged labour had on the patterns of inequality among the young women? How were these inequalities experienced by them and what impact had they had on their everyday lives? How important was the actual work they were doing and the kinds of work they wished for to them and their families?

We begin by noting that as traditional working-class men's employment has diminished, work has become more important to women. Previously, women's paid work was much more intermittent, taken up when domestic duties were lightest or at moments of national emergency, when women were brought into the labour force as substitutes for male workers. Until the powerful challenges of feminist writers such as Anne Oakley (1974) in the 1970s, women's domestic activity was largely hidden and certainly did not count as 'work'.[1] Their participation in waged labour was overwhelmingly viewed as marginal and the 'model worker' was a man with a dependent family (Goldthorpe, 1980; Jenson *et al.*, 1988). With such a strongly held model of the 'family man', trade unions in Britain and elsewhere bargained and demanded 'family wages' to support their dependants: their wives and children.

Theorists such as Giddens (1990, 1991, 1998) and Bauman (1991) argue that while waged labour once provided a focus for the development of class-based identities in industrial societies, the increasing instability of and flexibility in the labour market, alongside the increasing blurring of the divisions between work and non-work, are having an intensely weakening effect on the significance of class and status. Ulrich Beck (1992) argues that new forms of employment have produced an employment system fraught with risk, insecurity and underemployment, and in effect have resulted in an individualised society of employees. This combination of individual responsibility and accountability on the one hand and vulnerability and lack of control on the other means a heightened subjective sense of risk and insecurity. Giddens (1991) argues that conditions of doubt penetrate all aspects of social life and self-identity and the construction of a coherent biography becomes a reflexive project under constant reconstruction in the light of ever-changing experiences.

Discourses of endless possibility are certainly present in young women's narratives in relation to their working lives and the transition to paid employment. But as Furlong and Cartmel (1997, p. 109) assert, as young people struggle to establish adult identities and maintain coherent biographies, they may develop strategies to overcome various obstacles but their life chances remain highly structured, with social class, race and gender being crucial to an understanding of experiences in a range of life contexts. Our data shows that class location designated on the basis of parents' occupation and, importantly, educational credentials, is the most efficient predictor of life chances in the lives of girls and their families (Joseph Rowntree Foundation, 1995). Of course there are many inadequacies in these class schemes, not least the marginalisation of women. However the terms in which work is understood by most young women and their families is not framed in terms of class consciousness or action – we argue that this was always a wishful fantasy of the left. It is nevertheless one of the arenas in which we come to place and understand ourselves (the kind of person we are and the kind of person we can hope to be) in a complex permutation of possibilities and impossibilities. Meanwhile the actuality of employment and unemployment resonates, shapes, gives texture and colour throughout our psychic and physical lives.

Work still occupies most of the adult population aged 16 to 64 across Europe and the US – a point that is sometimes lost in 'post-industrial' arguments. It is crystal clear that for all of the women in this study, work remained crucial to the construction of their subjectivities whether their aspirations regarding work were realistic or replete with fantasy. Furthermore the material facts of their present employment or their aspirations regarding their working (or non-working) future had as much to do with class as they did with race and gender. What we want to do is move these debates on by exploring the ways in which different subjectivities are formed through a number of discursive interfaces that operate not only at the level of the social but also psychodynamically, in an effort to understand how everyday practices in relation to the school–work transition impact upon and produce gendered, raced and classed subjectivities.

It is important to note that arguments about the declining significance of work in relation to class emerged just at the historical moment when employment was becoming more important than ever before for women. The recession of the 1970s and 1980s did not result in a great decline in women's employment. In fact women have accounted for much of the growth of the labour force since the early 1980s, although it is important to keep a constant eye on the fact that many of the service sector jobs created as a result of economic restructuring have been low-level 'women's jobs' (Crompton, 1993; Eurostat, 1998). This does not appear to be a temporary situation: female participation in the labour market continues steadily to increase, signalling women's permanent attachment to the labour market rather than a reserve army status (Bakker, 1988; Wilkinson *et al.*, 1997).

The argument that 'work doesn't matter any more' and versions of it are all based on changes in the occupational market since the 1970s and 1980s, when employment in manufacturing fell dramatically. A sharp decline in the manufacturing base led to massive unemployment and a decrease in the number of what until then had constituted a large percentage of white, male, working-class jobs (Table 3.1).

Table 3.1   Number of employees in manufacturing industries, 1978–99

	Male	*Female*	*Total*
1978	4 656 491	1 968 468	6 624 959
1982	3 794 848	1 546 140	5 340 787
1986	3 349 142	1 414 235	4 763 377
1990	3 221 115	1 383 403	4 604 518
1994	2 689 703	1 132 942	3 822 645
1999	2 794 252	1 084 110	3 878 362

Source: Office for National Statistics.

Only in retrospect is it clear that the period of 'full employment' from the postwar period until the 1973 oil crisis could only ever have been an anomaly rather than permanent reality. Collusion in this fiction occurred on a grand scale and nobody wanted to give it up. Sociologists too invested their faith in the notion of unending good times for the masses, and social scientists operated as though concerned with the 'affluent worker', as if he would be affluent once and for all (Goldthorpe and Lockwood, 1968; Goldthorpe *et al.*, 1968). When overall unemployment began to rise (remembering that regional unemployment stayed in the 2–3 per cent range in the north and Scotland and was never less than 7 per cent in Northern Ireland) to over a million in 1975 there was a stubborn reluctance to admit to the permanence of such a high level (Hopkins, 1991). Meanwhile the enormity of change was unstoppable; transformations in the industrial landscape continued to erode the very foundations of the working class as it had traditionally been understood. Thus it turned out that the long boom was unique, not the long depression.

Traditional communities, no longer sustained by the industries that had created them in the first place, began to break up or reform, especially in the north of England and Wales. Meanwhile, the new jobs created during the economic restructuring of the 1980s were mainly in the communications and service sectors. Jobs in the white-collar service sector rose from 11.6 million in 1971 to 18.2 million in 1995 (Eurostat, 1996). The horizontal segregation of women's work is demonstrated by the fact that over half of all women in Britain work in only three occupational categories: clerical and secretarial; personal and protective services, including nursing, catering, cleaning and hairdressing; and sales occupations (Hakim, 1996). In our study the mothers' and daughters' working patterns reflected the massive increase in white-collar occupations, with the working-class mothers and daughters tending to participate in occupations at the lower rungs of status, security and pay. Of the nine (50 per cent) working-class young women who were not in full-time education and were working in paid employment, eight (44 per cent) were in the kind of work that constituted this increase in women's jobs – clerical work, VDU operator, receptionist, care work and catering.

Popular discussions on the feminisation of the workforce abound as increasing numbers of women enter the labour market relative to the decline of men's participation (Jenson *et al.*, 1988; Hakim, 1996; EOC, 1996b). Some would even argue that structural and social changes in occupations have 'feminised' much of the remaining employment for men (Wilkinson *et al.*, 1997). Two distinct camps have emerged in relation to this debate – popular, celebratory representations of successful 1990s women (ibid.) versus a far more cautious analysis by sociologists and economists (Jenson *et al.*, 1988; Callender, 1996; Hakim, 1996; Garcia-Ramon and Monk, 1996). Some feminists accuse politicians and analysts of simply ignoring or viewing in too narrow a way the gender implications of the global economic restructuring and political transformation, particularly across Europe (Garcia-Ramon and Monk, 1996).

Convergence and polarisation

While there is cause to celebrate the achievements made by and for women at work, there is still much to be concerned about, particularly the differential participation of women in the labour force. Women may be achieving parity of numbers in the workforce but they continue to experience great inequality compared with men in terms of working conditions. Sylvia Walby argues that the dual processes of convergence and polarisation mark the contemporary restructuring of gender relations and women's relationships to waged labour. Convergence between men and women is occurring in employment, particularly for some *young* women who have been able to take advantage of increased access to education and therefore achieve the same or better qualifications than young men (Walby, 1997). This can have a significant knock-on effect in a labour market context in which employers increasingly demand an educated and trained workforce.

At the same time Walby and others (ibid.; Bakker, 1998) note that there is a growing trend towards the polarisation of women in the labour market – a polarisation that was evident in our study. It is our contention that convergence and polarisation between the genders can only be understood in the context of social class, and that on the whole those women who are experiencing some convergence with men and those who are experiencing polarisation in the labour market do not come from the same social class.

Diverse transitions

For the mothers and fathers of the girls and young women in this study, their transition into the labour market was relatively standardised and homogeneous (though highly structured in class terms).

Changes in the youth labour market, particularly its collapse in the early 1980s, as well as the restructuring of existing employment opportunities within a framework that placed much stress on more training, workforce flexibility and reduced labour costs, served to make the transition from school to work more protracted, fragmented and unpredictable for their daughters (Ashton *et al.*, 1990).[2] This fragmentation was not as universal as discourses of individualisation might suggest however. As we can see from Table 3.2, at the time of the first interview the overwhelming majority (87 per cent) of the middle-class girls were in full-time education and did no paid work during term time (half of this group worked during the summer holidays). Only one middle-class young woman, Gill, a New Age traveller, was not in any kind of formal education. The changes that had taken place by the time of the second interview (Table 3.3) were due to two

Table 3.2   Employment and study by class and age at the first interview

| Employed | Studying | Working class | | Middle class | | Total |
		21 year olds	16 year olds	21 year olds	16 year olds	
Full time	Part time	1	–	–	–	1
Part time	Full time	–	1	1	–	2
Part time	Part time	–	–	–	–	–
No employment	Full time	3	3	11	2	19
No employment	No studying	1	–	1	–	2
No employment	Part time	1	–	–	–	1
Full time	No studying	6	2	–	–	8

Table 3.3   Employment and study by class and age at the second interview

| Employed | Studying | Working class | | Middle class | | Total |
		21 year olds	16 year olds	21 year olds	16 year olds	
Full time	Part time	1	1	–	–	2
Part time	Full time	–	1	–	–	1
Part time	Part time	–	–	1	–	1
None	Full time	3	2	9	2	16
None	Part time	1	–	–	–	1
None	None	3	–	1	–	4
Full time	None	4	1	1	–	6
Part time	None	1	–	1	–	2

of the 21 year olds graduating, Deborah beginning full-time work in her professional field, and Samantha doing a mixture of paid and voluntary work for her local newspaper in order to get some experience before applying for a postgraduate course. Another 21 year old, Abigail, was on overseas placement as part of her degree course, where she also taught part time. The pathways to employment demonstrated a considerable amount of stability across the rest of the middle-class sample regardless of race.

Diversity in relation to the school–work transition was very much the province of the working-class young women, who as a group occupied many more locations in relation to employment and study and were far more likely to move in and out of the labour and education markets. The middle-class sample could be seen as taking fairly traditional routes, in terms of social class, towards full-time participation in the labour market.

Unlike their mothers and fathers at the same age, of the working-class daughters 41 per cent (seven) had experienced periods of involuntary unemployment. Of these nearly half 18 per cent (three) had experienced redundancy. At the time of the study 12 per cent (two) of the working-class fathers[3] were unemployed and 35 per cent (six) had experienced unemployment and/or redundancy, compared with only 7 per cent (one) of the middle-class fathers. The effect of this on their children should not be underestimated and it must have infused their daughters with a lot of anxiety in respect of employment security. Whilst the growth of the insecure, temporary contract employment culture has made an impression on the professional labour markets since the 1990s, it is uncredentialled, semiskilled employees who have been most exposed to and powerless in the face of the vagaries of the market and poor employment practice. It is against this contemporary backdrop that the parents in the study, in particular the working-class fathers, depicted their own entry into the labour market during the boom years of the 1960s as an empowering experience of 'freedom to work':

> If you worked for a manager that was a right git, you told him to stick the job up his proverbial rear end. If you worked for a governor that treated you as a human being, you stayed with him. You had freedom of what you wanted to do (Sharon Cole's father, white working class).

> Well there's a big difference because when I left school I could walk into a job straight away, and if I didn't like it I could come out of that job and get another one in the afternoon. And I done that quite a few times

till I was 21. I couldn't count how many jobs I had. I must have had a good 10 or 12 jobs before I was 21 (Katy's father, white working class).

In relation to the current necessity for self-invention it is not surprising that the working-class fathers talked about the ease of their own transition into work, in a world where they did not have to transform themselves in order to fit in. This is precisely the issue that Sennett (1998) talks about. It is just such men who have taken the brunt of new work regimes that demand an entirely different kind of working-class masculinity – one that is groomed to meet the requirements of the service and information sectors – and who have found that they no longer 'fit'. Working-class women are more likely to have had to carry out this 'makeover' of the self to a greater or lesser extent in service and clerical jobs from the 1960s onwards.

In contrast to their parents, many working-class young people today perceive the transition into the world of work as filled with risk and uncertainty (Biggart and Furlong, 1996). The impact on young working-class women of unemployment and the threat of unemployment cannot be underestimated (Mizen, 1995). Jacky, who was employed as a low-grade clerical officer on short, temporary contracts, was acutely aware of her disposability and lack of employment protection:

> it's like any day they can say 'Oh, we'll keep you on for that week and then after that week we don't need you any more'. So that's a bit of a worry as well. Then I'll be unemployed again, and I don't really want to be unemployed (Jacky, 21, white working class).

Other differences emerge around race and ethnicity, with higher rates of employment for white women than ethnic groups. Studies of youth labour markets suggest that selection processes often present another layer of disadvantage to be faced by black and Asian young people, with much higher rates of unemployment than similarly qualified whites (Brown, 1992; Drew, 1995). While there are differences between ethnic groups and women of different ages within those groups, the main overall difference between ethnic and white women is that far fewer women from ethnic minorities work part time. In 1991 39 per cent of white women worked part-time compared to 26 per cent of ethnic women (Callender, 1996).

Not only are working-class young women entering a severely depleted youth labour market, but the consequences of voluntarily giving up employment are punitive to say the least. Katy's comment below highlights how changes in the laws governing unemployment benefit since the 1980s have affected those who deliberately leave their jobs:

> The first time I was unemployed [laughs], I'm an old hand at being unemployed, the first time I really hated it, 'cos I'd left my previous job of my accord, I didn't get any dole money.... Well in a way it was like a kind of a break [laughs], sort of like a nice long break from work. But it still used to get a bit boring. You'd sort of like be at home all the time. You'd go down the job centre and that, but there would never be anything there. So I did often wonder whether I would ever get a job (Katy, 21, white working class).

Katy was joking about having a nice long break from work, but her light-hearted comments hid how unhappy she had been in her previous job and how desperate she had been to leave. Knowing, however, that she would not be entitled to any benefits for six months after registering as unemployed, she had stayed in the job and saved as much as she could so that when she did leave she would be able to get by financially until she found another job. Most importantly for her, this meant that she would not have to ask her mother, who was a dinner lady, and her father, who was unemployed after being made redundant, for any money. Beneath the gloss of choice lay a great deal of insecurity. Katy had had to manage financially through periods of unemployment, had been forced to stay in a job she hated, and had had to cope psychically with the pejorative evaluation of her as not good enough to get work and as a 'skiver'.

In terms of young women's transition to financial independence, changes in social policy have contributed to a lengthened period of dependency, particularly for working-class girls (Furlong and Cartmel, 1997). When these girls parents were young, working-class youth became economically independent earlier than the middle classes, who often remained dependent on their parents until their early twenties (Roberts, 1984). This remained true for our sample in that the working-class girls entered the labour market at an earlier age than the middle-class girls. However the introduction of the 1986 Social Security Act (implemented in 1988) has meant that most young people under the age of 18 are no longer eligible for welfare benefits, even if they live away from the parental home (Donoghue, 1992). Other changes in benefit legislation have resulted in some young adults not qualifying for the full rate of benefit until they are 25 years old. These policy developments not only reflect successive governments' view that young people should be in full-time education or training, but also more generalised discourses that have been enshrined in educational and criminal legislation regarding parental responsibility.

Jenny's case illustrates the position that women who are married or cohabiting face when they become unemployed and are not entitled to claim unemployment benefit:

> I'm unemployed now, I don't get any benefits because I'm living with my boyfriend. They say he's earning sufficient money to cover both of you for each week which I don't feel what he's earning is adequate because he's paying for his little boy as well, paying the rent.... And we don't get any help with the rent or anything like that so – one step at a time. We miss out on a few luxuries and keep to the basics (Jenny, 21, white working class).

Gill, 21 years old, was the only middle-class young woman to have experienced unemployment, although her decisions about how and when she earned money were closely connected to her identity as a New Age traveller. She and her partner organised their year in relation to seasonal farming work and busking in holiday towns, and for a large part of the winter they claimed income support. As the only middle-class girl to have left school at 16 with few qualifications, and not to have returned to education by 21, Gill's assertion that 'I'm never going to have a job' reflects the strength of her attachment to the travelling lifestyle, however fraught with insecurity, difficulty and discomfort it may sometimes have been. Her assertion was quite different from Katy's fear (previous page) about not being able to find work. Both Katy and Gill were confronted with fictional 'choices', but in quite different ways. Furthermore the two 'choices' did not have the same status, and Gill's rejection of work was fraught with contradictions.

The development of flexible employment practices has been significant in the working experiences of young people and white and black working-class women. The Tory governments of the 1980s viewed the promotion of a flexible, efficient and competitive labour market as central to non-inflationary growth. In relation to business and industry, non-interventionist and voluntarist approaches to employment policies was the order of the day (Callender, 1996). Business responded by using a variety of strategies to rationalise costs, mainly through the workforce. These included reducing the core workforce and replacing them with part-time and temporary workers (Jenson *et al.*, 1988; Ashton *et al.*, 1990), which relieved employers of significant financial obligations such as sick and holiday pay. The introduction of new technologies, in particular microelectronics, in the pursuit of automated production was highly effective in downsizing work forces. Jenson maintains that working-class black and white women start at the bottom in low-paid, low-skilled jobs, many of which are the result of a deskilling reorganisation of the labour processes in workplaces:

> Cos our basic wages aren't very good, but we get commission on what we sell and we get like things now and again. Cos I've been there four years and I've never had a pay rise – I had one the first year. They're going to try and get us a pay rise this year (Kerry, 21, white working class).

Among our sample the overwhelming majority of working-class young women in paid employment were employed at the lower grades within their organisation, which is perhaps not that surprising, especially for the 16 year olds, given their relative youth and inexperience. What is more worrying is that half of this number could not expect to achieve a promotion, an increase in pay or an improvement in job security if they remained in their current post. '[Veterinary nursing] is not a very good job really, 'cos it's never much pay, and you can't really get very high with it' (Katy, 21, white working class).

Most of the working-class girls had relatively few academic qualifications and were in danger of becoming stuck in a 'job ghetto' (Hakim, 1996) of low-grade, low-paid work. Eleanor's situation most graphically portrays the kinds of effect, both material and emotional, that entering the labour market as an uncredentialled school-leaver can produce. Eleanor, a 16 year old white working-class girl, worked full time in a bakery and fast-food outlet earning £2.20 per hour with no formal employment contract and no pay for time off. 'And every Saturday at work, I work from 10 am till 6 pm, and they give me two hours' break and I go back at 8pm till 2 o'clock at night...' Her interview was peppered with references to work, but always in the context of how little she had been able to partake in previously enjoyed aspects of her life. In relation to seeing her friends, Eleanor said 'I haven't seen them for quite a while now, since I've been working, I haven't seen no one'. For many working-class people, paid labour remains an alienating experience that is something you do to pay for your 'real life'. Yet Eleanor's experience was producing a much darker, more despairing landscape in which, hope, one of the essential engines of life, seemed to have been lost: 'It's like when I have to, me having to work all those hours and everything. I think to myself "God, if I hadn't been born, then I wouldn't have to do all this", just, you know...'

Eleanor's response to her work environment seemed, in Baudrillard's (1988) terms, to be beyond alienation. Her despair was not mitigated by light at the end of the tunnel, for the only hope was to have been born a different person. For her the fault lay with her school, which had failed to give her the help she needed. She said that if she had got that help then 'I'd be doing something better with my life than working in a bloody bakery'. For Eleanor there was no possibility of reinvention. Psychically, she could not even sum up enough hope or fantasy to imagine her way out. People who cannot imagine things being different, cannot at least fantasise something else, cannot reinvent themselves. Eleanor never did get the help she needed at school. At least in her primary school, the resources available did not stretch to the psychological support she needed to cope with violence at home, the effect of which was to make her appear extremely vague in the classroom and unable to follow the simplest of instructions. It was clear from the interview with the 16 year old Eleanor that she was still preoccupied with violence. The implications of this story for those who are deemed to be members of the 'underclass' is instructive. Psychically, reinvention is far from an easy accomplishment.

Reskilling

New work identities emerged as the old trades, crafts and skills were lost during the running down and dismantling of Britain's manufacturing base. This decline of manufacturing undermined the traditional divisions between the non-manual, skilled and unskilled manual industrial labour associated with it. New technology resulted in the blurring of many traditional boundaries at work, with one person undertaking a variety of tasks where several would have been employed in the past. White-collar jobs, for instance, now demand a combination of sales, clerical and administrative skills. The great divide between mental and manual labour and between secondary and tertiary industries began to crumble with the use of flexible technologies.

The view that new skills are necessary for the transition to a modernised economy that relies on new technology is seen as particularly important for young people in Britain (Chisholm, 1993). But the very meaning of 'skill', once central to the notion of class and, importantly, the divisions within the labouring classes, has undergone profound changes. Skill is no longer related to manual crafts, but rather to a motley collection of practical abilities (keyboard skills, computer operation skills) as well as vague 'psychological' skills and aptitudes viewed as essential requirements for a whole range of service jobs where the relationship between service providers and their clients is formed increasingly through fierce market competition.

This change in how 'skill' is understood is especially important for women as they are viewed as possessing a higher 'natural' quotient of these skills – not only is the workforce becoming feminised but also the work they do. Some writers would argue that this reflects the growing recognition by organisations of women's adaptability, dexterity and skills (Wilkinson, 1994). These rather undefined 'social skills', which are 'transferable' and adaptable, are focused on and rely on an individualistic relationship between worker and company. For women in particular, it could be said that particular kinds of employment, particularly contemporary service work, require a particular kind of subject. Hothschild (1983, p. 37) refers to the increasing importance of emotional labour in work situations, where complex scripts governing interpersonal interactions have to be acquired. The policies and training programmes of organisations such as Mac-Donalds blur the boundaries between producer and consumer, and employees are instructed to treat every customer as an individual in sixty seconds or less (Leidner, 1993). Crucially however, this carrying over of the self seems to be a one-way process whereby an emphasis on such things as 'commitment' is not necessarily reflected in pay, status or conditions of work. All too often these discourses serve to obscure the intensely exploitative practices that persist in capitalist relations of labour and production, hiding their deeply classed and gendered inscription:

> I would get in [to the bank] at 8 o'clock in the morning, I wouldn't leave there till about 7 o'clock at night and, er, and it wasn't appreciated and in the end I just started doing my normal hours. I had enough. I wanted to leave there anyway. As soon as I started doing my normal hours they realised the work was piling up and they still tell me – they said well you've got to get this sorted out (Dawn, 21, mixed-race working class).

Optimists look to the opportunity to 'reskill' the entire workforce with the new 'conceptual skills' needed for computer-controlled technology. This reskilling requires a new system of mass education and training, which has been partly reflected since the early 1980s in the plethora of government training schemes for the mass of displaced manual workers and for those who had expected to enter industry upon leaving school. Since then, such training schemes have become crucial to understanding the school–work transition for working-class youth (Cohen, 1997). With very few jobs for young people and the systematic withdrawal of state benefits (Craig, 1991), 16 year olds have two official options: staying in full-time education or joining a training scheme. Young people have been fairly cynical about the advantages of youth training schemes and critical of both the content and the context of many schemes. It is interesting that only one of the young women in our study – Jacky, a white working-class 21 year old – had gone on a youth training scheme, but despite doing well during her work experience placement and being led to believe that there might be a paid position for her at the end of the training course, the company had let her go as soon as her placement ended: 'Because of the way I was treated on one of them, I wouldn't exactly advise anyone to go on them. It's good if you want to train or something. But if you're looking for a job, then it's not.' Even the Department for Education and Employment has found that youth training does not always improve the employment prospects of trainees, with only 56 per cent of former trainees still being in work six months after completing their training (DfEE, 1995).

There is a creeping assumption in the 're-skilling the workforce' arguments and in educational debates that we can all somehow do work that is 'clean' and interesting; a notion that if we open up higher education to working-class students we can all become professionals. This is the biggest fiction of all. Productive labour still occupies most of the population and technology has not become so sophisticated that flexible manufacture is the norm. There are still production lines, exploitative sweatshops, child labour and the regular flouting of a whole range of protective employment policies, such as the minimum wage, which is set so low that it does not constitute a living wage. It is also clear that the notion of permanent employment is a thing of the past, with those in employment often working only part-time or on short-term, insecure contracts:

> I'm looking to change jobs at the moment. What have they done? They've taken away a week's holiday and you've got to be off sick for a week before they give you any sick pay. There's all these cuts and whatever they're doing. And we had big rallies, whatever, a big demonstration outside the town hall. I nearly got arrested (Patsy, 21, white working class).

Our data certainly points to new divisions arising between the securely employed, multiskilled core of workers and the much larger periphery of insecure, semiskilled, part-time labour, to be used and discarded into habitual unemployment as required by the latest demands of production, although as stated before, women's participation in the economy since the early 1980s has had a permanence that was missing in previous eras.

The drive towards credentialism

As we shall explore in Chapter 6, the response of middle-class families to mass youth unemployment has been to lay greater and greater emphasis on the acquisition of academic qualifications, in order to ensure that their sons and daughters grab scarce places in what are seen as 'secure' professional jobs. We shall also explore how this emphasis on academic excellence is intimately tied up with the production and reproduction of the middle classes. In a climate in which the drive towards increased credentialism seems unstoppable, the idea that one can be credentialled enough, as a metaphor for being good enough, gets lost, opening up an emotional space where anxiety breeds. Although Samantha had just finished a degree in Art History she was planning to start a full-time course in journalism the following year because, as she said, 'I was quite keen to get another qualification after leaving university because obviously a degree isn't really enough'. In the meantime she was studying typing and shorthand in preparation for the journalism course, as well as working voluntarily at her local newspaper offices, all so that she would eventually be in a better position to get a permanent job.

In relation to the position of women in this changing educational and professional market, Barbara Ehrenreich, noting that previously only men had to scale the educational obstacles to a career in the professions, asserts that, 'today, almost no one gets in – male or female – without submitting to the same discipline and passing the same tests that were originally designed to exclude intruders from below' (Ehrenreich, 1990, p. 220):

> We'd be very happy if she'd finish the course, because you can always get work as a doctor, but it does mean going on doing more and more courses. You never really finish (Charlotte's mother, white middle class).

This kind of extended and ongoing commitment to education has major implications in terms of the nature and shape of working-class and middle-class young women's transition into the labour market. Very few working-class black and white families are in a position to meet the financial demands that such education requires.

Women at the 'top'

The 'feminisation of work' thesis presents problems but it also signals some important effects of the process by which women have entered the postwar labour market, especially since the 1960s and the onset of second-wave feminism. Since the early 1970s more and more girls have stayed on at school and gone on to further education to train for the expanding white-collar office-work sector. Some professions have opened up for the first time to middle-class girls, who can now join their brothers in higher education to train for such professions. By the mid 1980s just under half of all further and higher education students were female, and in the 1990s they became the majority (Ainley, 1993, p. 36).

Women may have increased their share of managerial and professional jobs (Callender, 1996) but relatively few have made it to the 'top jobs'. While one in four junior managers in Britain are women, they represent only 1–2 per cent (Summers, 1991) at senior management level. Women make up only 12 per cent of partners in law firms, 15 per cent of medical consultants (Hall, 1996) and 9 per cent of university professors or principal lecturers (Morley, 1999). So while women have had to work at least as hard as men to gain entry into previously male-dominated jobs, this does not necessarily herald a decline in occupational segregation (Rubery and Fagan, 1994). Mainstream media have a fondness for portraying the female worker of the 1990s as a 'self-assured, attractive, middle level manager, with two happy children (in school or day-care), a smooth-functioning household (thanks to all the new labour-saving household technology), and blessed with a supportive husband' (Bakker, 1988). The middle-class young women in the study, most of whom were, or would soon become highly qualified, were being trained to or had already entered professions where they could realistically expect to reach middle management level. In this respect they fitted the Cosmo image of the 1990s woman. But the majority could hardly expect to conform to the picture of glittering female success that the media likes to put forward, nor indeed would most of the middle-class girls' professional careers match the outstanding success of their educational careers (see Chapter 6). While organisations reproduce gendered power relations and prevailing notions of femininity, middle-class women still face vertical segregation in the professions (Cockburn, 1991; Hall, 1996).

Work and motherhood

As with social class, there is a desire to come up with one model that can explain and predict women's changing relationship to employment. But an adequate analysis must be multivariant in its composition to reflect the complex interrelationships and discourses within which women are located. We cannot hope to understand women's participation in the world of work in isolation from their social class, race, ethnicity and education, kinship and family structures, and, importantly, their relationship to childbearing and childrearing. Women's life courses are very different from those of men, and decisions about the gaining of qualifications, setting up an independent home, having children and taking care-breaks all have an immense and far-reaching impact on women's lives and the choices open to them in the future (Walby, 1997).

Within a popular 'women can have everything' discourse, what also gets lost are the emotional costs of combining caring for a family with a professional career. The majority of women leave their full-time jobs when they have children, but most return to part-time work. While the amount of time women take out to have their children has changed in recent years (McRae, 1991), childbirth is still associated with downward occupational mobility, especially when the mother returns to the same job but on a part-time basis. This was certainly the case for many of the mothers of the middle-class girls in the study, who had indeed left full-time professional work and returned to a lower-grade, often in a part-time capacity. Twenty years later it was likely that their daughters would face similar setbacks in their professional career trajectories. However, their high levels of educational credentials will make a significant difference to their return to the labour market.

In general, women with qualifications above A level are more likely to be in full-time work – 86 per cent compared with 50 per cent of unqualified women. But as labour market analysis shows, the effect of qualifications is most marked among women with pre-school-age children – only 27 per cent of unqualified women are economically active compared with 76 per cent of highly qualified women (Office for National Statistics, 1999).

Callender (1996) argues that an important factor in the expansion of the female workforce is the participation of women with young children, the majority of whom would previously have been full-time mothers and housewives. Marital status used to be the most important indicator of women's economic activity, but this is no longer the case. Responsibility for children under 16 is now the most significant determinant of whether or not and how much a woman works outside the home, especially the age of the youngest child, with the lowest rate for those with pre-school children and the highest for those with school-age children. At the same time the employment rates of all categories of women in the workforce are increasing, including mothers of young children. Lone mothers are the main exception to this, with significantly lower rates of employment compared with married or partnered mothers (Office for National Statistics, 1999).

It was during discussions of the future possibility of motherhood that an ambivalence towards the idea of investing wholeheartedly in a career emerged among some of the middle-class young women in our study:

> Um... [pause] well, I have got... there'd be quite a lot of time for me to have a job first. And I don't think I'd mind giving up my job to have children. I mean, you know, just for my own sake I'd want to do something, sort of a part-time job, but I wouldn't, I'm not really career orientated where I'd have to go back to my career at all (Samantha, 21, white middle class).

At least part of this uncertainty was closely connected to the young women's experience of their mothers being overworked because of the dual responsibilities of career and household. Quite simply, many of these young women did not want to have to work as hard as their mothers had done:

> I just remember, um, there was always a lot to do and it was always when mum was like, um, just fed up and didn't have much self-esteem, very low self-esteem (Liz, 21, white middle class).

> And she has, my Dad works really hard, he's quite a workaholic. Because he's such a perfectionist, everything has to be right, so he spends hours in the office and so my mother basically has to run the household and keep a job going and look after the children, all by herself. So that's quite stressful (Helen, 21, white middle class).

> Basically I think, it should be easier to have a baby and a career, and it basically is a bit hard to give up your career and have a baby and go back to it. Although it's possible, lots of people do it, but in the end it

shouldn't be quite so hard, it should be more equal role taking for men and women (Amanda, 21, white middle class).

Women in professional occupations have also seen an erosion of working conditions in recent years – although their salaries have stayed in line with living costs, they are generally expected to work longer hours and take more responsibility (Gee *et al.*, 1996). The contradictions this presents for middle-class women who want to have a family were summed up by Charlotte's mother (Charlotte was at medical school):

> all the women doctors I know feel guilty either because they're working and neglecting their families, or because they're not working and people say 'Well you've had all that money spent on your education and you're not using it.' So they live with guilt, one way or another.... I see people struggling and they don't do it. They get nannies and other people to do it for them.

As Charlotte's mother made clear, the choice is difficult and guilt-provoking. But it is also clear that some women, essentially professional middle-class women, can resolve such difficulties by employing other women, usually from the working class, to do their child-care for them, people such as Ruth, a black working-class girl who did extremely well at school and trained as a nursery nurse. But these working-class women are rarely in a position to pay for the sort of child-care they would like for their own children.

We shall explore in detail in Chapter 8 the young women's ideas about motherhood and how this might change their lives, but here it is important to consider why 'career' and 'motherhood' still do not fit together easily. In Chapter 5 we shall look closely at the enormous investment in the middle-class girls' education and their fear of downward mobility, reflected in fears of and fantasies about educational failure. Given the contradictions consistently produced by their 'femininity' in relation to work, how can these young women square the investment in their route to professional status with their desire for children? It was the middle-class mothers who most clearly articulated the difficulties these contradictions produced:

> You simply can't do all those things at the same time. Admittedly one or two women do, but the majority of women can't. So you've got to think in terms of having something that you can do, but different levels of intensity throughout your life really. I mean, I think the old idea of women just sort of stopping everything when they're married, and

spending the rest of their lives bringing up two children wasn't right either certainly. I think it's very good if women can get into something. But the idea that you can just carry on through your child rearing years almost as if they're not there, is obviously wrong [laughs]. Which you would need to do if you were going to get to the top in your particular profession (Samantha's mother, white middle class).

So I think that there's a right pattern that they should be supported during those years, but perhaps one doesn't get married, so you still need to support yourself then. Besides the heavy break up of marriage, there's also fathers do die, so it's important that if she needs to be able to support her family, then she can do so. And then there's the question of having something interesting and fulfilling to do academically. So there are several reasons for being able to support yourself, possibly your family, possibly part of the time, rather than being reliant on somebody else all the time (Charlotte's mother, white middle class).

The mothers' careers

The mothers' employment had involved many more shifts than was the case with the fathers over time. This was related to changes in the occupational structure, but also to social class. Like the middle-class fathers, the middle-class mothers' occupational mobility tended to be through promotion in professions in which they had qualified before having children, returning to those careers full-time as the children grew older. The majority of the middle-class mothers had careers in caring professions such as teaching, and all of these women had achieved promotion within these careers.

The expansion of the welfare state provided a big boost to women's employment, partly because of social policy on care for the elderly, children and the sick, which to some extent freed women to work outside the home. Paradoxically, because the expanded public sector provided much of this work, many women who were partially freed from caring in their homes took up 'caring' jobs. From 1960 onwards, jobs in the service and public sectors outstripped the manufacturing sector in number and economic importance (Gershuny and Miles, 1983).

Interestingly, in our study the main changes in mobility were found in the working-class mothers' occupations, with 10 (56 per cent) of them achieving occupational mobility in a different sphere from the one in which they had been employed when their daughters were six and ten, compared with four (27 per cent) of the middle-class women.

The working-class mothers' employment was overwhelmingly at the lower end of clerical work or as assistants to care professionals. However these moves, such as from a cleaner in a pub to physiotherapist's assistant, did represent a real improvement in working conditions for the women. Some of the working-class mothers had returned to college and upgraded their skills and qualifications as a strategy to get higher-paid work and work with better and more secure conditions of employment. Dawn's mother had been advised to do an NNEB course by the head teacher of the primary school where she worked as a classroom assistant, who had told her, 'You ought to go and get yourself qualified because later on in life when you want to earn some more money, you won't be able to because primary helpers won't get the choice'.

The fathers' career trajectories[4]

For the majority of the middle-class fathers, the expected trajectory of a career in 'the professions' had been fully realised, with promotion and/ or independent business ventures being achieved in their mid to late thirties. Eleven (73 per cent) of the middle-class fathers, all of whom had begun their professional careers in their early twenties, had achieved a significant degree of occupational mobility or promotion over the past 20 years. One had set up highly successful businesses in printing and publishing, others had been promoted to the senior ranks of the diplomatic and medical professions, and another had become a partner in a firm of solicitors. Two of the middle-class fathers' career paths were less clear; one had recently received a considerable inheritance and given up journalism to pursue his ambition to be an artist, the other (who came from a working-class family) had left the Greater London Council when it was dismantled in the early 1980s to set up his own small business, which had continued to provide a moderate income.

For the working-class fathers however, the picture was less uniform. Nine (53 per cent) of the working-class fathers had achieved some promotion in the same job, but as we discussed in Chapter 2 only one, Mr Green, could be described as having been successful in business. While none of the middle-class fathers had remained static at work (that is, stayed in the same position or job) three (18 per cent) of the working-class fathers had done so. Three (18 per cent) of the working-class fathers had become downwardly mobile, two (12 per cent) were unemployed and one had been medically retired in his late forties. Six (35 per cent) of the working-class fathers had experienced unemployment and/or redundancy while none of the middle-class fathers had done so.

Dreams of a working future

For the middle-class young women, their educational careers so far had been focused on their future working careers as professionals. They had a much more fixed idea of what a professional identity constituted and expected higher rewards in the world of work. It was unlikely that the majority of the working-class girls would have the same kind of financial reward, conditions and autonomy in their work, but this did not mean that they could not hope for a secure and interesting job. Jacky, who had been on a series of short-term, temporary clerical contracts but was unemployed at the time of the second interview, remained optimistic about her working future:

> My ideal job is something that I enjoy, definitely, with a good salary. I mean money isn't everything but it's just nice to have a – get on with life and that sort of thing. Some sort of job where I can get up the ladder (Jacky, 21, white working class).

Patsy was employed by her local council as a disability bus escort, but in the past, rather than sign on, she had worked as a cleaner for 25 hours a week, bringing home £55. Being a horse owner and horse lover however, her dream was one day to work with horses, perhaps even own her own stables. Patsy's fantasy for the future did not prevent her from being pragmatic about the present:

> Well I want to pass my driving test and then be one of the drivers for the council, and then in about a year's time I hope to pass my PSV, which is to drive the big blue buses about. Big 45 seaters and whatever. At the moment that's my aim. And when I've done that I don't know what I going to do, but I've given myself a year to do that (Patsy, 21, white working class).

Working-class Anna was an aspirational young mother who had had her daughter when she was 16 and left school, though not before doing well in her GCSEs. She was determined to improve her family's material circumstances and felt that she could work her way up to a job with intrinsic rewards in the catering trade:

> I manage a restaurant.... So it's a really good job and there's lots of rewards. Hopefully in about four or five years time I'll have my own

Beefeater, so it's very good, very good rewards. It's lot of hard work. Its long hours, like I go out the house at 9 o'clock in the morning and come home for a couple of hours in the afternoon and then don't come home till half past one in the morning. So it's a long day, but I love it, absolutely love it (Anna, 21, white working class).

In fact, by the time of the second interview Anna had had a change of heart about one day managing her own pub or restaurant. The demands of being assistant manager had proved too exhausting for her and she was unhappy about having to spend so much time away from her child and partner. Her comments reveal the downside of this kind of service work, which has so expanded in recent decades and occupies so many working-class women:

...and like the hours were ridiculous. Like sometimes I could do 16, 17 hours a day. . . . . I thought to myself well, it's a choice between either the Beefeater or John and Rosie really.

More usually however, and in contrast to the middle-class girls, who had constructed fairly rigid occupational routes through academic subject choice and exam success, those working-class girls who had not gone on to further or higher education tended to be more vague about the shape of their future:

I don't know what sort of job I'd have because at the moment jobs are so scarce, it could range from anything, apart from I wouldn't clean, because I do that at home and I'm fed up with it [laughs]. It wouldn't be – it could be a nine to five job, but it wouldn't be your normal nine to five pen pushing job. It wouldn't be that. Because I like to be out and about a bit more. It could be, because I do like my freedom (Jenny, 21, white working class).

And I don't really want to continue working in this field as a career. I want to do something either to do with – I want to do some voluntary work with animals. I want to do something that I really want to do, not something – at the moment I have to do what I'm doing. Although I do get benefits. But when I've actually done all my travelling and seen all I want to see, then I can leave the job I'm doing and do something I want to do (Kerry, 21, white working class).

I hope to [own my own house]. If I'm working I definitely will go for that. Because I mean it's cheaper than bloody renting anyway. It just seems daft. . . . I mean if I got a good enough job or good enough career and could move, in that way, then I would (Teresa, 21, white working class).

The middle-class girls were much clearer about their projected careers, the options open to them and the routes they could realistically take. This was especially so for those following professional vocational degrees in medicine and related fields such as pharmacy, where very clear training, registration and occupational 'ladders' are set out with options to specialise:

> Um I don't know. At the moment I – as well as you get more senior in pharmacy you can pick and choose where you go to, and the kind of thing you do, so because I've got like a rotational programme at the moment I've got a chance to see a bit more like what's on offer and then I can make a decision in a couple of years time about which way I want to go from there (Deborah, 21, white middle class).

For those middle-class girls who had done arts degrees the possibilities for work were far less defined and the girls tended to view their future as far more 'open'. Even so they expressed a clear expectation of finding work that was directly relevant to their training and appropriate to their level of education, and they stressed that they wanted 'fulfilling' and 'interesting' careers. It is important to remember that all but two of the middle-class girls had not had to think about their working future in such a concrete way before. This transition to the world of work had already been made by most of the working class girls who had left school by the age of 18, although for many of them it was partial and fragmented in the sense that it involved periods of part-time work, unemployment, a return to education and/or frequent jobs changes. For all but a tiny minority of the middle-class young women, their sights until that point had been firmly set on educational goals, but these had recently been or were about to be achieved:

> I mean I'd be quite happy doing anything that I sort of felt comfortable with and felt that I was, you know, reasonably good at I suppose. ... But unfortunately I'm not even quite sure what that is at the moment. Cos I mean up until now there's not, although I had year out after school I had something secure to do a year later, and so up until now you've always known basically what you were doing and had a sort of path to follow whereas now there's sort of sometimes this feeling there's this kind of endless stretch that you can sort of fill however you want. ... Sometimes it can seem quite an exciting thing and sometimes it's quite a daunting thing you know (Amanda, 21, white middle class).

> Just, I guess it's having a more a sort of wider outlook on things. In the sort of sense of a more, um – you know just being aware there's a

complete, there's a whole world, not just sort of getting out of Oxford, there's you know so many possibilities – or I feel there are (Naomi, 21, white middle class).

Conclusion

Everything is presented as a possibility today. But this also means that individuals are increasingly held accountable for their own fate (Giddens, 1991). The necessity for self-invention is imposed in extremely contradictory economic, social and individual landscapes, where everything is open to change but at the same time older patterns of gender practices remain firmly entrenched.

Of course the most obvious problems are to do with combining career with motherhood and creating a 'superwoman' who can do anything and has no choice but to do everything. This not only applies to the more glamorous stereotype of the powerful professional career woman. Most families in Britain are financially dependent on women's employment and most of this is part-time (Office for National Statistics, 1999). But something else is important here. The feminist discourses and economic necessity through which women as 'workers' have been constituted clash badly with other, older discourses that have powerfully formed feminine subjectivities. The expectation of and desire for independence can conflict with a deep-rooted desire to take time out to have children, to stay at home to rear them and to be 'looked after'.

It is interesting that in one discourse, class analysis, the importance of work in the formation of class identity and identities *per se* is being questioned, while in another, the feminisation of work discourse, the erosion of traditional male identities is very much on the agenda. Within this debate there is no questioning of the importance and impact of work on female subjectivities, while there is unquestioned acceptance that any changes in the male occupational structure will necessarily and without doubt have an impact on men's identity formation.

We do not want to present a completely bleak picture of the working-class families in our study and their relationship to work and education. There is no profit to be made by imagining that nothing had improved for them in the intervening twenty years, and indeed most viewed aspects of their material lives as having improved significantly. What we do want to explore, however, are the many contradictions that arose when attempting to map those changes in the lives of both middle-class and working-class people. Some things had not changed significantly for either class; inequality reigned with privilege and oppression persisting for the middle-class and working-class girls respectively. But there is more to the story of class than this; privilege is not a bed of roses for all middle-class girls, nor oppression a mire of hopeless despair for all working-class girls. What has impressed and intrigued us most is the ways in which people creatively live their lives – oppression, privilege, hope, despair and all.

Notes

1. Women involved in the domestic labour debate at that time (Seccombe, 1974) attempted to extend class theory in order to explain the oppression of women, with splits occurring over the question of whether the ultimate cause of gender inequality was capitalism or patriarchy.
2. See publications arising from the England and Wales Youth Cohort Study (Courtenay, 1988; Courtenay and McAleese, 1993.
3. One working class father had died some years before the last phase of the study, but prior to that his family had had no contact with him. These figures are based on 17 working-class fathers and 15 middle-class fathers.
4. See note 3.

Chapter 4

Working with Emotions

The transformations of class and labour in Britain have not only occurred at the economic level. As we argued in Chapter 1, social changes are crosscut by fiction and fantasy, which resonate and implicate subjects at the personal level. A central issue for us is what that actually means in terms of working with and attempting to understand the positioning of young women and their families. We are stressing the discursive constitution of the subjects in the new economy, but those discursive processes, those fictions in the Foucauldian sense, work in and through desires, anxieties, defences. In this chapter we want to explore our method of working with these issues as they arose in the interviews we conducted, and demonstrate what engagement with those processes has to tell us about the issues raised in the book. We shall be giving examples that both illustrate our method and make clearer why we think that working in this way is important and what might be gained from it.

Starting points

In an earlier phase of the work, Valerie and Helen, coming as they did from a different class position from the vast majority of middle-class observers, created a different discourse for reading both the working-class and the middle-class families than that which was usual (Walkerdine and Lucey, 1989). Working-class practices that in traditional discourses were routinely seen as evidence of a 'lack' or 'pathology' of some sort were seen as normal and understandable, while their non-recognition of middle-class practices allowed them to ask questions that were not normally posed. One of the issues raised by that earlier work was the anger felt by the authors about what was being viewed as pathology in working-class homes by middle-class observers who knew very little about working-class culture and practices.

Our class background has remained a central issue in this phase of the study. For example some of the middle-class girls initially evoked our envy, and through close examination of this feeling (which we describe below) we came to appreciate how contentious that envy was for us. What emerged was the extent to which this feeling was an expression of our own fears and fantasies that arose in relation to being successful. Using our own subjectivity and our experience of being envied by members of our own families was part of the process of understanding envy in a more useful way and being able to use it as a tool with which to examine the psychic aspects of the lives of the middle-class girls. We began to appreciate how, for the middle-class girls, living with privilege had its costs as well as its rewards: defending themselves against the envy of others was one of the psychic processes through which their classed and gendered subjectivity was formed.

During the collection and analysis of data in this latest phase of the research we had a number of starting points from which to develop our method of working. Firstly, research in the social sciences is overwhelmingly premised on the notion of a rational, calculating subject, but we wanted to posit a subject whose actions, behaviours and biographies are not solely determined by conscious will, agency or intent (or indeed the lack of these things). The subject of our discourse is altogether more irrational, anxious and 'defended' (Hollway and Jefferson, 1997). Following Freud and many others we embraced the idea that hidden aspects of human mental and emotional life are at play at the dynamic level of the unconscious. These unconscious processes, while remaining hidden, nevertheless profoundly influence and are intertwined with more conscious processes; not only individual and social ones, but also the very structures of collective human life – material and ideological institutions such as the state, education, the family and work; the organisation of biological processes such as motherhood; the lived experiences of class, race, femininity.

Discussions about methodology in the social sciences rest on the quest for the holy grail of the perfect method – a scientific method that will produce incorruptible data, uncontaminated by the research process itself. Our second point of departure opposes this position. We maintain that no matter how many methodological guarantees we try to put in place in an attempt to produce objectivity in research, the subjective always intrudes. Thirdly, we would assert that unconscious defence mechanisms such as projection, introjection and transference are all *relational* and *dynamic*. Despite violating the requirements of neutral observation (Kvale, 1999) they inevitably arise in the research interview, just as powerfully as in any other interaction. Put simply, in order to examine other people's unconscious processes you must be willing and able to engage with your own.

It is certainly not new for 'reflexivity' to be stressed in feminist research, and this is usually taken to mean reflecting upon, examining critically and exploring analytically the nature of the research process (Fonow and Cook, 1991; Ribbens and Edwards, 1998). Self-reflexivity has for some feminist researchers been an important part of the process of making visible the power of the researcher to interpret, represent and produce knowledge from the voices of her research subjects (Stanley and Wise, 1990; Reay, 1996). And yet, like most attempts to produce a solution, this strategy brings its own problems, not least of which is the risk of making the researcher's voice more central than that of the research subject (Wolf, 1996).

Aware of the potential dangers, we nevertheless wanted to use our own subjectivity in the research process, to regard it less as an intrusion than as a valuable aspect of our research data. But there are some important differences that we want to stress. Most qualitative research, including ethnographic research, is infused with a realism, with claims to an authenticity that purports to 'tell life as it really is'. Adding the researcher's voice in this case is designed to fill some of the absences that 'difference' produces in order to construct a more complete, more 'real' ethnographic picture. However, when attempting to take account of unconscious processes that are set in motion by all kinds of anxieties and fantasies, any notion of what constitutes the 'real' is seriously challenged. As Cohen (1999, p. 11) argues, 'the relation between the real and the imaginary is not fixed, but tactically determined. By the same token the imaginary is not a distorted reflection of the real, nor is the real simply a site for a projection of fantasy. We are always dealing with a process of *double inscription* whose articulation varies according to a range of social circumstances.'

Sociological fieldwork

In much of the literature on sociological fieldwork where the focus is on the interactional dimensions of the fieldwork encounter, relations between researcher and subject are examined through the effect of the researcher on the data gathering. In contrast to classical sociological research, existentialist sociologists recognise that fieldwork is not as rational as classical accounts depict and what appears as rational scientific action is in fact infiltrated with irrational feelings (Douglas and Johnson, 1997; Adler and Adler, 1987). However, although the existentialists recognise the importance of researcher subjectivity in fieldwork, the intrapsychic aspects are not considered.

The use of psychoanalytic concepts to theorise social phenomena and processes is growing in a number of disciplines. While the over-whelming majority of educational research is concerned with conscious processes, a growing and significant body of empirical work is concerned to explore the individual and institutional patterns of invest-ment and disavowal that enter into the formation of pedagogic identities (Shaw 1995; Britzman, 1995; Raphael Reed, 1995; Pitt, 1998). Oral historians have combined the techniques of life story research with insights from family therapy in order to explore the 'mixture of conscious and unconscious models, myths and material inheritance' (Bertaux and Thompson, 1993), which combine to shape individual and family narratives (Ginzburg, 1990; Thompson and Samuel, 1990). In the field of urban sociology and cultural geography, researchers and writers are drawing in particular on the work of the object relations theorists in order to explore the relationship between subjectivity, society and space (Pajaczkowska and Young, 1992; Rose, 1993; Pile 1996; Aitken, 1998; Cohen, 1999). In psychology, a number of researchers have begun to use psychoanalysis, for example Frosh (1999), Hollway, (1989) and Walkerdine (1996).

However, apart from a few notable exceptions (Kvale, 1999; Raphael Reed, 1999; Hollway and Jefferson, 2000), there is little sociological engagement with the intrapsychic dimensions of research methodologies. In the excellent volume *Psychoanalytic Aspects of Field-work* (1989), Jennifer Hunt examines the methodological implications of a psychoanalytic perspective for ethnographic fieldwork. She pays particular attention to the psychodynamic dimension of the re-search encounter, pointing to the issue of transference and counter-transference in fieldwork by examining the issue of projection of the subjects onto the researcher and *vice versa*. The essential aspect of using psychoanalysis as a research tool is that the researcher herself is the primary instrument of enquiry. This is in contrast to positivist research, which relies mostly on quantitative techniques and formal devices to study human and non-human phenomena. Using psycho-analytic techniques and theory in research involves the use of ideas that have been developed in the context of individual analysis and applied to something that is not taking place in the analytic context. Psychoanalysis, although a theory of the unconscious, has much to say about the conscious and rational aspects of our lives (Craib, 1989).

Psychoanalysis shows us the limitations of sociological and some forms of anthropological investigation. We are not arguing that sociology, psychology and anthropology should be reduced to psychoanalysis, but we are arguing that to get beyond conscious, rational explanations to a greater understanding of the influences and behaviour of our subjects, both the psychic and the social processes of how they have come about need to be investigated. In particular, we want to point to the debates within cultural and media studies in which psychoanalysis was first put forward as a theory of the subject and then discarded as too universalist and as not engaging with the specificity of the social practices through which people make their lives (see Cowie, 1997). While we would not dispute the undoubted and well-rehearsed problems with the universalism of psychoanalytic theory, we suggest that social and cultural analysis desperately needs an understanding of emotional processes, presented in a way that does not reduce the psychic to the social and cultural and *vice versa*, but recognises their imbrication. In light of this, we might mention that there is a postmodern turn in psychoanalysis that attempts to reinvent and transform the discipline. According to Elliot and Spezzano (1999, p. 28):

> The development of a postmodern orientation to psychoanalysis is intended to draw attention to the decline of traditionalist, modernist approaches to knowledge and experience. Such a decline, however, is not coterminous with its disintegration. On the contrary, we argue that what is emerging today is a kind of *psychoanalysis of psychoanalysis*: a running together of modernist and postmodernist psychoanalytical currents, the rediscovery or invention of psychoanalysis as a vibrant theory and practice, the sharpening and differentiation of models of mind, the restructuring of methodology, and the rethinking of interactional configurations in which the self is understood in relation to others.

They go on to argue three key points. Firstly, that the linear model of the subject is challenged by notions of multiplicity and· fracturing, notions which have had their effects felt in approaches to intersubjectivity that emphasises the link between unconscious desire and otherness. Secondly, while traditional psychoanalysis aims for the translation of unconscious fantasy into rational understanding, the postmodern version 'underscores the centrality of imagination, desire and affect' and intersubjectivity (ibid., p. 28). Thirdly, postmodern approaches critique the desire of psychoanalysis to be scientific and relate that critique to issues of epistemology and interpretation within the social and human sciences, aiming for a model of interpretation that is at once historical and personal. We would add to that: is at once social, cultural and psychic. Hence our attempt to produce a new methodological turn, one which recognises the critiques of psychoanalysis, of empirical work, of interpetation in the social sciences and tries to find a way forward. This is akin to the 'third space' that Cohen and Ainley (2000) characterise for youth research, in which the social, cultural and psychic are researched together and ways are found to develop methodologies that respond to the demand for inseparabilty at the level of explanation.

In a vain attempt to establish researcher objectivity it is common practice for anthropologists to record their fieldwork in the form of diaries and journals (Bohannon, 1954; Maybury-Lewis, 1965; Malinowski, 1967). However the separation between the objective and the subjective is problematic. For example Malinowski (1967) made racist remarks in his journals, though they were self-censored before publication. His followers were shocked when they later discovered his feelings and attitudes towards the indigenous people with whom he had been living. In an attempt to reproduce the myth of researcher objectivity it is common practice to separate the formal and subjective narratives of the research encounter (Van Maanen, 1988). Obviously there need to be boundaries between the researcher and the subject because doing social research is a very peculiar activity. Usually the researcher listens to a story or writes an account but has no place to intervene or do anything with the account except to produce an academic narrative. This can be both comforting and distressing to researcher and researched alike.

However, creating boundaries is quite different from being a detached observer. Detachment is often a form of defence. What are being defended against are intrusive feelings about the research process, the subjects, and the relationship between the two, including issues of transference and counter-transference (Walkerdine, 1997). We want to argue that transference, identification and fantasies do not disappear when we are engaged in 'rational' research, and indeed, as Elliot and Spezzano (1999) state, research as an activity of Cartesian rationality is itself to be critiqued. It is therefore crucial to acknowledge and attempt to understand what transference and counter-transference might be telling us as researchers. A psychoanalytic interpretation should be treated as a story amongst other stories. However the capacity to hear a story correctly requires the ability to pay attention to all aspects of one's experience (or counter-transferences). For the researcher actually to 'hear' what the interviewee is saying to her she needs to acknowledge her own fantasies. We hear what we expect to hear or feel comfortable with and screen out the rest. According to Moylan (1994), the ability of a mother to respond appropriately or otherwise to her baby's cries and to differentiate between a cry for food and an expression of loneliness is dependent on whether she is tired or preoccupied and able to contain the baby's distress. Similar processes operate in other situations, and if we pay attention to our thoughts and feelings during the research process we can often come to an understanding that might otherwise pass us by.

In an attempt to understand and overcome some of the complexities and difficulties of the research process and work towards an engagement with the unconscious, we will show how we applied psychoanalytic concepts such as transference, counter-transference, projection and projective identification to the collection and analysis of research data and, crucially, the relationship between the researcher and the subject. We will introduce our three levels of analysis, a method we developed using some of these theories. Through this we shall attempt to show that weaving psychoanalysis and autobiography into research and academic discourse through explicit investigation can lead not only to a richer narrative of the lives of our subjects, but also add crucial aspects to the understanding of classed subjectivities.

Defending against difficult feelings

Here we outline some of the concepts developed within varying strands of psychoanalysis that describe and analyse the ways in which subjects defend themselves against difficult emotions. But first of all it is useful to say something about how the 'anxiety' these difficult feelings may refer to and mobilise is understood. Classical sociological theory does not analyse the way in which anxiety circulates or the very powerful and material effectivities of that anxiety, though in recent times the importance of this has been recognised (Barbelet, 1998). In contrast, the concept of anxiety is central to psychoanalytic theorisations of the emotional development of the individual. Conceptualisations of anxiety are largely built around various forms of conflict. At the conscious level anxieties may be named and talked about. But at the level of the unconscious, rather than being 'out of sight, out of mind', anxieties continue to wield their considerable power beyond the rationalising influence of language. Object relations theorists such as Klein (1952) and Bion (1962) suggest that recognising that this is an *indwelling* fear makes sense of our constant striving but fundamental inability correctly to represent it. Hollway and Jefferson (1997, p. 55), in their work on fear of crime, note that 'The idea that anxiety leads to distortions and displacements demands a methodological strategy designed both to recognize and decode anxiety's many guises.'

Transference and counter-transference

Because of the complex nature of fieldwork and the fact that it does not take place in a clinical setting, transference and counter-transference are not literally translatable to the interaction between researcher and subject. However we have found the concepts immensely useful and in this chapter we shall explore how the transference and counter-transference of feelings had a significant impact on the way the participants in our study perceived, interpreted and influenced the research dynamic.

The concept of transference was developed by Freud in the analytic setting, where he discovered that patients unconsciously transferred other emotionally significant relationships onto the therapist. Freud (1905, p. 116) also theorised that many different kinds of earlier emotional experience were revived 'not as belonging to the past, but as applying to the physician at the present moment'. Freud believed every conflict had to be fought out in the sphere of transference, believing this to be an essential part of the therapeutic process.

In the clinical setting transference is generally defined as unconscious archaic images, usually from the patient's childhood, that the patient imposes on the analyst. Counter-transference can refer to an analyst's unconscious response to the patient or to significant people in the patient's life, or to the patient's transferences. In our setting, for instance, the interviewers were occasionally left feeling depressed after an interview even when the interviewees had presented themselves as happy, cheerful and always positive. These emotions, experienced as those of the researcher rather than the research subject, can be extremely helpful in pointing to and understanding what might not (indeed cannot) have been expressed by the subject. The fact that the researchers were all in personal analysis at the time of the research was helpful, as this gave them a heightened awareness of counter-transferences and personal conflicts.

Denial, splitting and projection

Central to our repertoire of psychic defences is denial. Denial involves a refusal to recognise or appreciate the inner significance of an experience, and like other unconscious processes it is linked to the management and regulation of anxiety. Perhaps the most poignant illustration of the power of denial came from Anna, who had hidden her pregnancy from her family for nine months. Denial, according to Klein (1946), is specifically involved in the 'manic defences, and particularly the denial of some part of the mind, or of psychic reality'. Denial is often followed by splitting and projection. This is where a person unconsciously splits off emotional material that is unacceptably anxiety-provoking, such as hate and destructiveness. By expelling these feelings from ourselves and projecting them onto someone else, we are able to deny that such feelings are inside us and instead assert that they belong to the other person.

What is stored in the unconscious is often painful and the individual sets up many defences to avoid feeling that pain. It is not surprising, then, that there is often resistance to accepting the existence of unconscious fears, fantasies and motivations. Also, our interviewees had parts of their lives that they understandably wanted to protect and hide from the prying gaze and questions of the interviewer, as well as from their own conscious awareness through defences such as denial, repression or rejection. During psychoanalytic treatment resistance refers to the opposition of the patient to making unconscious processes conscious. Freud used slips of the tongue and dreams as evidence of the existence of the unconscious. In retrospect it might have been helpful if the researchers had recorded their own dreams in a systematic way, and analysed their own and the subjects' jokes, slips of the tongue, parapraxes and so on as these could have provided important data in relation to unconscious fantasies in the research encounter that might ultimately have had a bearing on the activity of both researcher and subject. Thoughts that mean something at the conscious level may have a much deeper, possibly different or hidden meaning at the unconscious level.

It is through the mechanism of projective identification that one member of a family can become a kind of sponge for what may be seen as negative feelings of other family members. We frequently observed, for example, that when our subjects had siblings, either the subject or her sibling would be described as bright while the other was seen as less so, or that one might have been described as angry but the other as never angry. Consequently each person is described and related to with one or other of these characteristics being part of their identity. But as we shall go on to explain in our account of Angela's family, this is often an identity created for subjects by their families in order for the families to evacuate their own feelings onto another member, feelings that often stem from fear and a sense of inadequacy. And it is often the case that the person to whom these behaviours have been attributed also sees herself as this person and lives out the projection. What is crucial here is that these feelings and behaviours are as connected to the cultural and social as they are to the unconscious and psychological. So their subjectivity is full of complex contradictions that for many are terribly difficult and often painful to live with.

However any interpretation the researcher might make is very likely to meet with resistance. Where there is a lot of resistance the researcher needs to gather up all the evidence and make an interpretation later. But it is not just the interviewee who puts up resistance to difficult feelings. As we shall see with the examples of Anna and Mr Cole, it was the researcher who was trying to defend against difficult feelings. We also found that some of our subjects (mostly middle-class men) felt uncomfortable with the 'power' dynamics of the research encounter. It seemed that in some cases the researcher was perceived as having the more powerful role and the subject attempted to have an effect on the dynamic. In one instance a middle-class father who was financially and professionally very successful and spoke at length about his own religious interests wanted to know about the researcher's religious views. Another, an Asian middle-class father who was a highly educated professional, questioned Anjum Yazdani, the interviewer, about her family and her language, speaking to her in Urdu. It could be argued that they were both trying to establish a rapport, but this and cultural norms in the case of the Asian father notwithstanding, the regularity with which professional, middle-class fathers attempted to 'interview' the interviewer suggested that they were feeling vulnerable and their defence against this was to put themselves into a position that they perceived as more familiar, thereby reducing their vulnerability. A view that postulates that it is possible for researchers and subjects to be equal, becomes a fantasy. Looking at who reveals what to whom involves complicated plays of power.

Data-gathering technique

As a group we had worked for some years on the early data on the young women, listening to the taped interviews when the girls were four, six and ten and reading the transcripts many times. So it was with this background information that we came to interview the young women and their families. Each young woman was interviewed twice, one year apart, and the parents were also interviewed, separately when possible. Most of the interviews lasted between two and three hours and were based on a checklist of open-ended questions. After conducting a preliminary analysis of the first interviews and the video diaries (which are the focus of a second volume – Pini and Walkerdine, in preparation), the research team constructed questions for the second interviews. Here we aimed to explore some of the themes that had come up during the first interviews and in the video diaries, as well as things that seemed to be missing, such as topics that came up with the girls' parents or teachers that we felt needed further exploration, or omissions that we felt would be helpful to hear about in order to build up each girl's narrative.

Each young woman was assigned to a particular researcher for interviews and preliminary analysis, for example Anjum Yazdani interviewed three of the black and Asian 21 year olds. Further analysis was carried out by the entire research team over a period of several months. The interviews were recorded on audio tape. In addition the interviewer made written notes immediately after each interview. These notes not only recorded some of what the interviewer felt were the most pertinent points, but also the interviewer's feelings about the interview, its setting and evident omissions, such as things that were not said or were avoided. Although each interviewer tried to be as alive to these as she could at the time of the interview, it is our contention that because she was as unconsciously engaged in the interview as the subject, much of this may have been inaccessible to her at the time. It was through later listenings and readings of the interview, not only by the interviewer herself but also by other members of the research team, that the layered nature of the encounter became more visible.

We wanted to give the interviewees plenty of room to interpret our questions in whatever way they felt was important and appropriate for them. We used predominantly open-ended questions, which we hoped would enable us to hear the interviewees' narratives and understanding of what had happened to them during the ten years since the last phase of the research. Particularly useful for our method was our opening question, which was 'Can you tell me what has been happening for you in the last ten years?' We found that the most significant events were almost always spoken about first (cf. Sayers, 1995). Giving the interviewees the freedom to say whatever came to mind has similarities to the psychoanalytic method of free association. We wanted to elicit a narrative that was structured according to both the conscious and the unconscious, in which the associations were defined by emotional motivations. We hoped that this would give the subjects the freedom to express what was important to them and reduce the likelihood of their telling us what they felt we wanted to hear. Of course the context in which the interviews were set up, the expectations of the interviewees, the power-related dynamics of age, gender, race and class all had a conscious and unconscious bearing on both what was said and what was left out. However we were constantly impressed by the fact that what seemed to be the most important events were always talked about either directly or indirectly soon after the opening question. We avoided 'why' questions because they would invite or encourage what Hollway and Jefferson (2000) describe as 'intellectualising-type defences'.

Three levels of analysis

In this section we shall use a number of examples to help highlight the ways in which we attempted to develop and apply a framework of understanding that helped make sense of the sometimes puzzling narratives of various family members, and also to draw out the very real links between psychological, cultural and social processes that interacted in complicated ways through conscious and unconscious family processes. These were specific to class position and will be discussed from the perspective of class in Chapter 5. Interviewing a subject and other kinds of data gathering involved a dialogue that encompassed complex intrapsychic meanings from both the researcher and the subject: what psychoanalysts refer to as the 'inner world' of the researcher strongly influenced the whole research process. We needed to develop a way of understanding a large amount of complex, interview-based material. To assist us in this task we created a simple analytic framework comprising three levels of analysis. We used this framework not as a rigid formula, but as a reminder to ourselves to focus on things we might otherwise prefer to overlook or blur for reasons that the framework itself clarifies.

Angela was a middle-class, 21 year old high achiever who went to a prestigious private girls' school where she got 10 grade A GCSEs, and three As and one B at A level. She went on to Oxford to study medicine. Angela had a younger sister, Heather, who 'only' got eight GCSEs and two A levels (all at grades A to C). Heather was also a gifted musician and had won much praise for her musicianship. Although not as outstanding as Angela's, Heather's exam results had nevertheless placed her within the top 10 per cent of the 18 year old national cohort at that time. However, within the family the difference between the sisters was exaggerated into a huge gulf. Angela was seen as the success of the family, while Heather, despite her considerable achievements, was viewed as a 'failure' by her sister and both parents. They variously described her as 'not very bright', 'not very academic' and a 'slow learner'. She would not be going to university, even though her grades would allow her to, but to a catering college to do a diploma in hotel management. We learned from Angela's mother that Heather's identity as not very bright had germinated at the moment of her difficult birth. Her mother had carried extreme feelings of anxiety about Heather's intellect since that time, when she had been convinced that Heather had suffered brain damage through oxygen deprivation, though there was no medical evidence for this.

However the family narrative was very persuasive and June – who interviewed the family members – came away from the interview (at that point without knowledge of Heather's academic achievements) with the impression that Heather, whom she did not meet, was indeed an academic failure and possibly had learning difficulties. It was only when we analysed the data that the complexities in the family narrative were discovered. 'Triangulation' is a method developed within mainstream qualitative sociological research to deal with problems of validity (Denzin, 1978) and refers to the injunction to check pieces of information against at least one other independent source before regarding them as 'credible' (Lincoln and Guba, 1985). Using this method in the case of Heather and Angela, information on Heather's educational failure would have been amply 'triangulated' by the testimonies of three members of her family. This example helped us to point up the limitations of cultural and sociological concepts for understanding these interpretations, and this triggered our search for an alternative way of analysing and presenting our research.

Regardless of whether members of the same family can be regarded as independent sources of data for the purposes of arriving at some 'truth', we wanted to use the insights of post-structuralism and psycho-analysis to go beyond the mainstream notion of truth. The issue was not whether the statement 'Heather was slow' was true, but what that statement meant, and to whom.

Our starting point was an apparently unproblematic description by some family members of Angela as bright and Heather as slow. But to have taken this description at face value would have been to miss the complex dynamics that were going on, not only in this particular family but across the middle-class sample. For this family, as for many other middle-class families, there was a fear of failure, of falling off the middle-class conveyer belt. It was partly this fear that produced the 'Heather is slow' fiction: Angela's brightness was intricately linked to Heather's slowness. Of course it is crucial to acknowledge that, as we shall see in Chapter 7, in circles where only the top performance is considered good enough, Heather had indeed failed. The fiction, created out of the unconscious fears and fantasies of the family, thus became self-fulfilling.

Within our framework, at the first level of analysis – in common with much qualitative analysis (Strauss and Corbin, 1990; Silverman, 1993) – we looked at the face value of the individual narratives, first listening to them and later reading them to ascertain the overall plot, the 'story' that was being told, one containing events, characters and numerous sub-plots. Angela and Heather's case provided a stark example of how individual identities can be formed in relation to other family members. For this phenomenon we developed a second level of analysis that enabled us to problematise the family narrative through an exploration of the unconscious projections, introjections and transferences that were at play. At this level we paid close attention to words, images and metaphors; their occurrence and recurrence. Where in this narrative were there inconsistencies and contradictions; where did different parts of the narrative begin, stop, fade out, connect and disconnect; what were the omissions in the narrative and where were the silences; what tone and register of voice was used and how did this change? These are elements of what Brown and Gilligan (1992) refer to as the 'harmonics of relationship'. These observations prompted us to ask, 'Who is it that is speaking and who is being spoken to?' This was extremely important as it had implications for the identity of our subject, the family members and the relationships within the family and with others.

Let us return to the example of Angela and Heather. Although initially persuaded by the family narrative, June had a strong feeling that there was something wrong, that the narrative didn't quite fit. When the researchers felt anxiety, anger, annoyance, love, hate or

boredom they took these to be indicators of the presence of transference. These are the same clues that psychoanalysts use to help
themselves to recognise counter-transference in the analytic setting.
Briggs (1970, 1987) believes that feelings such as annoyance in a
fieldwork setting indicate a transference block that impedes empathy,
so she uses them as a research tool. In this case June felt very
uncomfortable and discussed her feelings with the team. Later, when
she reread her interview notes and listened to the taped interviews,
she decided to get a copy of Heather's exam results. These clearly
exposed as a fantasy the notion that Heather was an academic
failure. For all of the working-class girls in our sample, to get eight
GCSEs and two A levels Grades A–C would have been a cause for
celebration.

Questions of communication, of 'who is speaking and to whom',
cannot be fully answered without a detailed and thorough consideration of the unconscious dynamic between researcher and subject. It
was by moving to level three that we introduced the researcher as
subject to help us gain greater insight. Firstly, the interviewers paid
close attention to what they were feeling during the interview and
contemplated those feelings immediately afterwards in the writing up
of detailed fieldnotes. We asked, to which part or parts of me is the
subject speaking? Which part of me is responding? In other words,
who do I represent for the subject, and who do they represent for me?
Parent, sister, social worker, teacher, child? In the language of psychoanalysis, what transferences have taken place? It was by being aware of
and listening to the different parts of our own psyches, and to the place
in us that responded to a given message, that allowed us to tune into
the different meanings of our subjects. This gave us an important step
beyond Foucault's subjects as fictions. We could be discursively positioned as, say, social worker, but the defences and fantasies embedded
in that positioning were crucial to understanding the production of
subjectivities.

In relation to the Angela and Heather example, it was June's
relationship with her younger sister that helped us to explore the
research encounter at this level. In her fieldnotes she wrote:

> Although Angela and Heather come from an entirely different social class
> background from me there are very similar dynamics between the siblings.
> I, also the eldest was always seen as the clever one in the family, very much
> like my father, as Angela was described, and was always given the message
> that I could achieve whatever I set out to. Whereas my younger sister was

not seen as particularly bright and has spent most of her life feeling
inadequate especially in relation to her elder sister.

Although the circumstances of Angela's family and June's family were
quite different, there was enough in June's history for her to tune into
some of the fantasies described by the different members of Angela's
family. Of course what we tune into in our own histories may be a
projection onto the research subjects. This is where we need to check
out our own story and be aware of its place.

We were working on the premise that our experience of the dynamic
at that time could tell us something important about the persons'
relationship to the wider social world. So for instance, June's hunch
that there was something that didn't 'fit' in this family narrative threw
much light on other feelings that were coming up for all of the research
team in relation to the middle-class girls. Most importantly, it told us
something crucial about the seething anxieties that underpinned the
middle-class girls' success but also how this was masked by a hyper-
rationalism that would always construct and promote a rational
story.

It is important here to emphasise, through this example, the complete embeddedness of the social and the psychic. Within this and
other middle-class families there existed a particular understanding of
what constituted failure that was vastly different from the way success
and failure were judged by the working-class families. This understanding of failure nevertheless had its own 'real effects' (and affects),
producing 'objective' readings by which to understand performance
(on the surface), and at a much deeper level the subjectivity of family
members. In Chapter 5 we explore the ways in which an intense fear of
failure (of failing to reproduce oneself and one's children as bourgeois
professionals) operated to produce high levels of anxiety about educational attainment for many of the middle-class families. Heather's
'failure', then, was not only a projection by that particular family but
also an effect of the relationship between specific social and cultural
norms, discourses and family processes. This was neither a simply
social nor a simply psychic process but had to be understood as
working in a complex psychosocial manner.

One of the most important differences between the three levels
was the approach to perceived contradictions in the data. At level one
the emphasis was on 'mapping' the subject's narrative through plot,
sub-plot, chronology, place and event, as well as symbols, metaphors
and feeling. At level two the emphasis was on explaining any contra-

dictions in the account as an internal phenomenon of the person or family being studied. At level three the emphasis shifted to the question of why this apparent contradiction had been revealed to that researcher or research team. When a researcher in the social sciences interviews a teenage girl and her parents about such topics as education, class and pregnancy, the researcher is not simply presented with objective data, she is also presented with a number of narratives. These narratives are often emotionally charged, and always meaningful to the subjects.

In an attempt to move beyond both social and psychological determinisms to explain the nature of subjectivity, we took ideas from post-structuralism. This gave us the opportunity to see the experience of our subjects as a complex, usually contradictory mixture of unconscious desires, conscious rationalities within various available positions in a multiplicity of discourses. These discourses, in which the subjects positioned themselves in a particular relationship with the interviewer, existed at both the conscious and the unconscious level. The three levels of analysis helped us to explore and theorise responses that were not communicated in a singular or logically consistent way, as would be the case with the unitary rational subject assumed by traditional social science research.

From the following example we can see the way in which the research team worked with different interpretations of the same data and the ways in which these differences can raise difficult issues for the analysis and interpretation. However our aim should not be to reduce these differences in an attempt to find agreed meanings, but to make use of them to tell a more complex story, and to recognise that interpretive methods do not give greater proximity to the truth (Walkerdine, 1997). When June interviewed Jacky, a 21 year old working-class woman, June felt that the interview was a struggle, that Jacky wasn't 'giving' her much, and felt extremely irritated by this young woman. Margaret Lopez, our transcriber, talked about how angry she became with Jacky for feeling proud of 'pathetic achievements' such as passing her driving test, finding a boyfriend and getting a job. She couldn't wait to finish transcribing her tapes. Helen on the other hand liked Jacky, whom she thought 'was articulate and interesting and more giving than June had perceived'.

These very different interpretations of the same data can be traced back to the differing histories of the research team. This example shows us quite clearly the need for the researchers to be able to distinguish their material from that of the subject. When we analysed the responses of the research team it became clear that when Margaret was 21 her life had not been so different from Jacky's. June on the other hand saw Jacky's lack of vision and ambition and her minor achievements as being similar to her mother's and sister's, with whom she had difficult relations. Since her teenage years she had tried as much as she could to ensure that her life was as different from theirs as possible. This can be understood as a defence against a fear that they were too alike and that, like Erica Green, whom we met in Chapter 2, upward mobility had not completely erased the marks of working-class subjectivity. The transferences that took place during this interview made June aware of how afraid she was of ending up like them; their lives as she saw them had no sense of purpose or ambition, the very things that were both essential and crucial to her own identity. Deeply rooted conflicts about the researcher's sense of being were mobilised in this research encounter.

This example also shows the importance of acknowledging and examining our irrational feelings, which were clearly connected to the unconscious fantasies of the researchers. It allowed us, ironically, to be much more detached than we could possibly have been had we not been using psychoanalytic techniques. In fact the material might have been rather inconsequential if we had followed, for example, existentialist researchers who, although they acknowledge the role of irrational thoughts and feelings in fieldwork, avoid studying people about whom they experience deep conflict (Douglas, 1976; Adler and Adler, 1987). It needs to be emphasised that there were many disagreements about interpretation between members of the research team, and often a lot of discussion about our different responses and interpretations. This usually involved recognising aspects of our own subjectivity and the way in which our own histories influenced our interpretations. Thus unlike most other approaches we did not prioritise the pursuit of agreement amongst ourselves, because we were specifically interested in the interpretative processes through which a particular reading was made. It would have been a nonsense to stifle that aim simply for the sake of agreement.

By separating our projections and fantasies in a systematic way, the latest phase of our research enabled us to build upon earlier innovations (Walkerdine, 1991, 1997; Walkerdine and Lucey, 1989), taking the analysis further and deeper. We attempted to go beyond both classical and existential methods and used a psychoanalytic framework to explore some of the issues between the researcher and the subject and the implications of this for the production of knowledge, and then put this together with post-structural and cultural approaches. It was in this final stage of the research that we were able to bring some of these ideas together to analyse the data from within a psycho-social perspective.

Let us look at the case of Anna, a white, working-class 21 year old. Her mother had recently died of cancer; and she herself had had a baby whilst still at school, keeping her pregnancy hidden from everyone. Yet she responded to the first question – 'What has been happening in the last ten years?' – by shrugging her shoulders and saying that nothing significant had happened. After further questioning she rather tentatively started to talk about her daughter, who was now six, about her pregnancy, about taking her GCSEs two days after the birth and about the ups and downs of being a teenage mother. Only then did she rather matter-of-factly mention her mother's very recent death. In the second interview she was able to talk more freely about this extremely significant bereavement. June was amazed by Anna's story and her ability to keep her pregnancy a secret from everyone. She was also impressed by her incredible determination to make a success of her life (this was also the case for all of the young women who had children).

Anna's initial response could be seen as a defence against deep anxieties, which it was important for the interviewer to recognise and to judge whether or not they might be talked about in that or subsequent interviews. It seemed clear to June that Anna did not want to discuss her mother's death at that time. What was overlooked in this interpretation however, was that June's father was also dying of cancer. Furthermore June was obviously pregnant at the time and Anna talked quite a lot about her own pregnancy and her daughter as a baby. While Anna's reluctance to speak on the subject of her mother's death seemed at the time to be a manifestation of her defences against the pain of loss, it was also possible that June was unconsciously contributing to this silence because a part of her did not want to hear this painful story. At that particular time and in that particular context, pregnancy and motherhood was a subject that did not provoke such defences for either Anna or June, and it was on this basis that an empathic rapport was established between them.

Conversely the interviewer's defence mechanisms sometimes meant that they changed the subject or pushed the interviewee in another direction when what they heard was too uncomfortable for them to deal with. Consider the following example, in which Helen interviewed Mr Cole, Sharon's father. Mr Cole was so angry with his eldest son (or rather, as it transpired during the interview, his step-son) that when the

latter stole jewellery and money from Mrs Cole, Mr Cole threw him out
of the house. Mr Cole's feeling of betrayal went deep, as did his
reluctance to forgive his step-son. He said 'you can trust a thief, but
not a liar. As far as the family is concerned the boy doesn't exist.' Of
course the boy's existence was living proof for Mr Cole that his wife
had not always been with him, something that intruded into the family
dynamic. Treating him as if he didn't exist may have been a relief for
Mr Cole, defending against difficult emotions such as jealousy that he
would rather not have felt. During the early part of the interview Helen
felt that she had to struggle to get any rapport with him. Indeed
Helen's consistent impression of the whole interview, at the time and
throughout subsequent case discussions, was that Mr Cole resisted
going into any detail about what had happened with this son. It was
during one of the case discussions that it was noticed that Mr Cole had
asked Helen whether she had any brothers or sisters. This question
proved to be a crucial moment in the interview, because it was clear
that when she replied that she was one of eight children (he was one of
seven) his attitude changed noticeably and he became much more
forthcoming about his relationship with his step-son.

However at that point Helen suddenly stopped Mr Cole in his
tracks and changed the subject! How do we make sense of this
interaction? It is important to note that establishing rapport in
this particular interview was very important, as Helen had literally
had the Coles' door shut in her face, and when she was finally let
into the house by Mrs Cole she was left standing in the hallway while
they sat in the living room and ignored her. She felt extremely uncomfortable and was very pleased that he said anything at all at the
beginning. She wanted to answer his questions and wanted him to be
able to identify with and feel safe with her. Analysis of the transcript
shows that it was his knowledge of her as coming from a large family
that allowed him to project some of his own fantasies onto her and
make her a 'safe' person to whom he could reveal some of his history.
Simultaneously, however, events within her own family that resonated
strongly with what Mr Cole was telling her meant that she actually
didn't want to hear any more of his painful story and changed the
subject.

In this scenario, what can be seen as counter-transference was
the shift from not revealing things about herself and being an anon-
ymous interviewer to the temporary loss of her identity as a researcher.
What seemed to happen was that having slipped into a temporary
identification with the Cole family, she suddenly felt very uncomfort-

able and reacted by abruptly breaking the rapport. The fact that she didn't want to continue the conversation suggests that counter-transference took place and this family now represented someone else for her. It was difficult for her to keep the Cole and Lucey families separate. It was because it leapt over the boundary for her that it became uncomfortable. In an attempt to move away from these difficult feelings and to hold onto her researcher role she changed the subject. This is a very good example of the way in which an interviewer is different from a therapist. Psychoanalytic psychotherapists are trained not to reveal any aspect of their personal life to a patient, as this would interfere with the psychoanalytic process.

It was clear that the issues around surveillance and intrusion from outside that were current for the Cole family when Sharon was six were still there ten years later. But as the above example clearly shows, conscious and unconscious motivations were also in powerful play for the researcher. After many discussions about the data, Helen started to understand some of her own unconscious patterns, which became very apparent in this particular interview and was present in others. Because of some of the painful things that had happened to her family, she felt very uncomfortable when invited to discuss them by 'outsiders', and wanted to relieve her anxiety and pain by changing the subject. It was only after many months of interrogation and debate between the research team that this emerged. Ironically, while this particular interaction created more empathy between the interviewer and interviewee, psychically all Helen wanted to do was get out of the door that had previously been shut in her face.

Contrast Mr and Mrs Cole, who initially treated Helen as if she were a welfare agency 'snooper', with Mrs Falmer, a professional middle-class mother who treated June as if she were a counsellor. These transferences suggest that subjects from different social classes tended to present themselves differently in research settings, which significantly influenced the way the researchers viewed the differences between the social classes. While the most important and often most traumatic events were almost always the first to be revealed, such events were often played down or maybe not acknowledged as being particularly significant for the subject. It was only during the course of the interview or the analysis that the significance became apparent. Mrs Falmer, a middle-class mother, was very friendly towards June, served cake and tea before the interview and spoke freely about the Christmas holidays. But as soon as the interview began and she was asked about the last ten years she immediately burst into tears and said the questions were too difficult and she wasn't sure if she could continue with the interview. This took June by surprise as it was in complete contrast to the organised woman with whom she had just been drinking tea. After about ten minutes Mrs Falmer said she felt better and the interview continued. This was the first time the researcher had been in such a situation, she felt uncomfortable and wondered what was the best way to proceed. As she had only just met Mrs Falmer she didn't feel able to put her arm around her shoulder, and struggled to find words of comfort. In her fieldnotes she wrote:

> I didn't know Mrs Falmer, I could only guess what was causing her so much pain. I had previously interviewed her ex partner and father of her daughter so I knew that they had separated, although I had understood that it was at her instigation. I felt that her tears were something to do with that. [This was later confirmed.] I felt that if she needs to cry at this time that was okay. Her tears were very powerful I felt it was probably a good thing that she was able to express them. However, my overriding concern was fear that she wouldn't continue the interview, that I would be rejected, asked to leave the house and fail to get what felt like a very important interview.

Thinking about how to respond to this question proved to be a powerful cathartic process for this mother. Her 16-year relationship with Hannah's father had ended within the last year. She was finding this very difficult but had not allowed herself to feel the pain of the separation until that moment. As a successful professional woman who always had to keep up appearances and in some ways keep people at an emotional distance, including her daughter, she was not used to talking about herself. The more she talked about their relationship, the easier she seemed to find it and the more relaxed she became. At the end of the interview she thanked the interviewer for listening to her and said she felt 'much better'. Soon after she wrote to the interviewer apologising for her 'outburst'.

This is a good example of the researcher 'containing' the interviewee (Bion, 1967). To understand the notion of containment, Shelley Day Sclater's (1997) work is useful. She uses the language of object relations theory to talk about the emotional dynamics of the research process in order to understand the intersubjective production of subjectivity. In a dynamic container–contained relationship between, for example, a researcher and a subject, the concept allows the researcher, through feelings of empathy, to transform an unbearable feeling into something that is bearable and helps the subject make sense of her experience.

If we look again at the interview with Mrs Falmer, but this time put the analytical spotlight on the researcher who carried out the interview, additional insights can be gained. In this case the researcher felt trapped between being an 'observer' and not getting involved and wanting to comfort and reassure Mrs Falmer. But she was also worried that the interview might be abandoned and was relieved that Mrs Falmer wanted to carry on, relieved that she was accepted as someone who would be 'safe' to cry in front of. In order to interpret these feelings, we need to make some connections with the subjectivity of the researcher. At that time the researcher was taking steps to begin psychotherapy training and fairly spontaneously took up the role of therapist, not saying too much, giving Mrs Falmer space to cry. If we look at it from Mrs Falmer's perspective, unconsciously positioning the researcher as counsellor or therapist rather than researcher might have meant that crying in front of her was not such a bad thing to do. What was unbearable for Mrs Falmer was projected out and made bearable by an empathic researcher. Retrospectively, Mrs Falmer saw the event more in terms of therapy than as a research encounter. Perhaps she picked up (on some level) that the researcher had a leaning towards therapy and it was therefore both less embarrassing and safer to tell herself that June was a therapist. This was highlighted in the letter she sent to June a few days after the interview, in which she apologised for her outburst.

We can see that the researcher managed to hold the boundaries and maintain a high level of her own counter-transferences. Although she had the gratification of being put into this role she did not act it out. However she was very worried that things might become more difficult for Mrs Falmer after the interview and that a 'can of worms' had been opened for which she would be partly responsible. In this instance June imagined herself into the role of therapist. In her fieldnotes she wrote 'I imagined that having a good cry was what she needed, that it was good for her and was probably healing in some way.' The researcher could then feel some gratification about having something to do with this process, as well as having her fantasy of being a therapist partially fulfilled. In this sense, then, we can understand that the positions of, for example, 'benefits officer' or 'counsellor/therapist' are both created in discourse and work because the fantasy life of the subjects, researcher and researched, allows them to be mobilised as ways of coping with the encounter and defending against difficult feelings.

Ambivalence and unconscious processes

Social science research in general is premised on the notion of a rational, risk-avoiding subject, most of which is conducted within a cognitive or constructivist framework. However, as we shall explore in Chapters 5, 6 and 8, for many working-class young women there is much ambivalence about succeeding. Sharon Cole, whom we met in Chapter 2, expressed a strong commitment to her college course and aspired to become a lawyer. She also told the researcher that she regularly had sexual intercourse but did not use contraceptives, so the chance of her becoming pregnant fairly soon was high. Her parents said that if she got pregnant they would support her, although this was not what they wanted for her, or so they said. The anxiety and fear of both the parents and the daughter which the possibility of the daughter's success aroused, gave rise not to a conscious and active rejection of education, far from it. Instead, these anxieties provoked an immense ambivalence towards educational success, so that all three parties, whilst stating very positive feelings about Sharon's educational future, at the same time unconsciously desired her to become pregnant (we shall explore this example in detail in Chapter 8). As with the middle-class young women who wanted to stay middle-class, there was enormous fear among the working-class girls and their families of being uprooted, of the successful working-class girls leaving their home and family to enter the unknown middle-class world, a world that was alien to many of the working-class families. Hence the enormous ambivalence about success (See Chapters 6 and 8 for a detailed discussion).

Towards a new analysis

We want to point to the epistemological relevance and importance of subjectivity in the research process. We are not attempting to describe events as we consciously heard and saw them but to go beyond this to what lay beneath. Liz Stanley (1993) points out that description is a gloss that constructs a point of view. We realised that we needed an interpretive method that looked beyond the 'face value' account, a method that would allow us to identify the significant pieces of narrative as well as taking into account any avoidances or omissions. In addition we felt that the discursive and post-structuralist approaches offered no way of understanding how the subjects lived the contradictions of positioning, the demands of imposed fictions or the exigencies of everyday life. It is not without significance that the authors have all experienced psychoanalytic psychotherapy and were having therapy throughout the period of this research. This was extremely important for us in that, because the practice of psychotherapy is primarily concerned with bringing the analysand's unconscious mechanisms and processes to the surface and making them conscious, it gave us a discourse and practice in which to examine and record our feelings in a particular way. This kind of work requires training like any other methodology, so there is indeed an argument to be made for a form of training. Though extremely helpful for us, we cannot say categorically that a researcher would have to be in therapy herself for this method to be effective. What it requires above all is a willingness to engage (way beyond the point of 'comfort') in what are sometimes very difficult emotions.

Although in previous research we looked at the emotional relationships between mothers and daughters, we did so in a way that missed the richness of the social and psychic processes that we are now able to talk about. It has been important to construct narratives of working- and middle-class family dynamics and the relationship with educational achievement. In relation to our method, it has been important to be aware of the different levels through which we all operate. In some of the examples we have used these levels have been drawn out explicitly. In others they have been more implicit. However the point is not that the levels exist, but how we make ourselves aware of our own subjective engagement in any given example. It is because of our difference, of our different subjectivities, that particular examples connect to us as researchers. The richer in experience the researchers' lives have been, the more potential points of contact there are with their subjects, giving extra dimensions to the research. The challenge for those who talk about gender and class is being aware of the emotional dynamics within their own lives and finding some way of accounting for themselves, for their own subjective position. In the next chapter we shall explore the educational attainment of the young women in our study in the light of our research when these 21 year olds were four.

Chapter 5

Class and Educational Success

In this chapter we discuss the enduring importance of class in understanding the educational trajectories and life chances of young women. We shall briefly review the educational performance of the young women in our study and then look back at our earlier analysis of middle- and working-class mothering practices and the preparation of four-year-old girls for different modes of subjectivity. We shall then explore the ways in which a complex emotionality is bound up in the depiction of working- and middle-class girls as successful or failures. The ability to turn emotionality into rational discourse was, as we shall see, one of the factors in the success of the middle-class girls. On the other hand, for some of the working-class girls, emotional problems were usually interpreted as signs of lack of ability. In the case studies we present here, we show how emotional issues and problems, differently read and discursively constituted, were produced quite differently as an aspect of working-class failure and middle-class success, even though there was no less anxiety among the middle-than among the working-class girls. For the working-class girls, little was allowed to interfere with a designation of lack of ability, whereas the opposite was the case for the middle-class girls.

When the 21 year old group were four years old, each working-class girl was paired with a middle-class girl at the same nursery school. By the age of 10 only one of the original pairs, Julie and Patsy, remained in the same junior school. Five of the middle-class girls now attended fee-paying preparatory schools belonging to the Girls' Public Day School Trust, with the majority of the middle-class girls being in private schools from the age of eleven. By that point, the performance of the two groups had diverged significantly, with the performance of the top children in predominantly working-class schools being worse than the poorest in predominantly middle-class schools.

As table 5.1 shows, the majority of the working-class girls attended local authority comprehensives and the majority of the middle-class girls attended independent selective schools. This table also highlights how recent changes in the funding and financial management of schools has led to diversification in the comprehensive system. While a number of both middle- and working-class girls attended LEA-maintained, grant-maintained or voluntary aided comprehensives, we need to be aware of the anomalies and differences within the comprehensive system in order to make sense of parents' choice of secondary schooling and the comparative performance of middle-and working-class girls in state and 'opted out' comprehensives.

The schools that had chosen to become grant maintained or voluntary aided tended to be former grammar schools that had placed considerable emphasis on high academic attainment. The Catholic schools in the sample had also taken these options. The Catholic girls who attended them did well, but the non-Catholics did poorly. Importantly, the middle- and working-class girls attending grant maintained or voluntary comprehensive schools tended to attain higher GCSE and A level results than those in LEA-maintained schools. These schools were more selective in their entry requirements, as were a small number of LEA-maintained schools, which were prepared to take pupils from outside their catchment area if they had been designated as Band 1 pupils and showed particular aptitude for a subject the school specialised in. For instance Hannah, a middle-class 16 year old, travelled a considerable distance to attend an LEA-maintained comprehensive. This school had a highly reputable music department and for that reason the school attracted a significant number of middle-class pupils, who tended to do well in all examinations. Conversely, a minority of working-class girls who had attended LEA-maintained schools that performed relatively poorly in terms of national comparison, themselves achieved well by the same

Table 5.1 Type of school attended (per cent)

Type of school attended	Working class	Middle class
LEA comprehensive co-ed	61	27
LEA comprehensive or secondary modern for girls	11	7
Grant or voluntary aided comprehensive for girls	11	7
Grant or voluntary aided comprehensive co-ed	17	0
Independent selective school for girls	0	53
Independent selective co-ed	0	7

comparison. Overall the girls who attended independent schools held the top 12 positions in our sample in terms of performance at GCSE and A level. By the time of the study the trajectories and life paths of the two groups had diverged even further, as we can see from Tables 5.2.

Table 5.2   Participation in further and higher education by class

Level of education	Working class (%)	(No.)	Middle class (%)	(No.)
In or completed higher education	22	(4)	93	(14)
In or completed further education	28	(5)	0	(0)
Abandoned further education	6	(1)	0	(0)
Left education at 16 and has not returned yet	44	(8)	7	(1)
Total	100	(18)	100	(15)

Table 5.3   Qualifications of 21 year olds

Qualification	Working class (%)	(No.)	Middle class (%)	(No.)
Graduate	6	(1)	13	(2)
Undergraduate	11	(2)	67	(10)
Higher National Certificate	6	(1)	0	(0)
4 A levels	0	(0)	27	(4)
3 A levels	17	(3)	47	(7)
2 A levels	6	(1)	0	(0)
1 A level	6	(1)	0	(0)
Studying 2 A levels	6	(1)	0	(0)
Studying BTEC	6	(1)	0	(0)
BTEC	0	(0)	7	(1)
5 + GCSEs grades A–C	44	(8)	73	(11)
5 + GCSEs grades A–G	17	(3)	7	(1)
1 + GCSEs grades A–G	6	(1)	7	(1)

There was a uniformity of educational achievement among the middle-class sample while the working-class sample were far more diversified in terms of educational routes and performance. The performance of even the 'good' working-class girls at primary school and later at 16 and 21 simply was not of the same order of that of the middle-class girls. In the mid 1990s the debate on gendered

Table 5.4   Qualifications of 16 year olds

| | Working class | | Middle class | |
Qualification	(%)	(No.)	(%)	(No.)
Studying 3 A levels	0	(0)	100	(2)
BTEC	50	(3)	0	(0)
5 + GCSEs grades A–C	33	(2)	100	(2)
5 + GCSEs grades A–G	33	(2)	0	(0)
1 + GCSEs grades A–G	17	(1)	0	(0)
No qualifications	17	(1)	0	(0)

achievement shifted dramatically, with concern moving from the relative underachievement of girls to the low performance of boys in a context in which girls were now viewed as doing very well (Sammons, 1995; Epstein *et al.*, 1998). However the notion that all boys are now failing and all girls succeeding has served to mask deep and enduring class differences between boys and girls (Lucey and Walkerdine, 1999). Much research demonstrates that social class inequalities in education remain substantial and persistent, not only in Britain (Reid, 1994; Smith and Noble, 1995) but also across Europe (Muller and Karle, 1993; Shavit and Blossfeld, 1993). We found it striking and shocking that while all but one of the middle-class girls had completed their further education and gone on to higher education, few of the working-class girls had even approached it. How was it that such a homogeneity of success was achieved by one group, while the other took such diverse routes and most, but not all, had a comparatively poor educational record, especially as higher education had supposedly been opened up to make it more accessible to young working-class women (Ainley, 1993; Smithers and Robinson, 1995)? What were the technologies of institutional, cultural, family and individual regulation within and through which the girls, their families and schools were produced?

Just how might we understand the history of what happened to these two groups of girls? Is it possible to shed any light on the production of this distressing separation of the two groups? We shall begin by looking back at our earlier analysis of the data produced when the girls were four, as part of the book *Democracy in the Kitchen* (Walkerdine and Lucey, 1989).

Arguments about class and educational success have been somewhat muted in recent years. Indeed, such has been the interest in gender and attainment that it has overshadowed the former interest in class. That girls do well at school has recently been interpreted as a problem for boys, in particular working-class boys (Epstein *et al.*, 1998). However, of course, just as it always has been, girls' academic performance is cross-cut by class. The resounding success by girls that has been spoken of in recent years is primarily about middle-class girls and it has set in train a debate about a crisis of masculinity in post-industrial or deindustrialised societies. The effect of this on boys and men has been dramatic. It was formerly relatively easy for boys to obtain employment that did not require high levels of literacy, a particular accent, articulacy or stylish attractiveness, as the comments by the fathers in Chapter 2 made clear. (It was women who were previously employed in the service sector who came to require those things). However, far fewer of those kinds of jobs exist in affluent countries and so boys are now being pushed to remake themselves as literate, adaptable and presentable: it is this that has produced a crisis for 'working-class masculinity' and it is this that sets girls' educational achievement as a particular problem in the present.

In recent press reports the problem of low-achieving boys has been highlighted, but these boys are almost exclusively from economically disadvantaged communities, both black and white. It is as though the success of girls has somehow been responsible for the dramatic and distressing changes that have happened over the last twenty or so years. Yet, as we shall see, what is being overlooked here is that by no means all girls are doing well, though it would be difficult to guess this from the sensationalist headlines.[1] Indeed when the attainment figures are checked carefully it becomes clear that what is described as girls' high performance is in fact mostly the high performance of girls in 'middle-class' schools. In other words, then, what this debate is obscuring is that high attainment is still, as it ever was, a class-related phenomenon, even if that class attainment is cross-cut by gender (Smith and Noble, 1995; Plummer, 1998).

It is indeed the case that girls from professional, managerial and wealthy families are now performing very well at school, and in fact are going on in large numbers to do well at university and enter the professions. In that sense something has changed, but on the one hand it can hardly be the case that these girls are taking jobs from low-achieving boys, nor is it the case that all girls do well. As our research makes abundantly clear, there is still a huge class divide in attainment in Britain. What is clear, then, is that previous studies concentrated very strongly on the classed attainment of boys and rarely considered middle- and working-class girls (see Delamont, 1989, for an overview). However things have changed. Young women no longer rush to get married and settle down in their early twenties, forsaking career for the role of wife and mother. What has been the place of their preparation as subjects for the womanhood that awaits them?

The girls at four

When Barbara Tizard and Martin Hughes carried out the research that led to the publication of *Young Children Learning* (1984) they were particularly interested in demonstrating that working-class children were not linguistically deprived and that mothers provided a rich linguistic environment. While they did indeed demonstrate this effectively in relation to the mother–daughter pairs they studied, they also demonstrated that the nursery schools the little girls attended did not greatly enhance the language of the working-class girls, but attended more to the interactive style of the middle-class girls, which was more assertive. They wanted to argue against a theory of linguistic deprivation that had at its heart the idea that working-class children failed at school because of some fault in the linguistic practices of mothering. While agreeing with their argument about deprivation, in *Democracy in the Kitchen* (Walkerdine and Lucey, 1989) we argue that by ignoring the fact that their sample was composed of girls, Tizard and Hughes failed to examine aspects of gender and the classed work of mothering. If it is mothers who are supposed to prepare their daughters for school, what exactly are they supposed to do and how are they to do it? In *Democracy in the Kitchen* we discuss the classed nature of the regulation of the practices of mothering and the way in which this produces differences in the socialisation patterns of daughters. It is these arguments that we shall now review.

Sensitive mothers

Tizard and Hughes (1984) set some store by the idea that those mothers who are most sensitive to their daughters' emotional and physical needs will also be most sensitive to their linguistic needs, producing more advanced language and consequently intellectual development. This is in line with developmental models that mix together the psychodynamic work of John Bowlby (1984) and accounts of linguistic development that stress the intersubjective production of meaning, in which the mother provides a scaffold for the child's tentative meanings (see Walkerdine and Lucey, 1989, for a full discussion). Although Tizard and Hughes do not explicitly state that sensitive mothers produce children who perform well at school, the implication is there in the theoretical framework to which they refer. That is, that mothering is a natural process, through which child development is achieved, either normally, progressing towards rationality and achievement of academic success, or through the production of the bourgeois individual. We have discussed this at great length in *Democracy in the Kitchen* and this is not the place to rehearse the entire argument. We argue that it is women's domestic labour that produces what counts as natural and normal development and that women have been regulated very strongly as mothers, having the responsibility to produce normality, correct development and educational success.

Texts on education are constantly full of the need to make parents (read mothers, *pace* David *et al.*, 1993) responsible for getting it right for their children from infancy onwards. Women therefore bear an incredible burden and responsibility and we argue that it is middle-class women who are understood as the purveyors of normality and have to be strictly regulated, and indeed to regulate themselves through what counts as love and guilt (after all, who would want their child to grow up 'abnormal' or 'disadvantaged'?). By contrast working-class women demonstrate a number of tendencies in their child-rearing practices that are considered abnormal. This means that they have to be policed by educational, social welfare and medical agencies (indeed middle-class women) because they tend to utilise strategies of child rearing that have far stronger boundaries between work and play, make power differentials clear and do not value rationality at the expense of other ways of being. It is these women who for many decades have been held responsible for the educational failure of their children.

Proponents of the need for sensitivity assume that sensitivity comes from recognising and meeting emotional needs and thereby being sensitive to their meanings. It is from this base that mothers provide the grounding for educational achievement. However, if we examine the relationship between girls with sensitive or insensitive mothers, as defined by Tizard and Hughes, we find that the concept has no predictive power at all, especially when it comes to working-class mothers and daughters. What was quite striking in our study was that some of the highest-performing working-class girls were actually the daughters of 'insensitive' mothers, though the same did not hold true for the middle class sample: Tizard and Hughes do not designate any middle-class mothers as insensitive.

For example the girls we called Dawn, Nicky and Maura all had insensitive mothers, as defined by Tizard and Hughes, yet their performance was above the average for the working-class sample: all achieved more than five GCSEs between grades A to C and went on to A levels and higher education. While middle-class mothers are seen as 'sensitive' by Tizard and Hughes, and certain working-class mothers are especially picked out as not responding to their daughters' needs in the most effective manner, it is interesting that Dawn, Nicky and Maura did so well at school compared with the rest of the working-class girls. Indeed since these three girls were the only ones from the original group to go on to higher education, it is incredibly striking.

If the concept of sensitivity only has predictive power for those mothers and daughters whose subjectivity is constituted through the discourses of sensitive mothering, namely the middle classes, then while this is crucial for the middle classes, as we will show, it certainly does not determine working-class success or failure. This suggests that, at the social and psychic levels, something else entirely is going on. It is therefore crucial to understand precisely what that is. What can what Tizard and Hughes called 'insensitivity' be if it produces success in one group when the theory to which they refer would predict failure? It also points to the problem of using the middle class as the norm against which to judge working-class practices.

Let us examine once again what the two groups of mothers and daughters did at age four. In *Democracy in the Kitchen*, we argue that regulation by mothers varies according to class, with consequent differences in the regulative strategies adopted by mothers when bringing up their daughters. In addition to this, we argue that theories of socialisation assume a psychological subject made social through the taking on of roles and stereotypes, usually provided by significant others such as parents. Such approaches assume that the way children turn out is a fairly direct consequence of what parents do. We argued that such approaches not only invest parents with considerable power, but also place the most incredible burden of guilt upon them. Implicitly or explicitly, all approaches that assume that parents, especially mothers, have an educative effect on their children are socialisation approaches. We would not, of course, be so foolish as to imagine that what parents do is of no consequence for their children, but we would like to understand this in a rather different way, which we will explain with reference to our data.

We propose that social groups are produced and reproduced through strategies of regulation, forms of government and power that regulate the day-to-day practices of ordinary people. As we have

explained in the past (Walkerdine, 1988; Henriques *et al.*, 1998), in this
approach subjects do not pre-exist the discursive practices through
which what it means to be a subject are constituted. However those
practices are cross-cut by relations of fantasy, both on the part of the
apparatuses of regulation, *viz* the 'fear, phobia and fetish in colonial
government' referred to by Frantz Fanon (1969), and by unconscious
and conscious defences produced by family and cultural practices to
guard against the terrible fear that they might not survive, cope or
manage to get by (Pheterson, 1993; Walkerdine, 1997). What we aim
to do here, therefore, is to set out the practices through which the two
groups – middle and working class – are produced in relation to
educational success and failure.

In *Democracy in the Kitchen* we point to a number of practices through
which mother and daughter positions are produced, especially in
respect of the production of the normal or pathological bourgeois
individual. The apparatuses of social regulation, the 'truths' through
which a modern individual is assumed to be produced, demand a style
of parenting that stresses learning through play. Thus, we argue,
mothers are told to turn routine domestic tasks into opportunities
for playful learning. Potentially anything can form the basis of such
learning, from laying the table to preparing muesli, but what is clear is
that not only are the boundaries between work and play very fluid, if
not broken down, but mothers may find it very difficult to assert their
need to get on with their domestic work for fear of upsetting the fragile
regime of child development and education through play. For example
Sarah's mother set up the cleaning of the fish tank as a problem of
logic for her daughter:

Mother: Now, how are we going to get the fish out of the big bowl
           and into the little one, d'you think?
Sarah: I know, well, we get a thing and then put some water in it and
           then put it into there. Catch the fish.
Mother: And catch the fish?
Sarah: Yes.
Mother: How about something like that? [mother holds up a plastic
           pot.]
Sarah: Yes, I think that would do. Wash it out!

Notice how the mother treats the activity as pedagogic, as an educational task from which Sarah can learn about capacity, size and even
more complex mathematical concepts such as the effect of refraction

through glass and water on the size of the objects (Walkerdine and Lucey, 1989, pp. 73–4):

Mother: They look a bit bigger through their glass, don't they?
Sarah: Yes.
Mother: Even the small one looks pretty big, doesn't it?
Sarah: Through the glass.
Mother: Look over the top and see if it looks different.
Sarah: No, that one's little now, when I look from the top. And it's bigger when I look through the glass.

The mother sets up practices that aimed playfully to teach not only basic rationality but also the rationalisation of emotion. Such practices stress empowerment and autonomy of children to such an extent that sometimes young middle-class girls' behaviour towards their mothers can be tyrannical; that is, if a daughter manages to argue rationally for having or doing something that her mother does not want her to have or do, she usually gets her way, thus learning a very important lesson about her power and the power of rational argument. The belief about rational argument is founded on the very scientific rationality that underpinned post-Enlightenment science and a government of liberal democracy based on rationality and logic. Hence girls are not only learning a valuable lesson for their future as professionals active in the management of the liberal social order, but they are also being led to believe in the power of their own argument. The psychologists John and Elizabeth Newson (1976) argue that children should be given the illusion of choice and of their own power, because it is this that allows them to feel psychological autonomy. This principle enshrines the bourgeois agent of free will, economic 'man', who has grown psychologically independent of his parents and now operates as a free agent, with a strong and bounded ego. This concept is absolutely central to how development is understood as a path to rational, autonomous action, itself the centre of a definition of maturity. It is also central to the notion of the free, self-regulated, self-invented adult who is the cornerstone of Third Way policies. On the one hand we can now begin to see the very practices through which mothers are positioned to impart such lessons to their daughters, as well as how in practical terms, the practices work. On the other hand we can understand just what a threat is presented by family practices, especially maternal practices, that do not fit this norm. We might in fact conclude that once again it is working-class mothers who are held responsible for the failure to provide the kind of subject needed for the new economy. Subjects who understand the exigencies of power and the constrictions imposed by waged labour are not the remade subjects of the new democracy who understand that their advancement in life is their own responsibility, propped up by 'life long learning'.

This is achieved to some extent by the way in which girls are encouraged to be sensitive to other people's and their own feelings. Strong emotional responses are discouraged, just as powerful emotions are converted into rational argument. Powerful emotions have to be expressed as nice or not nice feelings. In this way girls can be both feminine and avoid what is understood as the worst excesses of 'animal passion'. For many of the middle-class mothers there are nice and nasty feelings, sensible and silly behaviour. These emotional strategies are produced through a variety of practices by which mothers regulate the emotional responses of their daughters. When daughters express violent emotions, and especially aggression towards their mothers, it is common for the mothers to respond with phrases such as 'That's not very nice' when in fact the daughter said 'I'll poke your eyes out'. In the following extract Julie talks to her mother (Walkerdine and Lucey, 1989 p.126):

Julie: I'll kick you in the face.
Mother: If you carry on saying that I'm going to ignore you . . . Taking no notice, yes. It's not very interesting. It's very boring.
Julie: Please! Please don't 'gnoring me.
Mother: *Ig*nore

We argue that practices such as these have a profound effect on what it means to grow up middle class and female, when rational argument wins the day and powerful emotions are at best not very nice. Such practices differ profoundly from working-class ones, in which the mother's power over her daughter is quite explicitly stated.

When we come to working-class practices, however, things change considerably. Not only are work and play strongly separated (or as Basil Bernstein, 1977, would say, strongly framed and classified), but mothers often insist that their daughters play on their own so as not to disrupt their housework. For example Nicky's mother insisted that she could not play with her daughter because she had 'got washing to do', 'got ironing to do', 'got altering to do', adding 'Yeah, well, it all takes time love' (Walkerdine and Lucey, 1989, p.81). Indeed it does, and not infrequently middle-class women employ others to do this work, which means that they may have more time to play.

In addition to this, the working-class mothers in our study were very explicit about power differentials and about their own position of authority, as well as allowing a space in which passionate emotions could be expressed safely. For example Nicky's mother managed to turn her daughter's desire to 'beat her up' into a game in which she pretended to beat her daughter up, getting her into a lock and tickling her (ibid., p. 135). In this sense, then, the practices they adopted threatened the rational autonomy and nice feelings that are central to the bourgeois order. It is not surprising, therefore, that working-class families are often blamed for the failure of their children within the education system by professionals who want to find some pathological practices that can then be put right. However, while it is true to say that these practices are outside the norm, there is no reason to suggest that there is anything wrong with them. Indeed more than this, if we look at educational success and failure, some of the most successful young women come from families in which the above practices are strongest.

However, if we argue that subjects are produced in and through the apparatuses of social regulation there is the question of how they have come to exist. In other words, although there is a great deal of surveillance and regulation of working-class family practices, the countervailing practices nevertheless survive, and on the basis of these some girls are even successful at school. It would be difficult to argue in some simple sense that these practices are forms of resistance to the imposed norm. Rather we would argue that they are cultural practices that have validity because they make sense in relation to the government of social relations of working-class life: actually two forms of regulation, the bourgeois order on the one hand and the regulation of working-class work on the other. While the professional and bourgeois order is founded upon the notion of the rational and autonomous subject, working-class life is at the same time epitomised by overt forms of power, in which employees are subject to exploitative and oppressive working conditions, overt authority and a strong distinction between paid work and play. It could therefore be argued that while these practices are pathological to the bourgeois norm, they are extremely well adapted to the conditions of working-class life. Are they, however, well adapted to the new social order in which the constant remaking of oneself demands a way of being that is far more akin to a mode of subjectivity that understands the subject as having a degree of control within the social world? How then do any working class girls succeed at school, where the demands of academic practices are far more similar to professional ones and therefore necessitate the learning of new forms of subjectivity?

As we argued in the Introduction, there is a crisis of working-class masculinity because the manufacturing base has been eroded in post-industrial societies. How, therefore, have family practices shifted to accommodate the change in what counts as working-class life and social relations? We shall answer these questions in a number of ways. In Chapter 7 we shall argue that for middle-class girls femininity is regulated in such a way as to ensure educational success and entry into the professions, once the nearly exclusive province of men. Secondly, we shall demonstrate that those working class girls who, against the odds, succeed at school, do so in quite different ways from middle-class girls. Working-class family practices, we argue, are not to be understood as pathological or abnormal versions of middle-class ones, but are produced in an attempt to adapt to much more difficult conditions.

Educational trajectories

We shall now look more closely at what happened to our sample of girls within the education system. We will not follow the tradition in the sociology of education that concentrates almost solely on working-class achievement (or the consistent lack of it), and has striven since the 1950s to explore the effects of affluence and embourgeoisement on the working class (Halsey *et al.*, 1980) while attempting to explore family processes as an explanation for inequality in educational success. As well as looking at the normative markers of educational success and failure, we want to highlight the complex and powerful ways in which subjective constructions of success and failure and, importantly, happiness, circumscribe their lives and set boundaries for what is considered possible or impossible at the present and in the future. These girls have been prepared for a world of work that is quite different from the labour market their parents entered. How have their differential relation to power, authority, passion, feelings and rationality stood them in stead as a preparation for the new labour market?

We argue that the production of educational success for working-class and middle-class girls is intimately tied up with emotional processes. But as we explained in Chapter 4, we do not want to restrict our analysis to only the conscious aspects of how families and young women organise and live their everyday lives in relation to education. We use a framework that can incorporate the complexities of unconscious processes and appreciate the power and creative significance (Raphael Reed, 1999) of the unconscious as a part of the fictions and fantasies through which subjectivities are created (cf. Walkerdine, 1997). By looking at what the girls, their parents and in some cases their teachers said about their educational achievements and how they felt about them at the time of the last interviews and in the light of the earlier phases of the study, we can explore the complex relations between the constitution of the girls as subjects within the social and cultural practices outside and inside the family and the psychic economy of those practices – the blending of fiction and fantasy. By these means we can explore in detail the complex processes of necessary self-invention.

A tale of two girls

Kerry was a white, working-class 21 year old who had not done well at primary school, where her teacher had described her as slow and of low ability. By the time Kerry was ten, things were going badly for her and she was having a real problem keeping up. Not only this but her class teacher also felt that she had a problem communicating with other children. She went on to a local co-ed comprehensive, which she left when she was 16 after doing badly in her GCSEs. Her experience of school from the very beginning was not a happy one. She hated school, always found the work difficult and was chronically bullied by one of her peers. However she never reported this to anyone, including her parents, who were completely unaware of the situation until she attempted suicide at the age of 15.

Kerry and her family felt that Kerry's struggle with school work and the mystery of why she found learning so difficult were made clear when she was positively tested as severely dyslexic after she left school. By that time, however, she had found herself a job in an office, had learnt to use a computer and had proved herself to be very capable; she was highly regarded, received promotion and many bonuses for her achievements. At the time of the interviews she was saving to go travelling around Europe.

At four Naomi was a confident, bright child. At five years old she went to a private preparatory school. At 10, although her performance in school was very good, she expressed, even at that age, significant anxiety about that performance, feeling that she 'didn't

work hard enough'. Naomi's teacher at that time described her as
'a little over-anxious', a child who constantly strove for perfection
but never quite got there. In her opinion these anxieties were
nothing to worry about as her performance at school was not suffer-
ing. Indeed, Naomi was achieving the standard expected of her in
a school in which one of the main objectives was to ensure a high
rate of transfer of its fee-paying pupils to public schools. To this
end, the school, like many other of the primary schools attended
by the middle-class girls, conducted regular testing in the classrom
in order to prepare the children for the public school selection
exams.

From 11 to 18 Naomi attended a prestigious and high-achieving
public school. She continued to do extremely well at that school,
but when she was about 14, what the family described as Naomi's
'sensitivity' and 'highly strung' nature began to topple over into
extreme anxiety. She began to have long episodes of crying
and chronic insomnia, and she developed obsessive behaviours,
including pulling her hair out and eating disorders. At 16, however,
she achieved 10 grade A GCSEs. She left school at 18 after sitting her
A levels, in which she attained three As. At 21 she was studying fine art
at Oxford.

After school Naomi had decided that she needed a break from her
studies and so, with money inherited from her grandfather, she had
spent a year in Italy to study the language and painting. At the time of
the interviews Naomi was not sure what she would do when she
completed her degree, but was considering going on to do a masters.
She had continued to pull her hair out and worry obsessively about her
weight, and sometimes returned home during term time in a state of
abject despair and panic.

The middle-class girls reported that their highly academic schools
were light on pastoral care. Naomi's problems went uncommented on
by her secondary school, because as far as they were concerned, and
within the remit of their 'job', Naomi was not a problem. She felt that
the only thing they were concerned about was that she should maintain
her high achievement levels:

> I just think I always took it a bit too seriously but I think that's the sort of
> school it was really, that it was very pushy and academic and it was never
> enough, you never did enough, or it was never good enough. You know,
> you could get 10 As at your GCSEs, but it wasn't, you know, there was no
> one whoever said 'well done'. You don't expect it.

Naomi's interviews contained many themes, but by far the most powerfully recurring one was the intense pressure to succeed. Her parents did not feel that the school had any part to play in helping Naomi to overcome her emotional problems. Indeed, they actively hid her emotional distress from the school. This had a dual function. On the one hand the appearance of everything being 'as it should be' was kept firmly in place. At the same time, keeping things quiet meant that Naomi was in no danger of being pathologised as a problem. Her parents, when they did seek help, went 'private' and took Naomi first to a behavioural psychologist and then a psychiatrist. This meant that Naomi and her family were saved from the deeply surveillant and regulating gaze of the 'caring professions'.

*   *   *

Kerry's struggle to keep up at school was becoming more and more difficult by the time she went to secondary school. Her poor performance was understood within a developmental discourse as someone who tried hard but would not get anywhere because she was slow and lacking ability. A teacher described her as a 'nice little girl, who just isn't very good'. Also, she didn't get on well with her classmates, was seen as different and felt isolated because of what her teacher described as significant communication difficulties produced out of knowing that she was not as able as the others.

Kerry's mother became increasingly worried about this and felt that Kerry had specific learning difficulties that the school was ignoring; she herself was dyslexic, as were other family members. She approached the school but the teacher assured her that Kerry had been given a test that showed she was not dyslexic. The only explanation left was that, as her primary teacher had said, she was of low ability. Kerry's learning problems dogged her throughout secondary school and contributed to her chronically low sense of self-worth. This lack of self-esteem was most dramatically manifested in her experience as the victim of long-term and severe physical and emotional bullying. (Despite increasing awareness of the problem of bullying at school during the late 1980s and the 1990s, many children remain trapped in institutional and social discourses and practices that have a profoundly silencing effect on the victim – Tattum and Herbert, 1997.) Attempts by Kerry to raise the problem with teachers were problematic; she even went to see the head teacher, but nothing was done.

Like many such victims Kerry's fury about her treatment by bullies was complexly intertwined with conscious and unconscious feelings of low self-worth, all of which combined to prevent her from finding a way to articulate her growing despair, either to herself or others. The feeling that her daily experience of bullying was a deeply shameful secret and indicative of her failure eventually broke down, and when she was 15 she finally told her parents something of what was happening at school. 'Because I got to that stage where I couldn't handle it anymore and then my mum and dad went down the school and they wouldn't do anything about it.'

The silence that surrounded not only her difficulties with learning but also the daily humiliation and terror that a small group of girls subjected her to eventually resulted in suicidal despair and Kerry took a barbiturate overdose. Only then did she receive any help, and this took the form of being admitted to a psychiatric ward. Once again she and her problems were in the hands of 'caring professionals' with powerful claims to know what was best for her.

*   *   *

Questions of resources and power resonate throughout as we look more closely at how these two girls' mental health problems were viewed and dealt with by their parents and schools. Here we have two young women who experienced deep anxiety, distress and despair. For both of them this was related to their educational performance. What is very clear are the different ways in which these problems were produced and understood discursively. Kerry's problems, within an educational discourse that centrally retained the notion of a working class 'lack' (despite competing theoretical discourses to the contrary), could only, in the end, be *her* problem – she quite simply did not have the ability to do well at school and so there was nothing to be done. The emotional consequences of being positioned within that discourse were hidden, emerging only as further evidence of her lack – as in her suicide attempt. For Naomi, one main source of her anxieties could not be attended to from within her class and cultural location.

These two cases also highlight some crucial issues surrounding educational achievement that relate to the whole group. Firstly, when the girls were 10 years old it was much more common for teachers to attribute poor performance to a lack of ability among working-class girls, while in the few cases where middle-class girls were producing the same poor results, this was far more likely to be viewed not as evidence of any lack of ability, but rather as a problem of motivation (Walkerdine and Lucey, 1989).

Patsy (working class) and Julie (middle class) were the only 10 year olds to remain in their original 'pair' since the four year old study, and they attended the same, mainly working-class junior school. Both had 'sensitive' mothers, although Julie expressed a furious envy of her younger sister, and both Julie and Patsy wanted to remain 'babies'. While both girls were doing equally badly at junior school, their performance was understood in quite different ways by the teacher. Julie was designated very much as boys tended to be, as having a 'natural ability' even though her performance at school did not indicate this. Patsy, who had obtained a high IQ score at four, at 10 was seen by her teacher as 'nowhere near as bright as the rest of them', very babyish and anxious. Like many of the poorly attaining working-class girls, she was viewed as unconfident and 'too sensitive'. All of the girls, including Kerry and Patsy, reported victimisation, dividing their acquaintances very starkly into those who helped them and those who hit, kicked, punched, pinched and bullied them. At 10 Patsy would hide under the desk, too afraid to face the class and the work she struggled with. Meanwhile Julie's problems with schoolwork were wholly attributed to a lack of motivation and the teacher said that she and Julie's parents were 'bending over backwards' to get her interested in maths, but to no avail. These different designations are important when looking at the same girls at 21. Julie's lack of motivation seemed to take on momentum rather than be overcome as she got older; she was one of the few middle-class girls to achieve poor GCSE results and not follow a straightforward educational path. What is important, however, is that Julie, despite her poor results and emotionally turbulent teenage years, went on to university and was later set for a professional career in fashion.

Patsy's mother was involved in work with teachers to help Patsy improve her performance, but she left school at 16 with very few qualifications and later worked part-time as an escort on local authority buses for the disabled. The point we are making here is that despite sensitive mothering and parents who did the 'right thing', two girls who went to the same nursery, infant and junior schools, and neither of whom did at all well in national examinations, ended up worlds apart. In spite of their parallel educational histories up until GCSE level they eventually conformed to their class-specific educational stereotypes: at 21 Julie was back on track and was likely to become a graduate professional, while Patsy, painfully aware of her lack of qualifications, was equally likely to remain in relatively poorly paid, low-status work. It is indeed a salutary lesson that Julie was categorically not doing better than Patsy, but that the differences in ability ascribed to each by virtue of their class status helped produce the stark and shocking differences in their trajectories and attainments. Seen in this light, no equal opportunities discourse can really get to grips with what it was that produced such shameful and painful differences.

Through the cases of Naomi and Kerry, Julie and Patsy we can also look at the very different relationships that middle- and working-class parents have to the education system and the schools their children attend. What came up strongly in the girls' and parents' narratives, as with Kerry's mother, was that working-class parents are often positioned within a professional discourse that locates them as 'not knowing' and the teacher as a powerful authority. Thus Kerry's mother deferred to the teachers' claim to 'know' that Kerry was not dyslexic, despite her strong internal knowledge, access to another set of discourses and the family history of dyslexia.

Fighting for your child

Of course we could ask, why did this mother not 'fight' for her child? Why did she not demand that something be done? While we must remember that some of the working-class girls managed to do well at school, failure in education was the norm for their parents, the majority of whom had left school at 15 without any qualifications. Jacky's mother said of school that she had 'walked out as I walked in – with nothing [laughs]. Nothing at all.' We would suggest that for many parents the anxieties, frustration and sense of powerlessness they expressed about the discursively produced space of 'the school' had deep and profound roots in their own schooldays.

'Fighting' for your child is something that middle-class parents are far more emotionally and materially equipped and discursively positioned to do. Reay (1998a), in her study of working-class and middle-class mothers' interactions and relationships with their children's primary schools, notes that working-class mothers have to negotiate difficult issues of difference that middle-class mothers do not have to go through when dealing with schools. Annette Lareau (1989) also concludes from her home–school relations study in the United States that they are characterised by separateness for working-class parents and interconnectedness for middle-class parents. Both

Reay and Lareau used Bourdieu's conceptualisation of 'capital' and 'habitus' to understand the very different social spaces that middle-class and working-class children and families occupy and the tremendous chasm that can separate their worlds. For instance the working-class parents in Reay's and Lareau's studies had no social access to teachers or professional educators, a separation of home and school that was linked to cultural and social capital. In contrast the middle-class parents had both cultural and social capital, which they exploited on their children's behalf.

The sense of inferiority felt by working-class parents – particularly the mothers, who are still the ones most directly involved with their children's schooling – may not manifest itself as that much of a problem, and may keep them at a safe and generally passive distance from the school. Until, that is, things go wrong. Parents who feel inferior to teachers find it extremely difficult to make the kinds of demands made by middle-class parents and in the manner in which they do it. A persistent theme in the working-class narratives was impotence in the face of what they viewed as the teacher's authority, as with Kerry's mother:

> And I said I'm sure Kerry is dyslexic. Um... and he said, oh, I've done a so and so test on her and she's not dyslexic. And that was just dismissed out of hand. ... So I thought, well, he must know what he's talking about, he's a teacher. Ha, ha, ha. So I didn't do anything about it. So she went through um... the first and middle school and she... she did have difficulties and then she went on to the comprehensive school and she still has um... the difficulties around the spelling.

However the interviews with middle-class parents clearly demonstrated that their power of negotiating with the school on 'academic' issues was considerable. Middle-class parents were quick to complain loudly if they perceived there was a problem with the service the school was providing (Bratlinger *et al.*, 1996). This extended to insisting on the removal of teachers whom parents deemed inadequate:

> There was one teacher, her geography teacher who was really pretty hopeless.... if there's enough parental pressure, then they'll get pushed out, and one had a bit of a conscience about that. But still you can't really tolerate people that are second rate (Samantha's father).

Other work has revealed the amount of pressure that teachers in schools with an intake from mainly professional middle-class families feel to be under from parents (Lucey and Walkerdine, 1999). Among the middle-class parents in this study there was an often unstated expectation that, should their daughters' performance slip, they would be listened to and heard by the class and head teachers, and together they would work out strategies to assist the child. As one professional to another, the middle-class parents in our study felt that they could communicate on an equal or almost equal basis. Often the parents had more qualifications and held positions of higher status than the teachers themselves, who could therefore be viewed as 'servicing' the family. Working-class mothers such as Kerry's and Patsy's did try to negotiate and overcome the emotional barriers that their own experiences had helped to construct, but lacked the certainty of entitlement that the middle-class women seemed to have (Reay, 1998a, p. 58).

In relation to mothers' involvement with their children's primary schools, Reay argues that cultural capital enters the process of raising issues with teachers at many points: it was middle-class women's confidence, their self-presentation as entitled, the certain conviction that their point of view was the correct one and their clearly articulated knowledge of the system and how it worked that counted (ibid., p. 113). While continuity and recognition characterise home–school and teacher–parent interaction for the middle classes (Vincent, 1996), parental involvement by working-class parents is premised on the notion that teachers must help working-class white and black mothers to support their children in the right ways (Walkerdine and Lucey, 1989). On an everyday, mundane level this different discursive positioning can be experienced by working-class parents as infantilisation. Being treated as though they are children themselves (Vincent, 1996, p. 96) and being fobbed off by teachers when they try to get detailed information about their child's progress (Reay, 1998a) can contribute to the construction of a deeply unsatisfying dynamic for everyone concerned.

But the contradictory positioning of teachers must always be kept in mind; some of the strategies that teachers employ when dealing with working-class parents are produced as a response to the teachers' own ensnared position (Walkerdine, 1989). While the meritocratic fiction persists that everyone, if they work hard and do well at school, can bypass the chronic ailments of late industrial capitalism, teachers are often painfully aware that there are no quick-fix, simple, pedagogic solutions to the inequalities that shape their pupils' educational and life chances. The impossible task of holding, being responsible for and reproducing that fiction can 'cause teachers to be

caught   up in a dance of denial over which they [have] little control' (Reay, 1998a, p. 124). In order to become teachers, they too
have to be produced within the same discourses that pathologise
working-class parents, whatever their own original social location.
In   Chapter 2 we saw that Erica Green, now living in Yorkshire,
was able to talk pejoratively about people living in council houses.
We can understand this as a complex defence against a split-off and
projected part of herself. It is quite possible for teachers from the
same   social location as their pupils to produce this kind of defence,
which may make them more, not less antagonistic towards children
who are too much like them. Just as for Erica Green, this may produce
complex defences that actually serve to oppose the working classes
even more.

While one set of defensive strategies often employed by the
working-class parents in home–school interactions included silence,
withdrawal or compliance, others mobilised feelings that allowed for
the possibility of a different set of actions. However those working-
class parents who did insist on voicing their concerns about their
children's education were in grave danger of being viewed as demanding and unreasonable. Feelings of inadequacy and unfairness were
coupled with a profound sense of not being heard, so it was not
surprising that some parents' attempts to defend against and overcome
those feelings manifested themselves in an angry way:

> ... she'd hate parents evenings, she'd say 'don't come', because we always
> ended up having an argument...or I'd start shouting at somebody
> [laughs]. I'd start having a row. It doesn't do any good, does it? [Laughs]
> (Zoe's mother).

The routes by which anger can be expressed depend on where the
individual is located in the discursive positioning of the subject, and
therefore the power and effectivenesss of their response. Zoe's
mother's anger drove her voice outwards in a desperate attempt to
be heard, and yet, as she said, 'it doesn't do any good does it?' She was
seen as stroppy and aggressive. Sharon's father tried to 'fight' for his
children, but he too was viewed as aggressive.[2] Zoe's mother also
invoked the shame of her daughter, for by showing her anger in this
public way she called into question her and Zoe's respectability, which
as Beverley Skeggs (1997a p. 1) states is one of the most ubiquitous
signifiers of class, with particular power to place, define and pathologise working-class women. For Samantha's father, a white middle-class
man who was heavily invested with both respectability and its close

companion – rationality – anger and aggression could be expressed in ways that would not be understood as pathological. Forcibly putting pressure on his daughter's head teacher to sack a member of staff was, we would suggest, an intensely aggressive act. But the structural, social and cultural networks in which he was so utterly normalised gave a quite different shape and force to an anger that on the individual level shared much in common with that of Zoe's mother – anxiety about his daughter's performance.

For many of the working-class parents, their requests for help were forcefully blocked by the school, and we suggest that this could have had a powerful negative effect on their daughters in a number of ways. Firstly, of course, the special needs of the daughters were denied, as with Kerry. Secondly, and perhaps more importantly in the longer term, the school's dismissal of the parent, and indeed of the parent's knowledge of the child, connected with the school's dismissal of the girl's own abilities and knowledge. By dismissing the parent, the teacher also dismissed the child; in some cases this meant that the success or failure of the child was dependent on the relationship between parent and teacher. Girls such as Kerry understood that struggle without help was the only thing on the menu. For such girls the possibility of asking for or receiving assistance was remote. This showed itself most dramatically in Kerry's experience of long-term severe bullying.

Who was the loser and who was the winner here? Kerry went to the very edge when she took her overdose and nearly died. But just when the school had given up on her and she had nearly given up on herself, something else came through. She faced her bully and left school. She found herself work and got help with her reading difficulties. She found that she was not 'thick' after all; that she could make friends and quickly earn the respect of colleagues through her competence at work. So the positioning of Kerry centred on two competing narratives: the school's narrative, that focused on her low ability, and her parents' alternative discourse of dyslexia. It was through that alternative discourse that they had been able to maintain some sense of self-respect. While she was at school the school's discourse and explanatory framework retained dominance, but the moment she left school that discourse was not the only one by which she was defined, and she was able to achieve modest success in a job she was good at.

Naomi supposedly had the best education money could buy and this country had to offer, and yet she felt strongly that it failed her. She appeared to be a confident, outgoing, autonomous and successful young woman, and yet she was racked by a fear of failure that those around her could not bear to hear about because they too held that fear.

Happiness: its constructions and functions

So far we have focused on the place and production of anxiety among the middle-class girls and their families in relation to the fear of educational failure. Of course anxiety about failure is not the sole province of the middle classes. However we wish to argue that just as anxieties about schooling had quite a different provenance in the case of the working-class girls and their families, so their shape, expression and effect were different. To this end we shall examine how 'happiness' entered as a construct for the working-class parents in relation to their anxieties about their own and their children's failure.

We would argue that their primary concern of wanting their children to be happy at school was for some working-class parents a response to extremely difficult but often unconscious feelings about their own unhappiness and failure at school. Teachers often express genuine puzzlement about parents who seem to set and accept low standards for their children and appear satisfied that their child is happy at school, despite the child's poor performance (Lucey and Walkerdine, 1999). This is sometimes understood by teachers as parents simply not being interested in their child's progress, although disinterest was far from what emerged from our interviews with working-class parents.

The starting point for our analysis of the girls' subjectivity was in many ways our own experience. We came from working-class families where to get good reports, to be described as 'bright', to be put in for selective examinations, to pass national examinations and to stay on at school past 15 or 16 (never mind go to university) was quite out of the ordinary. In many ways it was also beyond the comprehension of our parents, who struggled to understand and support these 'clever' children while we ourselves were struggling with a system entirely unfamiliar to those who loved us best. All they wanted was for us to be happy, as happiness was the most they could envisage in an education system that had only brought them failure and unhappiness. It was our examination of the interviews, as described in Chapter 4, that really brought these things to the fore in our analysis, not just in the last stage of the research but in the earlier phases too. For there it was, many working-class parents *did* express more concern about their children's happiness than they did about their performance at school, even when the children were failing badly.

But there is also a double-bind in which the emphasis on happiness can place working-class girls and their families. When Zoe was six her parents were praised by her teacher for their 'laid back attitude': they were more concerned with her happiness than with 'pushing her'. In a child-centred framework, making performance demands of children of that age created the danger of producing anxiety, and only happy working-class children who were less bothered about work were well-adjusted. Yet a family's desire for upward mobility and educational qualifications could not be satisfied without anxiety. Christine's parents' model of educational support, such as educational visits to museums or zoos every weekend, was thought far too self-conscious to produce the right kind of orientation or the right kind of knowledge. By comparison Hannah, who was in the same school as Zoe and six year old Christine from a professional family, could be deemed as both 'well-adjusted' and doing well because her parents did not display anxiety or appear (to the school) to push her (Walkerdine, 1989, p. 91). But the extent to which children like Hannah were pushed towards excellence and the activities that were to produce this excellence became hidden in a set of discourses that enshrined the notion of middle-class normality. In fact, as Hannah told us later in her educational career, she was expected to work very hard and was certainly expected to learn to play at least the piano and violin to an extremely high standard.

It is our assertion that psychodynamics within the family are a critical part of the matrix in which children develop their educational subjectivities. In Zoe's case the family were socially positioned in a way that produced, for her parents, educational failure. We suggest that their anxieties about their own schooling resurfaced when their children went to primary school, alongside an intense desire to resolve them. The ethos of child-centredness that Zoe's primary school embraced provided a framework in which to insert happiness as a strategy for ameliorating her parents' unresolved unhappiness about their own schooling experiences. It is important to note that, in this primary setting, the organisation of psychodynamic defences against the anxieties that were aroused in her parents worked to good effect, or at least in the school's terms – even if they did nothing to make Zoe an academically successful child, they did prevent conflict with the school, a not unimportant issue for working-class parents. However the move from primary to secondary schooling signalled a shift not only in the children's identifications, but also into an education system where the nurturing family ethos that characterised primary schools was replaced by the more impersonal and fragmented regime of secondary schools (Shaw, 1995). Moreover at that time testing was not a part of the primary curriculum in the way that it became in the 1990s. For girls like Zoe the emphasis on measured performance was encountered dramatically and relatively suddenly when they went to secondary school. We would argue that it is this arena, where the curricular focus is very much on examination performance, that an emphasis on the child's happiness can be seriously at odds with the demands of the curriculum.

At 16 Zoe still maintained a 'laid-back' attitude towards school and her prospects for GCSE success did not look good. She was certainly happy at school, but for her the social aspects seemed more important than doing well academically. Changes at the social level, namely the disappearance of the youth labour market, increased the pressure on young people to stay on at school until 18, and contracting opportunities for uncredentialled youngsters and older workers affected Zoe's parents' response to what was becoming clear would be her lack of examination success at school. Differences emerged between her parents in terms of their reaction to this changing situation and their daughter's education. While they were both very clear about the need for her to get some qualifications, for her father this conflicted with other conscious and unconscious desires; the conscious desire not to produce anxiety in her, and, we would suggest, the unconscious desire not to produce it in himself:

> I didn't want to lock her up in her room, so she got home from school and worked you know. Work, work, work, you know. I didn't want to do that. Just that when she was at school, pay attention, you know.... I just wanted her to be happy, that's all. She's not, er, ambitious. And I'm not ambitious [laughs], that's it. Willing to let things just float along.

Zoe's identification as 'laid back' may be only one side of the story. It would be too easy to say that Zoe did not care about education; she was full of good intentions. However she was unable to sustain the energy and motivation required to produce the kind of course work or examination performance needed for success. Her comments at the second interview, after she had left school at 17 to have a baby, also exposed the more defensive aspects of her outwardly relaxed persona; in retrospect she was able to articulate the possibility that this dreamy, happy-go-lucky persona was also a defence against her anxiety about being stupid and failing:

> I wasn't confident enough to ask for help. I was like, 'Oh, um.. they're going to think I'm stupid, they're going to think I've got to know this.' I mean, now I do look back and think why was I such a silly fool. If I didn't know it I didn't know it. You know, that's it, that's the way it goes. I mean, I'm not stupid and you know nobody's really stupid. . . . Because um . . . I've realised that um . . . before I used to sit down and, you know, let it fly by me.

Zoe's story also highlights how very ambivalent feelings about education and achievement are expressed in the family by various members and how these can have a powerful effect when communicated to children. While Zoe's father maintained his position as the 'laid back' one, her mother, who had a reputation in the family as 'a very determined woman' who could sometimes be 'stroppy' when crossed, was very keen for them to do well and tried to encourage them by example; she studied English and maths at GCSE level as well as taking a computing course because she had never done any O levels or GCSEs – 'I thought it would be nice to see what it involves really.'

We would suggest that one of the things that differentiates parental practice is the degree to which middle-class parents are prepared to push their children to achieve and maintain a high academic performance. We suggest that for the parents of children who are not doing very well and who themselves had a poor experience of school, it is very difficult to push their child and distressing to hear that their child may be finding school work difficult. Instead parents want to protect their child from difficult feelings and perhaps preserve their childhood as a time of happiness and freedom from worry and expectation. We are in no way stating that the middle-class parents in our study did not stress 'happiness' for their children; indeed when asked 'What would you like for your daughter's future?' nearly all the parents began with a version of 'For her to be happy'. We are arguing however, that happiness itself is differently constituted for working- and middle-class girls (David *et al.*, 1994; Reay, 1998b).

When the middle-class girls were four their mothers pushed them to discover the 'joy of learning', so that play and work became indistinguishable. By the time they were 10 the joy of learning was no longer enough and quantifiable achievement was firmly on the agenda. In this respect, one extremely powerful criterion by which to recognise and achieve happiness was above-average educational achievement. For the middle-class families, then, happiness was incontrovertibly fused with academic success in a way that it simply was not for most of the working-class families. What we must stress, however, is the enormous emotional, practical and economic task of ensuring that such happiness comes about. Furthermore we wish to raise the possibility that such intense and unrelenting labour may have unforeseen costs. In Barbara Ehrenreich's insightful analysis of the American professional middle classes, she argues that middle-class childrearing practices are characterised by ambivalence and anxiety:

> Middle class parents face a particular dilemma. On the one hand they must encourage their children to be innovative and to express themselves... But the child will never gain entry to a profession in the first place without developing a quite different set of traits, centred on self-discipline and control. The challenge of middle class childraising – almost the entire point of it, in fact – is to inculcate what the reader will recognise as the deferred gratification pattern. It is this habit of mind that supposedly distinguishes the middle class from the poor; and it is this talent for deferral that a middle class child actually needs in order to endure his or her long period of education and apprenticeship (Ehrenreich, 1990, p. 84).

Pat Allatt (1993) discusses the critical 'domestic transition' (Bourdieu 1984), whereby privilege is not automatically transmitted but depends on constant and purposeful activity by the family to maintain its class position and prevent downward mobility. The actual educational achievements of middle-class girls such as Naomi, Angela, Hannah and Liz make a puzzle of their anxiety about performance, enough for us to understand that there are some complex emotional dynamics bound up in this. Of course there is a material dimension to this anxiety too. The development of an increasingly competitive educational system over the decades in which these young women grew up has resulted in a drive towards the achievement of more and higher qualifications. While increased credentialism is one of the strategies with which professions have responded to the threat of invasion by the working classes, its impact has been felt throughout the middle classes:

> Once, only men had to scale these [educational] walls, devoting their youth and young adulthood to preparation and apprenticeship. Today, however, almost no one gets in – male or female – without submitting to the same discipline and passing the same tests that

were originally designed to exclude intruders from below (Ehrenreich, 1990, p. 220).

As several middle-class parents said, 'a good education is the only thing you can give your children'. In the interviews the parents' and girls' emphasis was sometimes on the value of education in fulfilling potential, extending choices and providing possibilities for the future. What was far less clearly articulated was the necessity for a set of qualifications as precursor to a professional career, which is the backbone of being and staying middle class, thereby achieving 'happiness'. Only by looking at what happened when these things did not seem to be firmly in place could we understand the worry and fears that surrounded educational achievement.

For working-class parents, sensitivity and the meeting of needs are impossibly at odds with one another on some levels. Schools, especially secondary schools, do not cater for the emotional needs of the individual; education is divorced from feelings (Shaw, 1995). Yet for all but a minority, how we perform at school and what qualifications we come out with will determine, at the very least, our social, material and economic future. Given the middle-class imperative to maintain and reproduce bourgeois professional status, being happy cannot be separated from good academic performance. We explored in Chapter 4 how Angela's family constructed a complex narrative about her younger sister to account for her poor (relative to Angela's) educational performance and to offset the anxiety her slowness provoked in all the family members. Angela's sister, although not nearly as successful as Angela, was hardworking and motivated in relation to school and did not arouse her parents' anger. In contrast middle-class children who did not demonstrate their commitment to education courted extremely negative reactions from their parents. Helen and Naomi both had brothers whose indifference towards school was reflected (in the families' terms) in their examination results and the fact that they had not lined up a university place whilst still at school. In both families this was a source of much conflict and was understood by the parents as a profound lack – of motivation, direction, ambition and, most crucially, self-discipline:

> So his way of doing it was like completely opting out, and was doing absolutely no work, doing nothing, just watching television, not having interests in anything. And my Dad gets really annoyed by that (Naomi).

When the children of the professional middle classes enacted their rebellion in the 1960s through resistance to educational institutions that would ensure they became just like their parents, they were charged with idleness and moral turpitude. The individual pathology that this lack of self-discipline is seen to represent, is perhaps more than anything else understood as the greatest threat to the maintenance of class position. Ehrenreich (1990, p. 15) writes that among the middle classes there is another anxiety: 'a fear of inner weakness, of growing soft, of failing to strive, of losing discipline and will'. We can begin to see, then, how the tendency towards constant purposeful activity in middle-class families (Allatt, 1993) could also have its darker, more defensive side – an attempt to ensure that the cultural and social capital upon which the middle classes depend is reproduced in each generation. Indeed we could see the growth of counselling to aid what Freud called 'ordinary unhappiness' and Rose (1991) refers to as 'governing the soul' as a counterpoint to this.

What we noted throughout the study was that a powerful fear of failure was operating within the middle-class families. For middle-class Naomi, then, it was imperative that she succeed educationally, despite the considerable emotional costs to her and her family, as we shall explore in more detail in Chapter 7. Naomi was powerfully caught up in this web of cultural, structural and class discourses – never able to allow herself off the roundabout of outstanding achievement, while never sure that she had made the grade – a fragile autonomy and confidence indeed. An autonomy, in fact, that was shown up for what it was: a constant need for reinvention in a deeply insecure era, a fiction of autonomy that papered over the defences mounted to produce it.

In the next chapter we shall explore the small group of working-class girls who, against all odds, succeeded in education.

Notes

1. See *Guardian* (1997a, 1997b, 1998), *Observer* (1998), Wragg (1997).
2. The construction of fighting as an aspect of working-class masculinity is explored in Walkerdine (1996).

Chapter 6

Doing Well at School: Success and the Working-class Girls

How can we understand the differences in educational performance among the working-class girls? It is extremely difficult to see any clear patterns that can explain both their failures and their successes. Concentrating on those working-class girls who did well at school, we can see how contradictory pressures shaped their educational outcomes, and how these defied current explanations of success and failure. Do working-class girls who succeed in education manage to negotiate hybrid subjectivities or other kind of self-invention and regulation? How do they inhabit the phantasmatic spaces accorded to them or the complex subject positions through which they are regulated?

Why should we assume that, if the modes of regulation of working- and middle-class subjects are different, the paths to success for working-class girls should be a copy of the middle-class ones? We have made it clear in the past that the injunction to be a particular kind of subject in education is quite different for children from different social positions (Walkerdine, 1991). We consider that the social and psychic economies, modes of regulation, discourses and bodily performances were all different for the two groups of girls.

Throughout the working-class sample there was a tendency for parents to talk negatively about their own experience of school, but significantly, not all of them did so. Interestingly there was no straightforward relation between working-class parents liking or doing well at school and their daughters' success. There was a complex link, however, between daughters' success and parents who, despite their poor experience of school, had later gone back into the education system to take up some kind of study, especially courses that would enhance their career or job prospects. But there were contradictions and anomalies at every turn when we looked at the working-class girls.

We have seen how the variations in the middle-class girls' educational careers were minimal in contrast to the diversity amongst the working-class girls in terms of pathways and outcomes. Compared with the educational success that characterised the middle-class girls' histories so far, the educational failure of the majority of the working-class girls was indisputable. Crucially, however, not all of the working-class girls reproduced the examination failure of previous generations, and in this chapter we shall look more closely at those particular girls in order to shed light on the production of their success (Table 7.1). We have taken as a baseline of educational success the government-imposed benchmark of five or more GCSEs at grades A–C.

Table 7.1   Working-class girls who did well at school

In higher education	In further education	Completed further education	Achieved 5+ GCSEs A–C
Nicky (21)	Rebecca (16)	Jenny (21)	Anna (21)
Maura (21)	Christine (16)		
Holly (21)	Teresa (21)		
Dawn (21)			

The only way we could begin to understand this without recourse to an easy pathology was to revisit our own experiences of education. After all, we were successful working-class girls from families in which there was no tradition of further or higher education or professional training. Until that point there had been an unspoken and relatively unexplored concensus among us that the fact of our difference from our families constituted a sameness between us. And yet, when faced with the task of trying to understand how and why we had managed to succeed in education when all around us had failed, we discovered the same kinds of variation in our stories as existed among the working-class girls in the study. Gradually, after many case discussions on the successful working-class girls and much reflection on our own accounts of educational achievement, the centrality of our families began to emerge clearly.

Although this is also the case for the production of middle-class educational success, middle-class families are discursively positioned in a positive way and are not subject to the kinds of pathologisation that have historically informed regulative and interventionist educational policies aimed at raising the achievement of working-class children (Finch, 1984; David, 1985, 1993; Vincent and Warren, 1999). While we wanted to retain the significance of the family in explanations of educational achievement we felt that we were in danger of becoming trapped by discourses that we felt were inadequate on two counts. Firstly, that a deficit model underpins conceptions of working-class families. While policies and initiatives designed to improve working-class children's educational performance have focused on precisely those interior spaces of family interaction, this has served to push responsibility further and further into the family and away from considerations of sociality (Vincent and Warren, 1999). Secondly, that sociological work that attempts to theorise connections between the individual and society (between agency and structure) is limited by an unwillingness to work with the notion of unconscious processes. In addition to this, traditional sociology invests much in an individual/ society dualism (Henriques *et al.*, 1998) so that the social and the psychic are understood as twin but opposite poles or forces. The psychoanalytically informed post-structuralism that guides our work assumes what Althusser (1969) called a position of 'absolute interiority' between the subject and the social.

We are trying to understand how some working-class children do manage to succeed educationally when it seems there is absolutely nothing in the social world to support that success. Educational statistics of every kind consistently demonstrate generation upon generation of failure for the majority of working-class pupils. How on earth is it that some, a small minority, of working-class children manage to succeed against such odds? As we argued in the Introduction, identity is produced in a phantasmatic space in which conscious and unconscious identifications form a dense emotional matrix through which events and processes – such as going to school, homework, taking exams, leaving school and so on – are made sense of, engaged in, given meaning and value. This is no less true for black and white middle-class girls, as we demonstrate in Chapters 5 and 7.

Our challenge is to understand and articulate what these girls' and their families' narratives tell us, and to try to make sense of the deeply conflicting complex of emotions and conscious and unconscious processes that emerged in and around their educational careers. Nor do we want to confine our analysis to individual and family dynamics, but instead to place the girls' narratives into a framework that includes and can take account of the very modes of regulation, discourses and practices through which these girls were constituted as educational subjects. How, then, did they inhabit the phastasmatic spaces accorded to them, and the complex subject positions through which they were regulated?

There are contradictions and anomalies at every turn when we look at the production of working-class educational success. Things that were clearly important to some of the young women in relation to educational achievement were unimportant to others; some had a positive experience of school, some did not; some did as they were told, others were rebellious and challenging; some found study easy, others intensely difficult. Importantly, some of the young women remained on a path that took them to higher education, others faltered and gave up after GCSE or A level. In the case of parents, some had high expectations of their daughters, but not all; some parents enjoyed learning and study and had returned to education as adults; for some (as we explored more fully in Chapter 5) their children's schooling provoked intense anxiety about failure. While some of the working-class girls had 'sensitive mothers' (see Chapter 5), it was certainly not the majority. These polarisations, although somewhat artificial, help to stress that scoring highly on the positive side of these dichotomies was no guarantee or predictor whatsoever of good educational outcome. We found no straightforward correlation between educational achievement, as measured by standard examination indicators, and what in educational research, policy and practice are continuously taken to be the weakest links between 'working class' families and schooling.

Family processes are implicated in both the success and failure of the working-class girls in the study, but we desperately need another model in which to understand their centrality. Whatever the educational outcome for working-class children, some have argued that issues of social reproduction are at the very heart of their experience. As Diane Reay argues in relation to mothering and educational success, 'Social reproduction is a process of achieving academic success for middle-class mothers and their children. For working-class families it is frequently about failing to succeed educationally' (Reay 1998a, p. 452).We have tried to explain why it is so difficult, almost impossible for middle-class girls to fail. Educational failure for them not only threatens the reproduction of their class subjectivities, provoking anxiety about loss of economic status, but the educational experience itself becomes a line of communication between parents and children, one of the routes through which such visceral (*not* rational) aspects of their relational lives as love, regard, dependence and disappointment are expressed and to some extent traded, as we showed in Chapter 4. In post-structuralist terms, we want to restate the reproduction arguments in a different way. In particular we want to focus on the production of subjects within the regulative apparatus of neoliberalism. In this analysis, as we stated in Chapter 2, the two classes are not simply the bearers of differing amounts of power and cultural capital, but the regulative apparatuses of particular modes of government at different historical moments produce different kinds of subject, and power is implicated not in the possession of capital but in the actual self-formation of the subject. We think this difference is crucial for our analysis, as we shall demonstrate.

First and foremost we argue that for all working-class young women, the fact that they are engaged in a process of transformation, of becoming different from their families, of producing a different and hybrid subjectivity, impacts powerfully on their conscious and unconscious lives. In this psychosocial landscape educational success can bring as many fears and anxieties as failure. However, as Reay (1997, p. 19) points out, 'the positive connotations invested in terms such as transformation and change mask an inherent negativity often overlooked in discussions of meritocracy'. There is no available or acceptable framework within which to raise the notion that educational success, most especially when carried on into higher education, may exact an enormous emotional toll on working-class children (Walkerdine, 1991, 1997). Furthermore, the significance of the difference that this success constitutes is not lost on working-class children as they move through the education system.

Nicky: finding out for yourself

While we certainly could not come up with any convenient typologies of the successful working-class girl, we can point to some complex trends in this sub-group. One way in which the girls discursively constituted their own narratives and biographies was as a 'struggle against the odds'.

Nicky was a white, working-class 21 year old in the last year of her biology degree. Nicky went to a mixed comprehensive which she described as 'very rough' and where she was consistently bullied. She was relieved to get away after her GCSEs, in which she achieved two As, two Bs, four Cs and one D, and went on to study science A levels at the local FE college. Having firmly decided that she wanted to go to university, she was aware that the competition was tough and she needed to get good A level results. She took a year out before applying, which gave her the chance not only to take an Open

University course in biology, but also, crucially, to work and save up for university:

> I try and help my parents a bit I suppose. I try not to ask too much. 'Cos I know they can't afford it, but they don't like that, they don't like me knowing that they can't afford it, which is fair enough.... I wanted to make sure that when I went to university I had enough money. I mean, I get a full grant, but I wanted to make sure that I had enough money, so I never came out of it in debt. I'm the same now, I mean, it's really tough trying to survive on my grant.

How do we explain this young woman's extraordinary determination to get to university? Her mother and father had both had a fairly poor experience at school and neither had returned to education since, though they were supportive of her studies and felt very proud that she was doing so well. Significantly, her younger sisters were also doing well at school (one had just finished her A levels at the time of the second interview) and both planned to go on to higher education.

It was common for the educationally successful young working-class women to express the view that their parents had little experience or knowledge to offer when it came to the navigating the education system. Nicky said:

> Well I talked to my parents about it, but my parents never went to college or anything, they finished school early, so. They always wanted me to get a good education, but they weren't able to give much practical advice. I've got an Aunt, my Dad's sister, that I had a few words with, she's umm, I think she went to college and she's got a really good job, and she gave me a bit of advice. Apart from talking to teachers, at college there's not much help. I had to make them on my own, and when I actually applied for my university degree, I didn't really know what I wanted to do at the time, apart from science. So I was a bit in the dark.

It may be difficult for those who take access to higher education for granted to understand just what this lack of knowledge actually means. Nicky's statement that she was 'a bit in the dark' understates the incredible problem many such people have to face. Often such young people and their families know absolutely nothing about university. When we explored our own histories, we realised that, in some cases, we lacked knowledge as basic as what a university was or why one would or could go there to do anything other than a vocationally oriented course. Having to find things out for themselves because their parents' knowledge could not be relied on was a common theme among these young women in relation to the complexities surrounding post-compulsory education in particular. Christine, 16 years old, was on a well-regarded music course at an FE college and had been made conditional offers by a number of universities for a music degree place at the time of the second interview. No one in her family had had any musical training or experience, and on going to college she realised how much her relatively informal musical education disadvantaged her:

> I just wonder where they learnt all the stuff they know, because some of them are grade 8 standard at 17, 18, and I was never pushed in any way at all, I just did it all on my own basically and it was like. So I'm a bit kind of behind compared to everybody else.

In fact Christine went to the same primary school as Hannah. At six, Hannah was learning the violin via the Suzuki method and was required by her father to practise every day. In common with the students from middle-class professional families on Christine's course, Hannah began moving through the musical grading system whilst still at junior school, whilst Christine was not put in for her grade 1 exam on the guitar until she was 13. This picks up and mirrors what we found, sadly and depressingly, when the 21 year olds were 10. That is, that girls who were doing well in working-class schools were in schools in which the overall performance was much worse than the middle-class schools. Thus it was impossible for a girl in a working-class school to be nationally competitive. It also demonstrates how much work is required to produce and secure the status of the middle-class subject.

For parents who attempted to provide the kind of continuity between home and school that was so firmly in place in the middle-class families, this meant going back to school themselves. Dawn's mother studied English and maths at GCSE level so she would be able to understand what her daughters were doing at school and help them with their work. But when Dawn went on to study A levels she had to say to her 'Look, now you're going into A levels, I'm not, I'm not up to that.'

Again, it is probably difficult for some to imagine the complex emotions caught up in that relationship, of parents who feel inadequate to help their children, especially as they progress through education. The parents may feel shame and the children shame and anger and pain. This is lived as psychic but it is produced socially and needs to be understood as profoundly psychosocial.

Conventional discourses to explain both middle-class children's success and working-class children's failure make a puzzle of Nicky's and her sisters' achievements. Looking back to the other phases of the study, when the girls were four years old the puzzle intensified rather than opened out for easier explanation. In contrast to the sensitivity of Teresa's mother, Nicky's mother was viewed as not following 'good' educational practice: she and Nicky were fractious, she refused to play with Nicky and regulated her behaviour in an authoritarian manner. She certainly did not encourage rational argument or nurture the 'puzzling mind of the 4 year old' (Tizard and Hughes, 1984). On the face of things it did not seem as if Nicky was in any way prepared for the practices of school and the production of educational success. And yet when she was 10, some of the resoluteness we witnessed at 21 had begun to emerge. Although her performance was not outstanding in her class, she expressed high aspirations for herself. A chord is struck when we recall her teacher's comments about Nicky at 10: Nicky was described as 'a steady, competent little worker...she's quietly motivated, she's not one of these that makes a great fuss about anything'. This resonates clearly with the adolescent Nicky, who never made a fuss about being bullied, quietly got on with her work, took an extra course when she did not get the grades she needed to get into university and never worried her parents about money.

A story of great determination, yes. But this leaves us with some unanswered questions about her achievements and the way she went about realising them. Nicky had certainly found great inner resources in order to achieve her goals, but her unwillingness to seek help from her parents, never to 'make a fuss about anything' also speaks of a massive psychic defence. Such defences are necessary to cope with the pain of family deprivation and poverty. It is not uncommon for working-class women who have gone through higher education to speak of the fact that their parents went without in order that their children might have something, often continually throughout their childhood (Walkerdine, 1991, 1997). Unlike the children of middle-class parents, who have a wealth of knowledge about higher education as well as considerable financial support and stability, Nicky knew that the path to her goal was a very lonely one. As she pointed out, nobody seemed to know anything that might help her and she had no financial resources to fall back on if she got into debt.

In this view, nobody was psychically or economically there to help her: there was no strong bounded autonomous ego (as in the picture painted of the normal middle-class four year old: Walkerdine and Lucey, 1989) but a painful separation, and she denied the anger, pain and loneliness by imagining defensively that she had need of no-one and could do it all by herself. Actually underneath all this pain may have been a powerful anger about her parents having nothing to give her, whereas, of course, they would have given her a great deal, or a fear that there was nothing to stop her falling apart other than her 'outer armour'. Going it alone protected her and them from the pain and the anger.

Nicky was somebody who was quite unwilling to show her emotional vulnerability to the researchers: everything had to be protected. It would be easy to argue that such defences are pathological and we could muster many a theory to sing a song of inadequate parenting. But in our view, such analyses would be wildly wrong. The defences Nicky exhibited were the very things that would ensure she got to and succeeded at university. The double bind is that while they may have been harmful to her emotionally, they were essential to her practically. Just as it is completely inappropriate to assume that working-class copies of middle-class family practices will make for educational success, it is equally inappropriate to assume that working-class psychic processes should, in the best of all worlds, mirror those of the middle classes. As Pheterson (1993) argues, systems of domination bring their own defences to dominator and dominated. We might argue further that the kind of dissociation that allowed Nicky to succeed can be seen as a way of coping with the terrifying differences in practices, subject positions, modes of discourse, performance and regulation that the two worlds provide. This kind of split and fragmented subjectivity is necessary to cross the divide. Whether a new position, that of hybrid, is formed in the process is no simple matter, either psychically or socially. Although the two worlds that Nicky kept so defensively apart could have been integrated with a great deal of hard emotional work; to suggest that this have been easy for her would be to deny the massive social inequalities that were at their foundation.

Teresa: a different kind of rebellion

Teresa's mother and father, who were Irish, had fairly fond memories of school (although they expressed little faith in their own 'intelligence'). Her father especially placed great emphasis on 'an education' as the way to get on in the world and had himself gone back to college as an adult to study electronic engineering. Teresa was considered bright at 10 and was expected by her teachers to do well in secondary school. After her GCSEs, in which she achieved three As, four Bs, one C and one D, it seemed realistic to assume that she was set for A levels and then university. Both parents were extremely supportive of their daughter's education and her father was proud that Teresa would be doing science subjects at A level. But something went terribly wrong at that point. After her GCSEs Teresa took an overdose. However she recovered and went into the sixth form at her all-girls school, but she quickly lost interest in studying and abandoned her A levels in the first year. Describing the school atmosphere as 'childish' she opted to 'go for a job', which she got in an insurance agency and enjoyed. Things seemed to be going well, with Teresa enjoying the adult status and financial independence the work brought. Nor did she feel that she had rejected education altogether; she thought she would probably go back to study once she had had a break from it. However that year she became pregnant and had a son just before her nineteenth birthday. She later went back to college to take a different set of A levels, but gave two of them up and failed the other.

Teresa seemed to come from the kind of working-class family that could promote educational success in their child. When Teresa was four her mother employed the kinds of practice that are taken to ensure educational success: she played 'learning games' with Teresa and was not an authoritarian mother (Walkerdine and Lucey, 1989). At 10 Teresa (like all the 'good' children) had a clear sense of what high achievers do in class and followed those practices herself. Her teacher described her very positively, but spoke in a derogatory tone of her father as having great expectations of his daughters and of pushing them, while her mother was described as a 'nice little woman who does not push herself'. These kinds of comment were exclusively reserved for working-class parents – the middle-class parents were never described in this way. Despite these deeply ambivalent comments from her teacher, Teresa did well at school and was expected to go to university. She attended a Catholic, single-sex, ex-grammar school that valued high performance and encouraged the pupils to go on to higher education. What happened to her to make her abandon these well-laid plans, which she had every chance of fulfilling?

We might explore the parental side of this by thinking about the investment made by working-class parents in order to have something 'different' themselves, to realise their own dreams through their children. Teresa's father had a massive investment in Teresa fulfilling his dreams of becoming not only a professional, but also one in a scientific profession – a particularly masculine fantasy of upward mobility and success (cf. Walkerdine, 1991). Her father was extremely proud of his 'little girl', who seemed to be so good at maths, physics and chemistry and could realise his own desire to escape from hard manual work. Teresa herself was the good girl, as opposed to her sister's rebellious 'bad girl' status. In relation to this sister, who would not do what her father wanted, Teresa said; 'actually I think a lot of the time I tried to make up for things that she'd upset them about as well'.

Making up for other people's failures and disappointments can bring its rewards, but feeling responsible for the happiness of others, particularly of parents, can become a heavy burden. For Teresa it became an impossible task in adolescence and she attempted to construct an identity that was distinct from her father's wishes and expectations. Teresa was very clear during both of the interviews that she had been (and to some extent still was) rebelling against her identification as daddy's little girl, which she articulated most explicitly when she spoke of dyeing her waist-length blond hair jet black when she was 15, but which was also present in her suicide attempt. This could be understood in part as a desperate desire to differentiate herself from her father and was all tied up with not wanting to go back to school to study three science A levels. In Chapter 9 we shall explore how her complex rebellion was further implicated in her having a baby at 19. At 21 she had distanced herself from everything scientific and her house was heavily decorated with artwork and poetry. Even though she had returned to college to study arts A levels, her enormous ambivalence about education remained in place. The struggle she experienced in committing herself to her studies is not entirely explained by the constraints of being a single mother. One interpretation is that she was caught in an unconscious desire to remain daddy's girl and make him proud of her by getting the education he had never had. But each time she did return to education – at 16 to do her A levels and then at 21 again to study at A level – she was never quite sure that it was entirely her choice. She allowed herself to be pushed back into education, only to find herself unable to sustain the energy and enthusiasm needed to complete the course. In relation to college and the idea of university she said: 'I start things, but I don't finish them very well. I sort of get lost half way.'

Teresa – whose mother had told her she was a clever girl when she was four, whose teachers had thought she was a bright girl when she was 11 and whose father could not understand why someone so brainy could not achieve educationally – had introjected this getting lost half way as an individual failing, an unfortunate aspect of her personality rather than as a way of defending against being taken over by the wishes of others. Paradoxically these were wishes that she might have longed to fulfil at one level because they might have brought her a better life and given a little happiness to her family, but the complex defences against this happening also made sure that she struggled to remain different and separate. In this way the ridiculous simplicity of a discourse that suggests we should all remake ourselves in the new democracy is shown up for what it is.

Clever girls

In *Democracy in the Kitchen* (Walkerdine and Lucey, 1989) we noted that some working-class four and ten year olds were placed in a contradictory position whereby they were seen by the family as 'clever' and constantly praised for the smallest achievement (whether physical or intellectual), while at school they were viewed as 'babies' who needed too much attention and failed to display the kind of independence appropriate for educational success. Obviously much development has taken place since then, but aspects of how designations of 'cleverness' and parents' pride in achievement remain complex and contradictory.

For example Rebecca, a black, working-class sixteen year old, chose to follow a BTEC nursery nursing course instead of going on to A levels, which her GCSE results and her teachers indicated she had the ability to do, but which she said she was not confident enough to tackle. (Heidi Mirza, 1992, describes the young black women in her own research as highly ambitious in class terms, although this often meant aspirations towards gendered and sometimes poorly paid careers in caring professions.) Despite her family's extreme pride in her studying this course, Rebecca became uncomfortably aware of how 'low-level' the course and the qualification was considered by employers and by other students at the college:

> Anyone can go into that course and come out of the two years with a – as long as you're prepared to sit down, probably every night and write a couple of sides, then you can be a qualified nursery nurse. Which is a shame.

Perhaps saddest of all, we can see that Rebecca's view of her own abilities had become implicated in her realisation that the course might not be, as she had been led to understand, of a value equivalent an to A level. Young women like Rebecca experience a painful mis-match between their parents' expectations for them (which can be unrealistic), their parents' and their own very real pride in what they achieve, and the value of those qualifications in a wider context (Bates and Riseborough, 1993). Rebecca's story also highlights a tendency among girls of Afro-Caribbean origin to follow lower-level courses than their teachers and past performance indicate they are capable of (Gillborn and Gipps, 1996).

Boundaries

While middle-class mothers are seen as 'sensitive' by Tizard and Hughes (1984) and particular working-class mothers are especially picked out as not responding to their daughters' needs in the most effective manner, it is interesting that two such working-class daugh-ters in our study (Nicky and Dawn) were the very ones who did well at school.

What these particular mothers do, and what they are implicitly criticised for when their daughters are four years old, is put compara-tively strong boundaries around their children's behaviour. There is an underlying assumption within the child-centred model of children's needs that boundaries are not good. However, perhaps this is exactly what allows children to achieve at school, because work and home are simply not the same and that difference has to be socially, culturally and psychically managed. However it might also be noted that, as we shall see in the next chapter, achieving the kind of excellence that middle-class girls uniformly do necessitates extremely strong, if not rigid boundaries in relation to schoolwork. In our study these bound-aries were enshrined in school and family practices that disallowed the possibility of failure – the girls had to work consistently well at school and homework had to be done, whatever else. In Chapter 5 we explored how, for some working-class parents, happiness enters as an emotional construct through which intense anxieties about learning are managed. While middle-class parents' anxiety about the reproduc-tion of educational success is likely to cause them to set up rigid boundaries in relation to schoolwork, white working-class parents are more likely to allow the in children to give up at the very point when learning is experienced as difficult, because of the complex emotions that are brought up for the parents in respect of their own school failure (see the section on happiness in the Chapter 5). Such a response, while completely understandable, does not help the children to succeed in areas where their parents have failed. What is necessary, then, is for parents and children to be able to manage a supportive relationship that allows the children to keep going even when the going gets tough, no mean emotional feat for families already in a socially disadvantagd position.

Holly was studying for an MA at the time of the second interview. But at 17, whilst at school studying A levels, she had become pregnant. Her mother, though supportive, had insisted that Holly remain at school throughout her pregnancy and sit her A levels. Holly felt that she had had no choice about this and, in a way that was reminiscent of the middle-class girls, said that she had not had an option when it came to education – dropping out of school, at any time, had been unthinkable.

Nicky had never found studying easy and became stressed and distressed when the GCSE and A level demands were heavy. Her father found it extremely difficult to see her tired and tearful, especially as he was in no position to help with the work. Despite the anxiety this aroused in him he never suggested to Nicky that she give it up: 'you'd have to pull her away from the books and say just leave your books alone for an hour. Go for a walk, go and do anything and *then come back to it*' (our emphasis).

We could also point out that, for most children, the practical and emotional aspects of schoolwork produce varying degrees of anxiety at one time or another. They represent hurdles that the child must be helped over if she is to learn and move on. The working-class parents in our study often spoke of how disturbing they found it to witness their children's anxieties about to schoolwork. Setting boundaries in what, at these times, can feel extremely unsafe is surely the best thing a parent can do. This may involve support, help and sensitivity. Crucially, it will also involve saying 'you have to do it'.

Being strong and independent

An our study, all of the working-class young women who were to varying degrees successful at school saw themselves as strong and independent, a self-identification that throughout their narratives was closely linked to their parents' struggle. Working-class parents often talked about how they had tried to give their daughters the message that life was a struggle and something that must be survived. For example Nicky's mother said: 'Well I always used to tell her as shewas growing up you've got to be hard in this world to survive.' One of the effects of the girls' sense of their parents being heavily burdened was that they did not want to add to their burden in any way. Holly had skilfully kept her misbehaviour at school a secret because 'I didn't want to give her too many problems because she had four children to raise by herself. I didn't want to create any more hassles.'

Parents had to be protected from some of the more difficult aspects of their daughters' experiences. Nicky endured chronic bullying at school, not only because she didn't want to bother her parents with it, but also because she felt that their interference would only make it worse. Maura, although she detested the sixth form where she had chosen to do her A levels, did not make a fuss about it with her parents because 'they had enough to worry about without that'. But as we also say, not being able to turn to parents, feeling that they might not be able to or, importantly, may be powerless to help can engender feelings of hopelessness. As we said in Chapter 2, no-one who feels hopeless is capable of the imaginative shift necessary for self-invention. To defend against feelings of complete isolation and hope-lessness, it is necessary to construct a scenario in which one only has oneself to rely on.

The narratives of Nicky, Maura, Anna and Holly were literally saturated with the desire for emotional independence. For Maura and Nicky, their financial relationship with their parents both symbolised and was the vehicle through which emotional dependency was often articulated (Plummer 2000). But along with this came an acute aware-ness, often since childhood, by many working-class girls of the lack of money:

> Yeah – I remember when I was younger thinking for some reason we – I don't know why – I think I've asked my mum since, she doesn't know what I'm talking about but – thinking that, um, being in the playground at school and getting really upset when I was really young in primary school and thinking we didn't have any money or something – I don't know what I heard my mum and dad say – I must have heard my dad say he couldn't afford something and then thought we don't have any money or we can't – [laughs] and feeling really guilty and kind of getting really upset about it. But, um, the only time I ever panic is whenever my dad says 'I'd give you some money and help you out but I can't afford it' and I think Oh god, you know I feel really guilty – I – I'm using my money say to go out and do something or, um, you know, and he won't ever say it unless he really can't give me any money.

What an incredible burden of guilt such young people have to bear. An important psychological issue is how precisely to understand the relation between the social and material and the psychic. These are very common feelings and experiences, but how are they produced, what do they mean, what are their social and psychological consequences and how does one intervene in them?

Due to lack of finances Maura lived at home when she first went to university. Even though the journey there took one and a half hours each way, she felt terrible when she finally had to ask her parents for money to pay for accommodation nearer college. While Nicky had resolved this by saving her money for years, Maura sought other solutions, including squatting in a flat in a run-down council estate and then sharing a small rented room with another female student. Maura finally changed to a university very close to her parents and returned home to live. Reay *et al.* (1999, p. 3), in their study of higher education choices among further education students, found a localism among the working-class white and ethnic minority students that was absent from the narratives of the more economically privileged students. We found a similar trend, with all of the middle-class young women going away to university, while all of the working-class young women, except Nicky, chose local colleges. We cannot underestimate the economic necessity of this and the financial burden that supporting children living away from home represents for most working-class families.

But money is not the only thing that keeps them close to home. The emphasis on localism relates to our ongoing argument about the difficulties that arise for working-class young women and their families in relation to the identity transformation and therefore loss that educational success consistently poses. At 16 Christine, who was about to make her applications for higher education but was still clearly ambivalent about it, certainly could cannot contemplate combining going to university with separation from her parents:

> But the thing is, 'cos if I went to a university, I wouldn't want to leave home, so I'd have to go somewhere that was quite easy to travel to in London. 'Cos I just wouldn't be able to leave home.

By the second interview Christine's position on leaving home had shifted somewhat, and she thought that she would probably find student accommodation because her preferred choice of university was just beyond comfortable commuting distance, but, importantly, still in London.

> Um I don't think so, cos it will be too much travelling and stuff. But that's the thing that's worrying a bit I think, it's a bit daunting just um knowing that you're going away – I'll probably come home for weekends and things, but it's just a bit, a bit frightening.

Very few of the working-class parents in the study had left home before they married, reflecting the working-class cultural practices of the 1960s and 1970s. In fact Christine's father said that he could not imagine Christine leaving home for any other reason than to get married. For the middle-class young women, going to university constituted a package of culturally supported rites of passage, including a highly regulated version of independent living and the 'gap year' spent travelling, which served to strengthen identifications between generations. Of course some of the middle-class parents did feel tremendous sadness when their daughters went off to university, but their comments in no way conveyed a sense of devastating loss:

> It was awful. It was as though someone had taken her away and she wasn't coming back. It was the first break-up of our family and we felt devastated. It was awful (Nicky's mother).

For the working-class young women, choosing a university close to home was a way of attempting to maintain a sense of sameness with their families in the face of an event that threatened to make them irreversibly different (see Chapter 8).

Holly

For Holly, a mixed-race 21 year old, being really strong and independent and not having to rely on other people was articulated through a powerful identification with her mother, who had escaped a violent relationship with their father to bring up Holly and her siblings alone. Heidi Mirza (1992) argues that a researcher's preoccupation with subculture, in particular the 1980s subcultures of resistance, had had a major effect on the study of black women. What emerged in this work was a core romantic idea that young black women were motivated mostly by and through their identification with strong black mothers. For Holly, whose mother was white, the discursive categories of strong woman and black woman, while there may have been mythical aspects to them (mirza, 1992), had nevertheless been ones that she had been able to make good use of.

I don't know, I think my mum's like a really strong woman and I think she's made us – like all of us are really strong and independent and we can just stand by ourselves, we don't need anybody else. And I think it's the way she's brought us up, so that we don't need to rely on other people.

For Holly's mother, the struggles that she and her children faced were more about race than class:

I can remember her [Holly's mother] telling us, were gonna have to work twice as hard as anybody else but that doesn't mean we can't do it, we can achieve whatever we want to (Holly).

It is interesting to note that Holly was the only young woman to sustain an educational career despite twice becoming pregnant in the middle of her studies: she had her first child during her A levels and her second child while she was studying for her first degree. Media- and government-driven moral panics about single mothers have suggested that their daughters will themselves go on to become teenage single mothers, producing generations who are locked into a cycle of single parenthood, low educational achievement and welfare dependency. But for Holly, who was in fact the most highly qualified young woman in the entire sample at that point, the spectre of poverty and racial pathologisation had in part at least, provoked and promoted the kind of motivation needed to stay on her educational course and not, as she said, 'be another case of another black girl being on social security'.

The white working-class girls who were at or heading for university shared Holly's determination not to be as economically or materially poor as their parents. This desire certainly seemed to be connected to their determination to embark and remain on their educational journeys and to divert if not halt the process of social reproduction:

I've always wanted to go to 'uni'. I don't know why. I have to do a bit better for myself. 'Cos a lot of people my own age in my family, a bit younger, a bit older or, all they've done is, well a lot of them have dropped out of school early and gone and got themselves a job that's got absolutely no prospects to it, like working in a burger bar or something. And I just did not want that for myself. I couldn't see myself spending the rest of my life stuck in a burger bar. I just knew I had to get out and do something a bit better (Nicky).

Christine, Nicky, Maura, Dawn and Holly shared a fantasy of escape in their drive towards higher education, while those young women had who left education at GCSE or A level, such as Teresa, Jenny and Anna, did not present the same vivid picture of what they needed to escape from.

Both Rebecca, who was Afro-Caribbean, and Holly, who was Afro-Caribbean mixed race, described how adolescence for them included a period where their identification as black and female was configured around notions of badness. As a mixed-race girl Holly had to walk a very thin and fluid line in relation to her colour identity, particularly when she moved school at age 11. At that time she transferred from a predominantly white primary school to a much more racially mixed secondary school, where in order to fit in she was required to adopt a completely different kind of racial identification:

> I can remember everybody used to call me white girl because I'd grown up in … and we went to an all-white school, I'd become like whitified, you know what I mean? So when I started the school I was very white, but they didn't like that because I wasn't being black enough. So then I went for a good few years trying to be as black as I could be, do you know what I mean? Talking in slang and just really hard and beating up white girls just for being white girls you know.

For Holly this subjectivity could only be played out at school, and careful attempts were made to protect her white mother from her rejection of whiteness. Holly managed to be both rebellious and resistant to the school's culture at the public level, while privately conforming to the demands and discipline of academic work (Furlong and Cartmel, 1997):

> Well I was quite smart actually, because I was doing all this at school, so that's probably why the teachers thought I wouldn't get anything, but then I'd go home and study. So I was having all the fun in the day and then I'd go home and do my work. I wasn't that stupid not to do any work (Holly).

Rebecca's rebellion did not stop at school, but also extended to home life: 'Just, like, truancy and being rude to my parents, staying out late, not doing my work, giving the teachers hell.'

What is significant about both young women is that there was a sea-change in their attitudes and identification as they approached their GCSE examinations. Rebecca said: 'and then I just from about the fourth year … I just buckled down and started doing my work'. It was around that time that both young women became conscious of how heavily failure was implicated in being a black subject and so became engaged in a different kind of practice: one which was less about conforming and more about seeking ways to resist getting caught up in some of the harsher aspects of that racialised subjectification:

> I like followed the crowd, just so I could hang out with my black friends and stay with them and stuff, but then I realised that I don't have to be acting like that to be black, because I am black no matter what I do (Holly).

Cycles of deprivation

Perhaps the most important precursor to the research described in these volumes was the National Child Development Study. This longitudinal study of 1600 children born in Britain during one week in 1958 provides a large and important data base with which to compare our work. The most important volumes are those by Essen and Wedge (1982) and Pilling (1990), who tested a number of theories of deprivation and disadvantage. The 'situational' view suggests that the behavioural patterns characterising the disadvantaged are purely responses to present stresses, and that people will be more willing to accept challenges when social circumstances improve. On the other hand there is the view that there is a 'culture of poverty', with its own way of life, handed down from generation to generation. This 'subculture of the poor' is viewed as 'an adaptation to the objective situation, providing a means of coping with it, but also preventing opportunities which do occur from being taken' (Pilling, 1990, p. 7).

Essen and Wedge (1982) argue against both these models, supporting an 'adaptation' theory of social disadvantage. That is, they argue that disadvantaged children do adapt to their objective situation, but often continue that adapted behaviour after the disadvantage has ceased. They do not believe that a culture of poverty exists in Britain.

In her study of the NCDS data, Pilling (1992) concludes that one of the central reasons for the success of working class children at school occurs when the social disadvantage is compensated by a psychological advantage – not so much from the practices of the parents but from the children's belief that their parents want them to do well, and to do better than they have done. Such beliefs allow children to keep going and succeed against difficult odds, no matter what. This is particularly interesting in view of the fact that in our study some of the working-class girls did succeed despite the fact that in their early years their mothers engaged in practices that were antagonistic to rather than compatible with the education system.

However, Pilling does not engage with the emotional consequences of parents wanting their children to have better lives than they did. Teresa's mother said: 'All we want is for our children to do better than we did. I think that's what everyone wants.' This desire was not articulated by those middle-class parents who had not had to scrimp and save for everything. For the working-class families, higher education and the subsequent possibility of entrance into a profession offered an escape from the grinding facts of ordinary-working class life. These working-class mothers and fathers did not want their daughters to have to do the kinds of work they had to do: boring, repetitive, dirty and hard, with little pay, status or security. As Pilling suggests, working-class parents' desires and dreams of a better life for their children act as a powerful engine that drives their children's motivation to succeed at education and helps to maintain them on the path to higher education. But the provenance of this motivation means that other, equally powerful messages are transferred in the emotional exchange between working-class parent and child.

We have seen how for middle-class families, educational success is the theme around which the reproduction of social class position revolves. Within this scenario, what is aimed at by children is becoming like their parents in the sense of having the same kind of career as them, the same levels of income, material comfort and lifestyle. For working-class daughters of aspirational parents the message is quite different; it is clearly about *not* becoming like them and it is this which is central both to the daughters' drive towards higher education and to the deep ambivalences that beset some of them concerning the same. In order to improve on their parents' lives they have to differentiate themselves from those who do not or can not improve (Skeggs, 1997a, p. 82). Wanting something different, something more than your parents implies not only that there is something wrong with your parents' life, but also that there is something wrong with them. This kind of dis-identification with one's parents and family can engender a deep sense of shame, which is itself so shameful that it must be psychically regulated through repressive mechanisms.

Perhaps most importantly, and which might explain why so many of them give up, this dis-identification with their parents means that the leaving involved in going to university and perhaps becoming a professional hits at a very deep level (Plummer, 2000). These are separations on a grand scale that middle-class young women simply do not have to tackle. Of course psychic separation from parents is an issue for everyone to a greater or lesser extent. But for able working-class girls who do well at school, education is the arena in which it is played out.

A recurring theme in the working-class young women's narratives was that of profound difference – from their parents, families and friends. Nicky and Maura spoke of not having anything to say to friends who had left school at 16 or 18; of there 'not being much similarity between us anymore'. This kind of distance and loss of friends could usually be borne by the girls who had stayed on the educational course because they had inevitably made new friends with whom they did have something in common. But parents and family were a different matter and could not so easily be traded in. The working-class parents had no reference points through which to understand what their daughters really did at college or university and were frequently intimidated by the level and volume of work they were required to do. Mothers in particular also expressed amazement and fear about their daughters' foray into unknown territory:

> I don't know if I could cope in that environment. Of all those new people and having to give presentations and things you know (Christine's mother).

> It's like when she went off to America, no I couldn't imagine myself doing something like that. I'd be petrified. I mean I get lost when I go out of Broadwick [her local town] let alone anything else (Nicky's mother).

Conversely the working-class young women at university were routinely infantilised by family members because they were still studying and not in full-time waged labour. Maura, in the second year of her degree, was occasionally asked by relatives if she was still at school: 'because I'm still studying, some of them think that you only study when you're like 15 and everything, so they associate it with being like 15 or something, or 16', Negative constructions of students further served to isolate and distance the young women from their wider family: 'My uncle is a definite Geordie man. He's very biased about a lot of things and one of them is students so he doesn't believe I do anything at University except go out and get drunk (Nicky).

The opposition between play and hard work was not so stark in the middle-class families, where going to university was a rite of passage that most family members had undertaken. For them, student life should be both a time of serious study and a youthful sabbatical in which to experience and experiment with the new. The working-class young women, however, had on some levels introjected the notion that students did indeed do what they wanted which was usually taken to mean very little. Maura had consciously changed the way she dressed when she attended family functions as she was anxious to dispel the notion that she played around all day. But throughout these young women's stories there were tangible threads of guilt; the guilty feeling that perhaps these relatives and friends were right – that they *were* idle, immature and indulgent. Parents tended not to appear in these damning indictments of study and students, and were viewed as much more supportive and understanding of the demands made upon their daughters, typically because they had actually witnessed the hours of labour their daughters invested in their studies. But parental support was not quite enough to banish the constantly re-emerging feelings of guilt among these young women, and in a way the support itself became heavily implicated in the construction and constitution of that guilt. For indeed the young women were enjoying themselves at university; they were having fun and doing what they wanted; they did not have the responsibilities that their parents had had when they were the same age, and they were looking forward to a better life than their parents currently had.

While the parents gave a strong message that this better life was exactly what they wanted for their children, envy was sometimes aroused, an emotion with such negative connotations that few would give voice to it (Plummer 2000). Nicky's mother said: 'I must admit I get jealous sometimes, you know, and thinking, cor I wish we'd had the chance to do that when we were younger.' Teresa's mother had had to leave school at 16 because her family could not afford the cost of her staying on. When she said that she envied Teresa because Teresa had had chances that she had been denied, it was her anger and frustration that was communicated most clearly.

Whether envy and anger are spoken about or not, the knowledge that they are being given a chance that their parents (or siblings) have never had is embedded in the experience of educational success for many working-class children. Recognition that one might be the object of others' envy may not happen at the conscious, rational level, precisely because it is so irrational to think that a parent with whom we share a loving relationship could harbour such negative feelings towards us. However at the unconscious level, fear that this envy may cause us to be the target of our parents' aggressive feelings continues to operate and may in turn provoke our own aggression. In an object-relations model (Klein, 1959), aggression towards the parent (typically the mother) can be notoriously difficult for a child to express or even acknowledge because of intense fear that the parent will retaliate by an equally aggressive rejection of the child. So what happens to all these negative, outlawed feelings?

We want to suggest that these feelings are turned inwards and transformed into an acceptable emotion: guilt, which meandered through the successful working-class young women's stories like a river with many tributaries and was most transparent in their discussions of money and financial dependence on their parents. Maura, Christine, Nicky and Holly felt so guilty about taking anything from their parents because on some level they felt it was supporting a period in their lives that their own parents would like to have had but which had been denied them. Not only that, but there was tremendous guilt in the knowledge that their parents were supporting something that was having an unforeseen consequence: it was pushing them further apart from one another. 'Survival guilt' is a common experience among people who have survived a great trauma – for example genocide – in which others died. The families of these young women had not perished of course, but there was a sense in which their new lives as upwardly mobile women had been produced on the back of the, sometimes self-imposed, deprivations of their parents, as in the case of Christine's parents.

Elsewhere, one of us has explored survival guilt among a group of working-class women who went on to higher education (Walkerdine, 1992). Several of these women felt they did not deserve to survive what their parents had not been able to survive physically (in some cases fathers had been injured or killed in work-related accidents) and this translated into a feeling that they could not survive psychically even though they were now in professional work. This kind of almost unbearable guilt is, we suggest, a consequence of the experience of extreme deprivation. While it contains complex patterns of envy, as we suggested earlier, these are produced out of the situation itself and are not reducible to a universalistic model of mother–child relations. This demonstrates the crucial need for a different kind of psychosocial work that recognises the intricate imbrication of the psychic and the social (Walkerdine, 1991, 1996, 1997). The feeling among these women that they had no right to the life they had worked so hard for was more easily expressed as a sense of masquerade or fear of failure or exposure contained in 'passing' as middle-class than as aggression towards a parent's self-denial, when it was that very action which had helped assure their own path to changed status.

It would be quite simplistic to conclude that parental support and belief in something better is what needs to be pushed in working-class parents. Conversely, this account demonstrates the incredible pain and difficulty associated with the transformations that success in education can bring for working-class girls.

Conclusion

Liberal discourses ask 'what can we do to make working-class children succeed at school?' and focus on pedagogy and the practices of teachers and parents, particularly mothers. Those on the left, in the meantime, are hooked on theories of reproduction. Neither of these frameworks can really address how or why some working-class children succeed. The more recent 'conformist' literature on working-class children who do well at school is replete with problems, with the 'conformist' category set up as an opposition to the 'resistance' literature (for example Willis, 1977). We are advocating an understanding of working-class girls' success as not a simple conformity at all, but then neither could it be understood as an easy rebellion or resistance. Why some girls would long for something different and have the strength to make this happen through what is an emotionally and socially terrifying shift while others feel safer staying within the well understood and maintained practices of school failure is a question that demands to be asked, but it is not usually addressed in the educational literature.

Middle-class children receive the message from birth that not only are they able and clever, but also that their destiny is to go to university and become professionals, a destiny that is pushed hard and has its own real constraints (see Chapter 7). This is certainly not the destiny of working-class girls, nor is it presented as such – is this why girls like Teresa, Jenny and Anna, who have achieved examination success at school, give up even when they have a sure footing on that path? Because it is not the working-class girls' destiny, the motivation to remain on that path must be generated from within. There are no structural reasons why they should succeed and therefore they have to rely on their own inner resources. However we also wish to stress that if such success is achieved by a working-class girl, the hopes and aspirations of her and her parents become intertwined with the pain of separation, and therefore a loss or shift of identity (Walkerdine, 1991, 1996, 1997; Reay, 1996). Girls who have not done so well at school at least do not have to face the difficulties that choice can bring. We therefore want to stress the great emotional costs of success, costs which, as we shall see in the next chapter, are huge but differently produced in the middle class. So how do any working class girls at all succeed in education when they are regulated to become 'docile subjects', but in the present 'government of freedom' must remake themselves as autonomous, reflexive subjects? Firstly, we argue that this regulation is double-edged. It is precisely the strong boundaries between work and play that are crucial for understanding the production of a subject who is capable of recognising the absolute separation of home and school (cf. Walkerdine, 1991) and coping with it psychically by complex defences. Secondly, the very inner resources that are necessary for success can also be self-destructive, and this contradiction needs to be understood in order to assist children and adults in this transition. Thirdly, there are no easy hybrids. Hybridity may be a cultural and social fact but it is never lived easily in a psychic economy. Fourthly, this work suggests the absolute necessity of examining the emotional costs of self-invention.

Chapter 7

The Making of the Bourgeois Subject as Feminine

The production of middle-class success

In the literature on middle-class pupils, apart from some notable exceptions (Walford, 1984, 1986, 1990; Delamont, 1989; Roker, 1993; Allatt, 1993), there is remarkably little research on their experiences in the education system. Frazer (1988, p. 344) notes that 'overwhelmingly researchers have concentrated on the experience and position of working class girls, neglecting middle (let alone upper) class girls. Even research projects which include middle class girls in the sample tend relatively to neglect them at the reporting stage'. Middle-class girls' educational 'success' seems to say it all, confirming the 'healthy normality' against which all other performances should be judged. But what does educational success actually mean, and what proportion of young people can be said to be successful? How do we disentangle success within the normative process of education from the subjective meaning of success in every other sphere of our lives? It is important to consider how, in the numerous strands of 'youth' research, educational performance remains a starting point from which sociologists and psychologists go on to study the problems of young people (Cohen and Ainley, 2000). In 'problem-centred' youth research, the assumption remains that those who are achieving well at school, staying on at school and going on to higher education do not need to be explained. There is nothing more to say about them, they simply 'are', and the conviction that they are the norm renders them invisible.

Why should we want critically to examine middle-class practices when they clearly work, producing success for middle-class daughters? The very fact that so little has been written about middle-class youth, and especially middle-class girls, makes it important to take a much closer look at their experiences. Bates and Riseborough (1993) point to the importance of considering how the invisibility of the 'conformist' in educational research has led to a 'theoretical trivialisation of the process of their schooling [and] . . . is all the more remarkable given the centrality of the concepts of social and cultural reproduction in the armoury for understanding schooling and society'. However we consider that the opposition conformity/resistance is itself a problem and one that we would want to oppose in its easy certainty and resistance-theory-driven position. Social scientists interested in examining the processes by which systems of stratification are produced, reproduced and transformed cannot do so by focusing only on one section of what may be described as the 'class continuum'. An understanding of the production of disadvantage requires a corresponding investigation of the production of privilege. What kinds of subject are being produced inside this changed globalism? Are class differences the same as they ever were, and if so, what does this mean given that the conditions are so different?

Sarah Delamont's (1989) study, based on a Scottish public school for girls, with data collected between 1969 and 1975, is one of the few detailed works on middle-class girls' education. As she aptly points out:

> The lives of middle-class girls at home and at school are probably the least researched topic in the whole of the sociology of education, despite being the group who have been, over the last century, the most influential group in rearing and marrying the men who are the most successful products of the British education system. (ibid., p. 61).

We might add that in more recent years it has been middle-class girls who have been viewed as the success story of our education system, indeed given the furore about their success relative to that of boys, they have been too successful for some in this changed economy. What guidelines, therefore, does this study, conducted over twenty years ago, offer to our own research? Delamont differentiates between groups of girls within the same class, between daughters of the intelligentsia (professionals, the new middle class) and daughters of the bourgeoisie (business people, entrepreneurial, managerial, the old middle class). The academic girls in her study came from professional families and were highly regarded by the school. The others were less concerned with academic attainment and were less liked by the school, possibly because their parents had 'money rather than class'. As Delamont puts it:

> the debs and dollies were from entrepreneurial homes (the old middle class in Bernstein's (1973a) terms), and St Luke's was preparing them to

take their place in that sector of the Scottish elite. The swots and weeds . . . were representative of Bernstein's 'new' middle class, and were preparing to enter the intellectual elite of the country (ibid., p. 58).

She argues that it is the intellectual group who have more cultural capital and are therefore more set to succeed through their own efforts in the bourgeois world rather than by making a good marriage. This is interesting in the light of our research, in which almost all of the middle-class girls succeeded spectacularly at school. If like Delamont we divide them up according to parental occupations, all our young women came from the new and none from the old middle class, which reflects both the sampling criteria used by Tizard and Hughes (1984) and the change in class composition from the time of Delamont's study. In addition to this, Penny, Gill and Julie came from upwardly mobile working-class families, in which their parents had been the first generation to go on to higher education or join a profession.

Delamont explains her findings with reference to cultural capital and the way in which the middle class is reproduced. However what we wish to do is to examine the place both of rationality and of the feminine in the making of the bourgeois subject, a subject who, in fact, typifies the norm of the modern subject and possesses certain characteristics that appear as 'middle class' but are not confined to the middle class (Rose, 1992; Henriques *et al.*, 1998). In this sense our approach here is different from that implied by the reproduction of the middle classes in Bourdieu's sense. In this analysis the technologies of the social produce modes of power and regulation through which a particular kind of subject is produced at a particular historical moment. Our aim, then, is to understand how, at this particular historical moment, this subject is remade as feminine. Our aim is to demonstrate that what is so impressively achieved by girls and their families is the production of practices through which the bourgeois subject is assured, and that this requires a great deal of hard work on the part of a lot of people. It is not achieved easily or without a struggle, a struggle that defends against Otherness, the Otherness typified by the unreason of the masses.

Additionally, we wish to argue that the academic success of middle-class girls is historically specific. We want to show both how it is produced and what it means. Given that there have been so few studies of the middle classes, it is relevant to note how difficult it was even to address this issue. Throughout our research and analysis of the data we engaged in a process of 'making strange' things that on the surface and in popular and/or traditional discourses are often 'taken for granted' and therefore do not seem to require an explanation (Bourdieu, 1984; Smith, 1988). As part of this we began to ask what success means and what is invested in its production. For instance high educational performance and achievement for girls is presented as an indisputably good thing, which on some levels it may well be, certainly in terms of the production of certainty and the maintenance of financial and social location. But as we have said, this certainty can been understood as operating against its Other: loss of money, position, status. The strategy of academic success can therefore also be understood as a defence against uncertainty. When we interviewed the middle-class girls we became aware of a growing sense of our own confusion and contradiction: we were presented with apparently seamless success but at the same time deep anxieties surfaced, anxieties that increasingly seemed to underpin that very performance, supporting our view of success as part of a defensive organisation. Within a celebratory discourse of girls' attainment in the 1990s there is little room to make sense of the defences that produced that very performance.

Both the statistics (see Chapter 3, p. 62) and the middle-class families' narratives told a story of outstanding examination results, university entrance and an intended professional career path. Of the middle-class 21 year olds, 93 per cent were engaged in or had completed a higher education course (all at degree level) compared with 22 per cent of the working-class young women (and only 17 per cent were studying at degree level). Eighty-seven per cent of the middle-class girls had followed an undeviating pathway, moving from GCSEs to A levels to an honours degree, while 44 per cent of the working-class girls had left school at 16 and had no plans to return to education in the near future. The homogeneity of the middle-class girls' educational pathways would seem to contradict theories of individualisation that assert we can no longer understand educational experiences in terms of class-based divisions (Beck, 1992). Indeed the similarities between them were so striking that a sense was strongly evoked of them not only following well-trodden paths but also of being on a conveyor belt. Educational experiences may have become more diverse, but this diversification had impacted most powerfully on the working-class girls, as we saw in Chapters 3, 5 and 6.

Among the middle-class sample it was the daughters of parents from working-class backgrounds who were the first in their families to go through higher education or, as in the case of Penny's father, join a profession via a more informal route, who presented as a quite distinct group. Penny, Julie and Gill all deviated from the norm of the other middle-class girls in that they were not able to sustain their footing on this tightly circumscribed educational path. Gill did badly at GCSE level, dropped out of school at 16 and did not later return to education; Julie also did badly at school and left at 16 to train as a dancer, which she then gave up; Penny's otherwise good performance faltered at A level and later she gave up her degree course after only one term. Importantly, however, both Julie and Penny did regain their educational footing and went on successfully to complete university degrees.

We need to ask why this should be. Why should these young women be different from the other middle-class girls? This cannot be explained by differences in wealth or the social position of their parents, except for Gill, whose parents were divorced. We therefore need to look at the effect that the class transition made by the parents had on the psychic lives of their daughters. Evidence from other work, and indeed from the previous chapter on academically successful working-class girls, suggests that immense emotional problems are associated with class transition through education, problems that manifest themselves as problems of identity. This appears to have been in some way – not necessarily consciously – transmitted to the daughters of these upwardly mobile parents, since the daughters' success was at best ambivalent and at worst led to a conscious identification with the poor and transient, as in the case of Gill, who became a New Age traveller and lived in a converted bus. She eked out a living doing seasonal agricultural work and busking, but was the object of quite strenuous and nasty police surveillance and was continually moved from place to place. In a simple sense, these young women were not 'reproducing' anything certain that had gone on before, and they revealed the inherent instability of becoming the embodiment of the bourgeois subject.

Black and Asian middle-class girls

Serious inequalities in the educational achievements of black, Asian and non-white ethnic youth in Britain continue to be of concern to educationalists (Mirza, 1992; Griffiths and Troyna, 1995; Sewell, 1997; Tomlinson, 1999). Among the working-class sample, Dawn and Holly were Afro-Caribbean, mixed-race 21 year olds, and Sarena (21 years old) and Rebecca (16 years old) were both Afro-Caribbean. Among the middle-class sample there were two young Asian women: Atiya (21 years old) and Satinder (16 years old). Although our group of black and

Asian young women was small and it is difficult to make general-
isations, we can raise some observations relating to the complex
intersections of race, class and gender within the sample. As with
class, qualitative work in the field of race and education concentrates
on the problems of ethnic underachievers, with far less attention being
paid to successful pupils. Gillborn and Gipps (1996, p. 16), in their
review of educational research on the achievements of ethnic minority
pupils, argue that there is usually a direct relationship between pupils'
social class background and academic achievement: the higher the
social class, the higher the achievement.

Sudbury's (1998) analysis of British black women's achievements in
education and employment demonstrates similar tensions to those we
have explored in relation to the white community. She argues that
there is a popular black discourse presented in newspapers such as
Voice that 'African Caribbean women are doing better than "our" men'
(ibid., p. 156). She argues that this is often attributed not to the men's
lower qualifications but to women's lower levels of aggression and
their willingness to

> put up with the everyday racist backbiting endemic to educational institu-
> tions and office environments shared with white people. Accordingly
> African Caribbean women's advances in the field of education and
> employment are presented as the outcome of their willingness to ignore
> hostility in return for qualifications, status and money (ibid., p. 157).

This hostility towards black women's success is further illustrated by
the easy slippage from successful career woman to single mother/
matriarch:

> The assumption that African Caribbean women are 'doing better' in
> educational and economic terms is frequently meshed with gender politics
> to create a discourse which resonates with black male insecurities. The
> compliment of the professional woman who dominates the office is the
> single mother who dominates the household. Resentment toward socially
> mobile professional women can therefore be seen to build on the ambig-
> uous feelings of men of African descent towards single mothers who are
> portrayed simultaneously as the 'backbone' of the community and as
> matriarchs denying African Caribbean men their rightful position as
> heads of households (ibid., p. 158).

Sudbury argues that this position builds upon sexist assumptions that
black women house slaves had an easier time than their male counterparts and that black women's success can be seen as contributing to

black men's emasculation and white supremacy. She further suggests that the predominance of black women in service sector jobs, when discussing these women get such jobs not because they are less threatening than black men but because they are cheaper to employ. We would also add that this is part of the economic trend towards the 'feminisation of the economy' discussed in this book.

Sudbury also recognises the difficult and important class divisions which exist between black women. In our study we found that the singularity of direction and purpose that characterised the majority of the middle-class girls' educational routes or pathways and the expect-ations that shaped them were undisturbed by race. 'It was always, I would do my A levels and go to university, get a job, travel, get married and have kids or whatever' (Satinder, 16, Asian middle class). Black feminist writers have argued that in Britain, black people are mostly viewed as a homogeneous group, as automatically working class, a universalising process that prevents class differences from emerging (Reynolds, 1997; Sudbury, 1998).

Using the category 'race' can also mask deep historical, cultural and religious differences and divisions within and between black, Asian and non-white ethnic groups in Britain (Mirza, 1992). Satinder's and Atiya's families were both engaged in class processes that appeared on the surface to be very similar. Atiya's parents were educated professionals whose families occupied a social position in Pakistan that would be understood as middle class in Britain. Despite this privileged position in Pakistan, the powerful and endemic circulation of racist discourses and practices throughout British institutions – social and professional – presented the possibility of a serious erosion of previously enjoyed class advantages, and Atiya's parents had there-fore faced the threat of downward social mobility when they emigrated to Britain, although Atiya's father was a well-established member of the medical profession at the time of the research. Satinder's father had been a village school teacher in India; a job that had carried some social status but little financial reward. He was not a graduate himself and decided against teacher training in Britain because of financial restrictions. He also felt that at that time the job prospects for teachers in Britain were not good, so he and Satinder's mother put their energy into developing small businesses, first running a post office and then a nursing home. Emigration for this family repre-sented an opportunity to engage in a process of upward mobility through business development and by investing in their children's education.

What is interesting in the case of Satinder and Atiya is how both of their fathers pushed them forcibly to take science subjects at A level so that they could go on to study medicine, and therefore secure professional employment and status, despite both daughters being much more interested in and, especially in Satinder's case, showing more aptitude for arts subjects. Atiya, who did achieve the grades needed to get into a high-status medical school, wanted to do an arts degree but was heavily dissuaded from this with the promise that she could do anything she wanted after she qualified:

> They were keen that I had a very academic career, because I wanted to do journalism to start with and anthropology and all sorts of things like that, and they said – it's a typical Asian thing – they want me to do a very vocational career and like get a skill, so that I'm always self-sufficient, so that's the only other thing there's been clashes about. But in the end I did what they wanted me to do and I did medicine. But then they've always agreed that when I've finished the degree I can do whatever I like. So I'm just waiting to finish the degree now.

This focus on medicine and the medical sciences began early: when Satinder was six years old her father spoke of wanting her to study biology, maths, physics and chemistry when she got older. Both sets of parents stressed the importance of a university education, which would provide academic and professional qualifications and vocational skills that could be taken anywhere in the world and, as Atiya's father said, be marketed at short notice – both of which are essential to the migrant's survival. Some research suggests that pupils and parents of ethnic minority background demonstrate a greater commitment to education and value qualifications more highly; young people from ethnic minority backgrounds report more parental encouragement to remain in education (Drew *et al.*, 1992). Satinder's parents were very keen that all their children should develop professional lives, which included entrepreneurialism:

> We would prefer her to, yes, to go into medicine or pharmacy, as probably we might give her some finance help to develop her private business or anything like that. So that's in my mind anyway, put it that way (Satinder's father).

The very idea of becoming a doctor, psychiatrist or pharmacist seemed to reflect the desire and necessity to complete the fragile project of becoming the Western bourgeois subject within the constraints of racism and racist practices. Gewirtz *et al.* (1995) argue that recent immigrants to Britain may 'possess considerable cultural capital, but that it is in the wrong currency'. For Atiya's and Satinder's parents perhaps, their daughters' joining a prestigious, high-status profession such as medicine represented a means to convert some of their cultural capital into the right currency.

Early practices

Let us examine how these young women were prepared to be the bourgeois subject. In Chapter 5 we made it clear that when the middle-class girls were four years old there were a number of practices in which the girls and their mothers were engaged that were specific to this group. For example the lack of clear boundaries between work and play, the turning of domestic work into educative play and the import-ance of rational argument as a means of power for the young girls themselves. Alongside this was the classification of passionate emo-tions into nice and nasty feelings, sensible and silly behaviour. What place did those early practices have in the production of the middle-class girls' educational success? Why was it case that these girls suc-ceeded and how does this relate to the socio-economic debates with which we began this book – the feminisation of the economy, changes in the global division of labour, and how these global trends are manifested in class-ridden Britain? How did the girls manage to invent themselves as professional subjects in the new labour market? What bodily performances were expected of them? As we shall see, it is the female body and its child-bearing capability that have to be so intensely regulated in this new economy. To step up the professional career ladder, work must assume a central place in a young woman's life. The possibility of having children is therefore seen as a great threat to straightforward progression through education and up the career lad-der. Management of this is central to the making of the bourgeois subject as feminine.

We want to explore just how the production of these girls as subjects who could gain power through rational argument, the epitome of the bourgeois individual, was made to work as they progressed through the education system. What does it mean, in this new context, that the bourgeois subject may be defined as masculine but that these young women were allowed entry in increasing numbers? Their mothers were 'sensitive mothers' and facilitators of the 'knower' – the rational and autonomous child of child-centredness. When their daughters were four, if these mothers were employed at all they were mostly employed in the lowest levels of professional work. This changed over the course of their daughters' growing up and most of them entered full-time professional work. What is often covered over, as we pointed out in *Democracy in the Kitchen* (Walkerdine and Lucey, 1989), is the work such women put into transforming their housework into a playful learning exercise for their children and the effect this has on themselves. The mothers in our study turned routine activities such as cleaning the fish tank or preparing the muesli into the basis of an invisible pedagogy, one which taught their daughters to argue for their own power through the use of reason (even to the detriment of their mothers, who could sometimes be rather oppressed by these 'suburban terrorists'), and which allowed them to talk of nice or nasty feelings, but tended to reason them away rather than encourage them to be expressed or contained. At the time of the last interviews, their daughters were set to enter the professions, to become the bearers of that bourgeois rationality. How had those early lessons served them as they grew up and what effect had this had on their mothers, as well as the daughters' view of their mothers' lives in comparison with their dreams for their own?

The mothers did not have established careers: most had had their children at a relatively young age and later struggled to develop a career and bring up their children at the same time. It was this that their daughters wanted to avoid. Liz, whose mother had worked and studied law when the children were young, said: 'I just saw how much hard work it was [laughs], I don't know if I really want that much hard work'. There was also the knowledge that despite their mothers having full-time jobs there was little redistribution of domestic labour in terms of gender:

> And she has, my Dad works really hard, he's quite a workaholic. Because he's such a perfectionist, everything has to be right, so he spends hours in the office and so my mother basically has to run the household and keep a job going and look after the children, all by herself. So that's quite stressful.

They had seen how difficult their mothers' lives had been and did not want to repeat this pattern. This is interesting because their mothers had in fact put so much invisible work into providing them with the sensitive learning environment considered necessary to produce the bourgeois rational subject. now, In the following discussion Naomi's mother looked back on that time:

Mother: I don't know, well when I first started working I think I sort
            of thought well I'll … um. I don't know quite, I didn't think it
            through. Because I also always, I got married as I started
            work, and so I was always going to have children, but I sort
            of, somehow always thought I would be capable of being
            head of, definitely being head of department, head, whatever.
            I enjoyed it.

H: So what held you back in reaching that?

Mother: 'Cos I've um, well, put more into the family.

H: Mmm, you've got more demands at home.

Mother: Yes, a lot. I've got four children and there's no way I would
            put myself through, um, I mean going for it in a career way,
            at all.

The mothers' invisible work was clearly a huge investment in their
daughters' future, one which offered important returns now that the
economic situation was changing to accommodate greater female
participation in the professional labour market.

   Having documented the kinds of practice that, when the girls were
four years old, produced the mothers and daughters as particular kinds
of subject, what were the practices through which their production as
rational bourgeois subjects were accomplished? This accomplishment
was not simply due to the family alone, but was participated in by the
school and by the wider middle-class culture at large. In the next
section we shall document some of the ways in which socially and
psychically it was accomplished.

   How, as the young women grew up, was the relationship between
their production as the bourgeois subject and as feminine lived? Did
the two clash or live alongside each other, or did both have to be
transformed in order for the bourgeois subject to become feminised?
As we have already seen, professional men have been feeling threatened by the increasing number of women who are doing well educationally and entering the professional and business labour market. This
has been met with a post-feminist assertion of 'girl power' and the idea
of an active and powerful femininity, This whole cultural and discursive trend fits well with the growing opportunities for women to make
progress in the rationally ordered public space without losing or
demeaning their femininity. Indeed, the discourse describes well how
many middle-class young women want to present themselves and to be
understood. In this chapter we shall investigate, as well as examine the
detailed patterns – educational and otherwise – that emerged as each

young woman developed a unique overlay of her intellectuality and femininity.

The bourgeois subject as feminine

In order to understand the historical production of the bourgeois individual, we need to examine the family and cultural practices that contribute to this production. However, it would be foolish to suggest that these practices were in any simple sense the root cause of success of the girls in our study. In this chapter, then, what we are talking about specifically is the making of the bourgeoisie and the fictions upon which it is founded.

It might be argued that we are mistaken to examine and criticise the middle-class's strategies when they so patently produce success for their daughters. Why should we want to take that apart, criticise it even? We wish to argue that the production of that success – that is, success for middle-class girls – is historically specific. We want to show both how it is formed and what it means. As we said earlier, there have been very few studies of the middle classes and in the educational literature they are often regarded as the norm. In order to examine middle-class practices we had to 'make strange' those practices which are so often taken for granted. However, because all of us grew up working class, to some extent they were already strange to us and this gave us another take on what was going on. Part of this was that we began to ask what success meant and what the price was paid for it. Why, we asked, do middle-class girls seem to follow a path that looks a little like a conveyor belt and why must they be kept to that path at all costs, with so much fear that if they diverge from it, or allow themselves to be left behind, they will find themselves abandoned in a desert, lost without a map? Because there seemed to be something keeping the families in our study on this track at all costs, we began to ask ourselves about the nature of their desperate investments, what it was that was being so studiously and relentlessly avoided. It was addressing these questions that enabled us to produce the account provided in this chapter. Now that girls can, in principle, take the place previously accorded to their brothers, their production as the bourgeois subject is a huge struggle and is never simply or entirely achieved, and certainly not without terrible penalties for body and mind. This view of what happens to the girls is in complete opposition to a simplistic notion of a genderquake as a freeing feminist triumph!

There is a creative tension in our argument about girls being made as particular kinds of subject. On the one hand we argue, following a position first expounded in Henriques *et al.* (1997) and developed in our later work (for example Walkerdine and Lucey, 1989; Walkerdine, 1989, 1991, 1997), that in order to understand the production of subjects we need a blend of Foucauldian post-structuralism and psychoanalysis. It is this creative tension that allows us to understand both the place of subjectification (the production of 'the subject' in discursive practices) and subjectivity (the lived experience of being a subject). It has been argued by many (for example Rose, 1999) that Foucault's later work can be used as the basis of an account of the 'care of the self', which perfectly describes the autonomous subject of neoliberalism, making any recourse to arguments about unconscious processes unnnecessary, and in fact counterproductive in the sense that the experience of an unconscious or interiority is one of the significant psychological fictions of the twentieth century. Yet this fiction functions in truth, as Foucault put it. We are created as modern subjects with an interiority and it is through that interiority that we live our emotions. Our aim here, then, is to recognise the powerful place of those emotions in producing the very practices and subjects we are talking about. Such emotionality is completely absent from the hyperrationality of Foucault and his 'Others'. A creative tension between these two positions helps us to imagine what a psychosocial account might look like. We realise that we are taking a risk, but we believe that the explanatory power of our work will be greatly reduced if we do not take that risk, no matter how unconventional. We need to find a way to talk about subjects being made and subject-making, in a way that goes beyond accounts of structure and agency, precisely because those accounts make modernist psychological and sociological assumptions that we need urgently to move beyond.

Reason and emotion in the production of the post-Enlightenment subject

As we have argued elsewhere (Walkerdine and Lucey, 1989), a central strategy in the regulation of middle-class girls has been a form of rational argument which converts powerful inner feelings into apparently rational positions. To understand why these particular practices became widespread we need to look not only at the recent history of class, education and psychology, but also at the way in which the rational and the feminine have been understood in the move towards the production of a rationally ordered bourgeois liberal democracy. In an earlier volume (Walkerdine, 1989, p. 27) we argued that:

> in a nutshell...ideas about reason and reasoning cannot be understood historically outside considerations of gender. Since the Enlightenment, if not before, the Cartesian concept of reason has been deeply embroiled in attempts to control nature. Rationality was taken as a kind of rebirth of the thinking self, without the intervention of a woman. The rational self was a profoundly masculine one from which woman was excluded, her powers not only inferior but also subservient. The 'thinking' subject was male; the female provided the biological prop both to procreation and to servicing the possibility of 'man'. Philosophical doctrine was transformed into the object of a science in which reason became a capacity invested within the body, and later mind, of man alone.

Foucault (1979) calls such developments 'fictions which function in truth'. They are not essential truths about science or men or women, but because they have been enshrined since at least the nineteenth century in scientific debates about rationality, science and woman, especially the science of woman, they have come to be understood as matters of fact, statements that can safely be made and empirically supported about women and about reason. It was during the nineteenth century that 'human nature' became the object of scientific enquiry and the female body and mind the objects of a deeply patriarchal scientific gaze. Ideas about female nature included a female body suffused (from the hysteria of the womb) with madness and irrationality, whereas the upper- and middle-class white male body was the natural embodiment of the rational mind: a rationality not only naturally given, but also extremely necessary to the civilising process. Europe, with its immense colonial powers, presented itself as the natural progenitor of civilisation, keeping at bay primitive animal irrationality, be it invested in colonial peoples or the European masses. We wish to argue that the 'truth' about rationality embodied a deeply held fantasy of its opposition to the powers of unreason, everything contained within that fantasy from the masses, to colonial peoples, the mad, women and so on. Bhabha (1984) conceptualises this well when he writes of the 'fear, phobia and fetish' with which colonial peoples were viewed in the discourses of the coloniser. In other words, our argument is that not only is reasoning held to be a supreme and important power for the production and maintenance of a particular form of government, but also that this form holds within it deep fears about Otherness, the price to be paid for the loss of reason, the fall off the edge of the bourgeoisie. Foucault argues that alongside the rise in human and social sciences there was a change in power and government, in which population management became a central and strategic mode of government (Henriques *et al.*, 1984). This ties in with what sociologists have described as the rise of the 'new middle class' (Bernstein, 1977; Abercrombie and Urry, 1983; McNall *et al.*, 1991) – that is, a professional class that is central to the management and government of a liberal democracy in which power operates not through coercion but by autonomy, free will and choice. Thus, it can be seen that as well as the middle-class as owners of capital, the professions have become important for the management of neoliberalism. The professions, of course, must have a strong and clear grasp of reason above all else in order to take their place as the governors of those Others.

Of course in all of this it is difficult to understand how women, who became the object of science, should become the bearers of rationality. We have argued elsewhere (Walkerdine, 1989) that typically girls and the feminine have been understood as antithetical to the playful, masculine child of reason, yet also necessary in order to provide the essential feminine caring context in which rational development can occur. This is precisely what middle-class mothers do: they provide the basis for rational argument, and more than this, they make emotions safe. Emotions can be understood as part of the irrational, the dreaded animal passions. It follows, therefore, that the bourgeoisie have to tame these in some way. We suggest that this is just what these mothers do. But what has happened in the last twenty years or so to allow girls to become rational subjects, taking places in the professions once occupied by men? Feminism has certainly stressed that women can accomplish the same as men and has fought long and hard for the erosion of sexism. This has had a particular effect on the education of girls and the entry of women into middle-class male occupations.

However, as we shall see, the entry of middle-class girls into masculine norms of rational academic excellence comes at a price. It is not achieved easily and indeed is produced out of the suppression of aspects of femininity and sexuality. In that sense, in our view the discourses of 'girl power', which stress the possibility of having and being what you want, provide an ideal that it is almost impossible to live up to, and through which young women read their own failure as personal pathology:

I had musicianship classes, orchestra, I actually had more orchestra, choir, quartet, quintet, piano lessons, violin lessons ... if you do something and you don't do it well ... I didn't do it well, you didn't want people to think that I couldn't do something well. If I can't – if I couldn't do it well I wouldn't do it at all (Hannah, white middle class).

The production of excellence

What we found in our study was that the middle-class girls' educational lives had been rigidly circumscribed by expectations of academic success, often to such an extent that quite outstanding performances were only ever viewed as average and ordinary. It was so much harder for the young women to feel that they had done well by getting 10 grade A GCSEs and four A levels when they went to a school where this was simply the norm and to get anything lower was tantamount to failure:

I actually complained to them [her parents] a few times about not feeling, like, I had any kind of recognition for my achievements, it was just, like, that it was expected that that's what was going to happen and I was going to do well and we didn't need to talk about it because it was just a foregone conclusion (Abigail, 21, middle class)

Hannah, a middle-class 16 year old, achieved nine A grades and one C grade at GCSE:

And I was really pleased. Yes, I hoped that I'd get a B in science, I knew I wouldn't get an A but I hoped to get a B but I was really pleased to get a C. And ... so I rang up my mum and I said 'Oh, mum I got a C.' And she said, 'Oh, well, congratulations on the A's anyway.' Fine. Bye.

It is difficult to overstate the way in which very high academic performance is routinely understood as ordinary and simply the level that is expected. This and its attendant anxieties are, we will show, major factors for the understanding of middle-class girls' educational attainment.

Working-class girls who have achieved reasonably good exam results typically received a lot of praise from their parents, and seemed to take pride in their own achievements. In contrast, middle-class girls, many of whom achieved outstanding exam results – typically much higher grades even than the most successful working-class girls – found it considerably more difficult to be proud of their performance, or to hold on to a sense of what they had achieved. We had already witnessed anxiety about educational performance among middle-class girls who were doing very well at the age of ten, and this anxiety had largely remained with them during the intervening years – believing that they were not 'good enough', despite the evidence of their grades. Angela was studying medicine at a top of university:

> it's difficult at Oxford because you've got the, kind of, top few people from every school in the country, and I mean, I was in the top five or ten at school, but it's so different. I mean, you're always kind of, in the middle. I just try and stay in the top middle...I mean they're so quick on the uptake, it makes you feel, that's the one thing that's bad about it, it makes me feel a bit stupid sometimes. I mean some of these people are just so amazingly bright, you just think 'God, I shouldn't be here, I shouldn't be with people like that at all'.

If we accept that a complex relation between preparation for the labour market and the production of practices of subjection and subjectivity is central to the process of schooling, then we must also recognise that a significant part of achieving high performance must be carried out at the emotional level. Despite evidence of their success, the feeling of not being good enough was endemic among the young middle-class women. This anxiety typically surfaced as an individual pathology, an indication that the young women had internalised this failure as a personal one that could only be overcome by working harder and harder. Very few of the middle-class girls made a connection between their sense of inadequacy and their social and economic location. We suggest that it was difficult for them to step outside this individualising discourse precisely because doing so would threaten to expose and undermine the sense of rightness and impenetrable normality contained in following a strictly circumscribed educational trajectory that would lead naturally to a professional career. For the middle-class girls, failure was simply not an option: whatever else happened, they were compelled to succeed educationally. This placed them in a terrible psychic dilemma: to struggle with both the feeling that one is not good enough, the equally powerful feeling that one must fail can be expected to lead to difficult psychic consequences. It was in the context of their production as proto-professional subjects that the middle-class girls had to prove themselves to be self-regulating, a process that began in the early years and was integral to and inextricable from the processes through which this level of educational success had to be achieved (Allatt, 1993; Reay, 1998b). However we wish to argue that the routine nature of that success and the apparent ease with which middle-class girls like Angela, Naomi and Charlotte consistently performed well above the average, may have masked a deep fear of failure, a fear that was driven underground because it threatened the very bases upon which available subject positions were founded.

It was common for teachers in the schools the middle-class girls attended when they were 10 consistently to use terms such as 'natural ability' to describe top pupils but rarely to describe high-performing girls, even girls like Angela who were doing very well in terms of their test scores and teachers' ratings. We noted how an opposition between 'flair', 'ability' and 'hard work' was set up; an opposition that down-graded the 'quality' of girls' good performance because it was not produced in the right way (Walden and Walkerdine 1985; Walkerdine and Lucey 1989). Child-centred discourses and mathematics education have implicitly contrasted the 'old' ways of hard work and rule-following with 'new' concepts of development, activity and discovery. The implications of this are serious – suggesting that children who make their work visible are rather lacking in 'flair', 'ability' and 'brilliance', the most prized qualities in the production of good performance. Paradoxically, while the term 'hard work' was used pejoratively in the case of the middle-class girls, it was praised in the working-class schools.

When Angela was 10 her teacher said of her: 'If she comes across something new it needs to be explained to her whereas some of these [other pupils] will just be able to read what they're to do and do it'. Angela was certainly a 'good girl' and an 'ideal pupil', and indeed her performance throughout her educational career was outstanding, so wasn't it extraordinary that she was never attributed with 'flair', but rather was viewed as a good girl who only came top through sheer hard work? Extraordinary yes, but by looking back to what was said about her as a child we can begin to understand how and why girls like Angela consistently denied themselves the accolade 'clever'. By the time she was 21 Angela had introjected the 'truths' told to her about her performance; that it could only be sustained by the kind of unremitting, exhausting and anxiety-provoking labour that she did indeed display. The opposition between flair and hard work she had encountered at primary school continued to exert its influence into higher education. In the intensely competitive environment of medical school, being seen to be working hard signified a lack of brilliance and so had to be denied and hidden. 'And then it's a kind of big competition and a game you need to make out they've done the least work and get the best results. Which I find quite hard. I mean, I don't work that hard, but I do need to put quite a few hours into an essay.'

We therefore argue that the new professional femininity is certainly not produced through a simplistic and easy notion of a female future, but through the painful struggle of constant reinvention. What looks easy on the surface is devastating beneath. Just as we argued in Chapter 3 that women cannot easily take up masculine subject positions in the workplace, so it is just as difficult to do so in the classroom. Girls are damned if they do attempt to be assertive, facing being described pejoratively (as a 'madam' by one teacher, see Chapter 3 and Walkerdine, 1998), and damned if they don't: a plodder versus a madam is not a great choice.

Many of the middle-class mothers (including Angela's) pushed their daughters to intellectualise to a very high degree when they were four, but later we were presented with girls who, for the most part, had succeeded in the education system and yet it was taken (either by themselves or their teachers) that there was something wrong with how they had achieved that success. It is not surprising, then, that they were anxious about their performance, an anxiety that their teachers had not been able to see when the girls were 10.

There is something else to be added to 'hard work'. For the 16 and 21 year old middle-class girls and their parents, working hard, particularly at school was stressed constantly and while the working-class parents and girls also spoke of the necessity for hard work, its object was different: hard work was something that had to be done to become a willing worker who would be employed and paid, whereas for the middle-class families hard work was necessary to ensure the continuity of privilege in times of economic uncertainty and when men and marriage could not be relied upon to maintain class status and lifestyle in the new and uncertain labour market. At the unconscious level, did the latter also offset the guilt of privilege, becoming a 'virtue' that would allow them to enjoy the fruits of success without the aftertaste of guilt?

We want to show how the story of rationality as natural and normal, the new middle class as given through the destiny of their intelligence, is produced by a great deal of work, some of it social and cultural, some of it psychic and defensive. As we have seen, the majority of the middle-class girls in our sample did extremely well at school and went on to 'good' universities to prepare to enter a profession (most of them did not wish to go into business).

Let us examine how this was produced. We have already documented some of the work that went into preparing the four year olds. We have also seen that, according to Tizard and Hughes (1984), nursery school staff paid far more attention to the language styles of the middle-class girls, thus reinforcing what had already gone on in the home. By the time they were 10 the middle-class girls' performance outstripped that of the working-class sample to such an extent that the performance at the top working-class school was worse than at the bottom middle-class one. In addition to this the majority of families had taken their daughters out of state schools and put them into preparatory schools run by the Girls Public Day School Trust (see Chapter 5). Such schools were all single-sex, and while behaviour was split along gender lines in the state schools (for example boys were understood to possess a playful rationality while girls were seen as possessing the ability to work hard) it was organised quite differently in the preparatory schools. There, both of these subject positions were available to girls, which meant that the top-performing girls behaved and were treated far more like the boys in state schools. In addition to this, excellence was the expected norm. Nobody was supposed to do poorly and girls were expected to work as hard as it took to produce excellence. Anything less was simply considered as failure.

When we began work on this phase of the research we had a hard time figuring this out. After all, we were used to understanding excellent performance as exceptional, to be praised and congratulated. Yet what we were met with was something quite other. Exceptional performance was treated as quite ordinary, as expected and unworthy of comment. We felt dumbfounded. After all, we were far more used to hearing the elaborate praise accorded to working-class girls for a performance that was far, far inferior, a performance that would have been the object of ridicule or shame in middle-class households. To understand this we might contrast the example of Heather given in Chapter 4 – Heather's examination performance was considered too poor for her to pursue an academic career, even though she achieved eight GCSEs and two A levels (all grades A to C) – with the case of Jacky, a 21 year old working-class young woman who left school at 16 but whose father was proud of her achieving seven GCSEs grades D to G. We asked ourselves why it should have been the case that only the highest performance would do and anything less produced considerable distress among middle-class parents. What function did excellence serve and how was it achieved?

Clever but feminine

Of course academic excellence is precisely what ensures the production and reproduction of the new middle class. It gets girls places in the right universities and ensures they do well there, getting the right jobs afterwards. In difficult economic times excellence acts as a form of insurance as graduate unemployment is very high and competition fierce.

The road trodden by such young women may lead to success but it is straight and circumscribed indeed. To attain their goals they have to perform a balancing act in respect of cleverness and femininity. To maintain an acceptable subject position in both requires them to perform not only as an academic, but also as feminine. To our eyes, many of the middle-class young women in our study at first glance appeared to have everything. They were brainy, successful and extremely good-looking: the epitome of 'girl-power' indeed! Perhaps for these young women the elaborate manifestations and displays of femininity (good looking, great social life, plenty of boyfriends) served as a defence against the fear that, clever as they were, they were somehow incomplete as women. This defence brings together Butler's (1990) notion of 'performativity' and Riviere's (1985) notion of masquerade. There are several examples of girls' anxiety about trying to be clever and feminine being pushed to extremes, such as Naomi who pulled her hair out, and did not see herself as being allowed to do anything other than well and go to a good university. In fact, despite her quite extreme emotional problems she achieved 10 grade A GCSEs, two grade As and one B at A level and went on to Oxbridge, still feeling that she was not allowed to fail. Her mother said that the staff at her expensive private school had paid little attention to her emotional problems, caring more that she should achieve the highest academic standards. Being feminine cannot be allowed to interfere with academic success, indeed nothing can. This is illustrated graphically by the difference between working- and middle-class attitudes towards pregnancy and motherhood, which we shall explore in the next chapter. While working-class parents tended not to like their daughters becoming pregnant, they often came round and would accept a baby in the household if that was what the girl wanted. However middle-class girls and their parents simply could not contemplate a baby. Several of the girls mentioned that having a baby would 'kill' their parents. So birth was equated not with the beginning of life, with something new, but with the end of it, with dying.

Nothing is allowed to get in the way of ambition (and the dreaded drop into the abyss that it defends against). Naomi had a problem with academic success – not a difficulty achieving results as such, but a difficulty simultaneously sustaining emotional well-being – and of course if she broke down, she could not continue achieving these results. A middle-class girl, such as Naomi, who has any kind of problem with academic success is typically presented with a number of costly therapies to allay the problem and produce or sustain the required success. Compare this with the experience of working-class Kerry, discussed in Chapter 5, where her subjectification and her family's investments in education are entirely different.

For Naomi and her parents, the high grades she achieved were merely expected, not exceptional. While Naomi's parents felt that they had not pressured her, her interview made it clear that she felt extremely pushed to achieve a high performance (which was simply the norm), and this anxiety manifested itself as both hair pulling and anorexia, of which the school took little notice. In fact, the time at which she was achieving success at school was the very time she was most unhappy about her self-image, as became evident when she looked at some photos of herself taken at that time:

> all the pictures of myself there I absolutely hate at that time, I just really look so awful, and that one [looking at photos of herself] I seem quite happy but – like, I mean, quite sort of smiling and – but I think I felt really drained after.

We can see from the above examples that the production of the middle-class girl as the rational bourgeois subject requires a huge investment. The right kind of schooling has to be provided, in which she will be made to feel that an exceptional performance is merely ordinary and therefore is never enough. She may also be made to feel that femininity is to be struggled over, sometimes renouncing sexuality because the onset of womanhood is too painful to contemplate when pitted against the extraordinary academic efforts she has to make. So it is not difficult to see why the anxiety displayed by so many of the girls when they were ten had escalated. Some coped with it, but others did not and professionals had to be brought in to help keep them on track. Naomi was kept on track even though she was clearly extremely disturbed. What, one may ask, would she have to have done to herself to be allowed to get off the conveyer belt? Certainly anorexia and pulling her hair out were not enough for anybody to give her permission to stop.

What is the huge psychic and economic investment, then, which goes into making young women into the bourgeois individual? Why must they succeed at all costs? Why is their emotional state at all times subsumed to rationality, to excellence, to brilliance? We suggest that the huge investment in success covers over the terror of its opposite. That what is defended against is the fear of falling off the edge of middle-class life and culture, of falling off the edge of rationality and into the darkness of those held to be in the pit of unreason, the dark forces of the masses and the equally dark forces of their own passionate desires, so easily projected onto 'the great unwashed'. If nobody can let rationality go, there must be some powerful emotions and it is so easy to locate them in all of those feared Others who appear to threaten civilisation. After all, if the working class is rapidly splintering and changing, with part of it becoming the non-working underclass, with the middle class containing complex defences against falling off the edge, these young women's impossible rebellion must carry all those defences – they cannot be allowed to be seen to fail. It does seem as if their only course is to become both very clever and very beautiful. So, as Riviere (1985) argued and Judith Butler (1993) reiterated, gender can become a performance, a masquerade, a set of practices and bodily dispositions, as realised by the 'I can have everything' girls. Yet this heady normality, this utopian success, hides the opposite: a defence against failure, a terrible defence against the impossibility that the supergirl identity represents.

In the next chapter we shall explore the production as subjects of those Others – working-class girls who have babies – because they are the very antithesis of these young women: they are allowed to become pregnant and are allowed – indeed expected – to fail educationally. These two issues go together to help us understand both the differential regulation of sexuality and femininity and the way in which young women come to take up such polarised positions.

Chapter 8

Pregnancy and Young Motherhood

The pressures of the fecund female body present a problematic path through education and life, whatever the class position. What is important is how that fecundity is regulated and lived. For middle-class young women it is their inscription as the bourgeois subject that counterposes fecundity in a way that simply does not allow the possibility of pregnancy. The two positions are incompatible, and that incompatibility must be lived by the girl herself as, we suggest, a psychic struggle from which she never escapes. Conversely the position of working-class girls is to be the fecund Other to the middle-class girls, a designation that is difficult to escape in order to follow a career or manage upward mobility. In both cases self-invention is demonstrated to be a complex and difficult path, along which the woman herself has to hold together, psychically and socially, the contradictions of the positions in which she is inscribed. And of course these contradictions are quite literally embodied – fecundity or lack of it marks and scars the female body. The increase in infertility technologies and methods of assisted conception points precisely to the increase in some demand for motherhood by older women who have been caught inside this struggle in one particular way, the career path of middle-class girls. What we want to demonstrate in this chapter are the complex psychosocial processes through which young women live the contradictions of the discursive positions. We shall do this by exploring young motherhood among the group of young women with whom we worked.

As can be seen from Table 8.1, 28 per cent of the working-class girls became pregnant: of these four gave birth (one young woman had two children), one had a termination and one had a miscarriage. The one who miscarried had a second pregnancy that resulted in a live birth. Of the middle-class girls 20 per cent became pregnant: these pregnancies resulted in two terminations and one miscarriage. None of

Table 8.1   Pregnancies, terminations and live births among the young women in the study

		Girls getting pregnant		Girls having babies		Girls having terminations		Girls having miscarriages	
Class	Total number	*(No.)*	*(%)*	*(No.)*	*(%)*	*(No.)*	*(%)*	*(No.)*	*(%)*
Working	18	5	28	4	22	1	6	1	6
Middle	15	3	20	0	0	2	13	1	7
Total	33	8	24	5	15	3	9	2	6

these pregnancies was planned. Clearly a higher percentage of working-class girls become pregnant (28 per cent compared with 20 per cent of the middle-class girls). To understand this we need to examine the sexual activity and contraception practices of the two groups. From the interviews at least, it did not appear that one group was more sexually active than the other. However it was the case that the working-class girls expressed more doubts about contraception. None of the middle-class girls decided to continue their pregnancy, whereas 6 per cent of the working-class sample had a termination, 6 per cent had a miscarriage and 22 per cent gave birth.

Although middle-class girls are expected to regulate their sexuality and fertility in favour of academic attainment, it is not because they have less sex or start it later, but because of the regulation of the consequences of their sexual activity. No middle-class girl serious about her academic attainment would be allowed or would allow herself to get pregnant. This makes teenage motherhood a mainly working-class affair. What is it, therefore that allows working-class girls to have babies and how does this relate to changes in femininity? It seems that the regulation of femininity works quite differently upon the bodies of working- and middle-class girls. Indeed it is the fecund body of the middle-class girl that has to be regulated at all costs in favour of the predominance of the mind. It is this regulation that produces, we argue, the bourgeois subject as feminine or the feminine as a masquerade of the bodily performance of the bourgeois subject as masculine. This masquerade is never fully successful and it is a painful problem for such women at all stages of their educational and professional lives. On the other hand the fecund body of the working-class girl does not represent a threat to bourgeois masculinity but rather contributes to a discourse on welfare scroungers.

Discourses on young motherhood

In order to understand this we need to examine just how young working-class mothers are constituted discursively. We need to understand the relation of this to the current practices and emotional, psychic relations through which the girls' subjectivity is constituted. The figure of the unmarried mother is less subject to moral sanction than in previous generations. The popular regulation of female sexuality in recent years has concentrated not on unmarried motherhood but on two other issues: welfare-scrounging single mothers and AIDS. Such negative discourses on teenage single motherhood are sufficiently pervasive to constitute a discursive formation (Foucault, 1972), where frequent and various pronouncements on single motherhood fit together to construct these young women as deviant and problematic. Executed and popularised by the media, such constructions begin to be seen as objective reality, eventually becoming regimes of truth (Foucault, 1980; Hall 1992). John Redwood, former Conservative cabinet minister, illustrated the germination of such truths in the following comment:

> The assumption is that the illegitimate child is the passport to a council flat and a benefit income. If no one in the family can help, maybe the girls should consider letting a couple adopt her child to provide the home the baby needs. (quoted in the *Guardian*, 5 September 1995).

This was almost the same statement that Margaret Thatcher made at the 1988 Conservative Party Conference. It was in this context that the Child Support Agency was set up to pursue fathers who were not paying or paying too little to support their children. Conservative ministers even implied that the number of young single mothers was such that they constituted a threat to the welfare state through their 'lifelong dependency': 'Teenage pregnancy often leads to a whole life of state dependence, with few luxuries. The teenage mother is rarely able to gain a full education or develop a career', so said Michael Portillo in 1993 when he was Treasury Chief Secretary (quoted in the *Guardian*, 5 September 1995). Peter Lilley, the Social Security Secretary, made a speech that implied that young women get pregnant for the sole purpose of getting council accommodation: 'I've got a little list [of] young ladies who get pregnant just to jump the housing list' (Peter Lilley, 1992, quoted in the *Guardian*, 5 September 1995).

This was enough ammunition for the green paper on housing, which aimed to restrict housing entitlement for lone mothers and was announced by Sir George Young in 1993. Michael Howard, then Home Secretary, made a speech in which he claimed that children of lone mothers were likely to become criminals, implying that the solution was for 'young single mothers [to] have their babies adopted!' (Conservative Political Centre Conference in Blackpool, cited in the *Daily Telegraph*, 10 October 1993).

To explore the effectiveness of these modes of regulation we need to examine how single mothers are created as subjects by the practices used to regulate them. Current legislation provides for a number of practices – such as the work of the Child Support Agency – that form a clear regime of meaning, organising what teenage motherhood means, at least in the public sector. Our evidence suggests, however, that young women's behaviour is not inhibited or altered by the 'scrounger' discourse. Women who do get pregnant clearly do so despite the disapproval of Conservative politicians, while those who do not get pregnant have other and perhaps more important reasons for avoiding pregnancy than merely avoiding the disapproval of Conservative politicians. However all young women are clearly aware of the scrounger discourse, and the young mothers in our survey, while distancing themselves from the scrounger stereotype, seemed nonetheless to experience the discourse as an additional burden.

Phoenix (1991) asserts that there is no evidence that teenage mothers get pregnant in order to get housing in either Britain or the USA (where studies have attempted to find a link between the incidence of teenage and lone motherhood with welfare policies and dependency on benefit). Clark (1989) asked young women whether they had got pregnant for such reasons. They expressed their 'disbelief' that anyone would get pregnant for such calculated personal gain. Also, as Phoenix (1991) points out, calculated pregnancy resulting in birth contradicts the other popular stereotype of such young women as irresponsible because they have unplanned pregnancies. In fact others (Morrison, 1985; Simms and Smith, 1986) have shown that mothers under 20 have a high rate of accidental, unplanned pregnancies. Just as Oakley (1981) argues that (older) women become pregnant for many reasons, Phoenix (1991) suggests that this is also the case for teenagers.

Clark (1989) and Phoenix (1991) state that their subjects claimed they had not deliberately got pregnant in order to obtain accommodation. However, as we have argued above, while this may indeed be the case in general, it does not examine the effect of these modes of regulation on teenage sexuality itself. AIDS-prevention campaigns stress the use of 'safe sex' and the dangers of sex without contraception, in fact downplaying the risk of pregnancy. When speaking about teenage sexuality our subjects did mention AIDS:

> I think, as long as you are not promiscuous, I think it is alright...people that I met, yeah definitely take it [*AIDS*] seriously...'cos so much has been made of it. It is at the back of your mind so you just, you know, you just are careful (Naomi, 21, middle class).

> I am really, really worried about HIV but I am not as worried about falling pregnant because it's happened before.... And I am really worried about HIV, but you always think it's not going to happen to you.... And in your subconscious you know you're just sort of saying, 'Don't worry what happens' (Emily, 21, middle class).

> I'd rather be, you know, pregnant again than have AIDS.... Generally people don't talk about Aids, they talk about pregnancy. I mean pregnancy is a big issue, yeah, but Aids is more important...there's no way of escaping it is there really. Even if you use condoms you can't be absolutely sure...the safest way is don't have sex basically.... I think I am more concerned about AIDS definitely because that could kill you. AIDS is just a frightening thing and it's so easy to catch (Zoe, 16, working class).

> There's a lot of sleeping around at university. I don't think it's [AIDS] stopped that at all...although people I do know generally take precautions (Samantha, 21, middle class).

The working-class young women appeared to be more frightened by the AIDS discourse presented by the media than did the middle-class young women. They also seemed much more concerned about the possible risks than did the middle-class young women, and at least one young woman's comment betrayed the influence of government propaganda, through which she had understood AIDS as 'easy to catch' and always fatal, which medical evidence suggests is not the case at all. The working-class young women were more likely to admit the relevance of perceived 'risks' even when they did not alter their behaviour. The middle-class girls, on the other hand, were either less taken in by the propaganda or had a tendency towards omnipotent fantasy, denying that AIDS could ever happen to them.

What is created, therefore, is a climate of moral regulation in and through which teenage sexuality is lived and in which teenage pregnancy is less important than avoiding risky sexual practices in relation to AIDS. In past decades the moral and social regulation of female teenagers depended almost exclusively on the regulation of their sexuality. Although this may have shifted in the 1990s (Wilkinson and

Mulgan, 1995), girls are still seen as being in danger and in need of protection (Holland *et al.*, 1998). Hudson (1983), argues that the intrinsic belief about and attitude towards the adolescent girl is that some girls are unable to control their sexuality and sexual behaviour, and therefore it has to be regulated and controlled authoritatively – preferably by their parents, but if they fail then the state should intervene.

It is therefore not surprising that in the case of working-class girls (who are most likely to feel the impact of regulation by social work agencies), preparation for sex – that is, carrying condoms for safe sex – while acceptable within an AIDS discourse, damns them within the discourse of 'easy availability'. Janet Holland *et al.*, (1998), in their study of power in conventional heterosexual relationships among young people, looked in particular at sexual risk-taking by young women. The young women in their study were neither ignorant nor irresponsible with regard to contraception and condom use, but nevertheless 'repeatedly failed to fulfill these intentions – most had at times had unprotected vaginal intercourse whatever their plans' (ibid., p. 5). No wonder, then, that one working-class young mother revealed that she was terrified of being seen as a slag. In the 1980s, feminist researchers such as McRobbie (1982) and Lees (1986) pointed out that preparation for sex was seen as what slags did, while not having sex provided no escape because of the counter designation of 'sexual drag'. In the 1990s it would seem that constructions of conventional femininity were putting young women at risk. As Holland *et al.* (1998, p. 6) assert, 'To be conventionally feminine is to appear sexually unknowing, to aspire to a relationship, to let sex "happen", to trust to love, and to make men happy.'

In Britain, less than 4 per cent of all births are to teenagers and within this figure there are enormous regional variations (National Council For One Parent Families, 1994). In a study looking at the rate of pregnancy and the outcomes for teenagers in different socioeconomic circumstances, Smith (1993) found that there was a higher pregnancy rate amongst teenagers in more deprived areas, but that the proportion of pregnancies ending in abortion was greater in affluent areas. However Smith's study only used data from NHS hospitals. In relation to teenage abortions this presents problems because the NHS is not the only provider of such operations. Consideration needs to be given to the fact that a significant proportion of middle-class teenagers who become pregnant and wish to have an abortion opt for the private medical system (OPCS, 1995). On the basis of these studies, we can reasonably assume that our data reflects national trends. Even though our data reveals that a small proportion of middle-class young women do become pregnant as teenagers, teenage pregnancy and low socioeconomic status are almost always lumped together and the evidence suggests that teenage motherhood is 'overwhelmingly a working class affair' (Hudson and Ineichen, 1991). While confirming the above, Phoenix (1996) points out that, even among the working classes, only a minority of young women under 20 actually have children – and this is true even in the USA, where the incidence of teenage motherhood is higher than in Europe.

However, the social problems often associated with early motherhood such as poverty are not necessarily caused by giving birth early in the life course. Teenage motherhood is not a cause for generalised concern as the majority of young mothers and their children fare well. What is a cause for concern is the negative social construction of teenage motherhood, where 'correlation' and 'causation' are confused. Similarly, studies that have followed up women who give birth in their teenage years indicate that motherhood in the early life course is not uniformly disadvantageous. Some of the women who have their first child in their teenage years go on to gain educational qualifications, to be employed, to obtain independent housing and to raise children who fare well (Furstenberg *et al.*, 1987, 1992; Kiernan, 1995).

Phoenix (1991), when exploring the attitude towards conception by young mothers-to-be, found that they could be divided into two groups: the first had not thought about the possibility that they might conceive; the second had not wanted to conceive when they did. Moore and Rosenthal (1993) suggest that girls falling into the first group have limited knowledge of the reproductive process and fail to use contraceptives because they believe they are unlikely to suffer from the negative consequences of their behaviour and hence take risks. In an Australian study, Littlejohn (1992) found that 20 per cent of teenagers did not believe they could get pregnant and therefore did not need to use contraceptives. This confirms the view of others that around half of all adolescents have erroneous beliefs about their fertility (Morrison, 1985). The other type for whom unplanned pregnancy occurs is the 'unprepared' young woman who responds spontaneously to the 'heat of the moment'. Morrison suggests that a large number of young women fail to use contraceptives because they have not planned to have sex. What is not mentioned in this work is that it is working-class young women who are being discussed, for whom taking contraceptive pills or carrying condoms means they are seen as being prepared to have sex. Our interviews suggest that many young working-class women feel considerable anxiety about being seen as a 'slag' or a 'tart' and go to great lengths to avoid such designations.

Clearly, previous research supports our data in as much as it demonstrates that teenage pregnancy is overwhelmingly both working class and unplanned and that middle-class young women are more likely to have abortions. However no previous research has specifically examined the class aspects of this phenomenon. To account for and explain working-class teenage pregnancy, therefore, they have had recourse to explanations such as failure to use contraceptives, having friends who are young mothers, being in a stable relationship with a partner and whether the young woman's own mother had a child as a young teenager (Morrison, 1985; Simms and Smith, 1986; Phoenix, 1991).

These previous studies took working class teenage motherhood as a phenomenon demanding an explanation, as if the lack of middle-class teenage motherhood somehow didn't need an explanation. Our methodology attempts to explain both. For example, we can point to the prospects of a professional career, which acts as a contraceptive for middle-class girls. In addition to this, regulation of the professional middle-class means that a daughter's assumption of middle-class status acts to maintain and pass on the family's status. The regulation of feminine sexuality for middle-class girls has to be understood as part of a wider regulation of their achievement and academic success. Nothing is allowed to obstruct the academic path – certainly not motherhood, which is seen as the ultimate failure, to be avoided at all costs. Indeed many of the girls in our study described the effect that their pregnancy would have on their parents in terms of death: 'it would kill them', thus making clear the necessity and parameters of vigilant self-regulation.

Three of the middle-class 21 year olds expressed this as follows:

> It's just something I've never thought about. I've never even contemplated having a child ... I think it'd kill my mother.

> I think even if I became pregnant now and I had an abortion I don't think I'd tell them. ... I think it would be almost more traumatic for them than it would be for me.

> I know many of my parents friends wouldn't be happy if their daughters became a single mother.

Almost all of the middle-class girls said they would have a termination if they got pregnant. It has become clear that teenage motherhood cannot be allowed onto the agenda of most middle-class girls in Britain today. The regulation of working-class female academic success is quite different. And it is in this light that we shall go on to consider the 'clever' working-class girls who become mothers.

As we argued in Chapter 6, for working-class girls who do well in education, higher education represents a move away from the familiar, the family, and into a strange, hostile and often frightening new world (Walkerdine, 1991, 1996). For working-class girls, to become the bourgeois subject does not involve maintenance or reproduction of anything, but a significant transformation of the self (in the sense of Foucault's care of the self, 1987, p. 88).

It is in this light that we might begin to understand how motherhood functions quite differently for these girls than for their middle-class counterparts. What is it that allows them not only to contemplate pregnancy and motherhood, but also to be supported by their parents in a way that is quite opposite to the situation with middle-class girls and their parents? Three of the working-class girls expressed this as follows:

> My Dad, was like brilliant, he was 'don't worry, we'll help you out' and everything. ... I've always been the little girl because I'm the younger one anyway. But I've always been Daddy's little girl type of thing. So he was really supportive (Teresa).

> My Mum, towards the end [of the pregnancy] was really supportive. She was really getting into it and really getting excited (Zoe).

> Like my Mum and Nan said like 'we will help you get through it'. If they hadn't said that I think I would actually have put her up for adoption. ... I would have done it, but like now I would have regretted it so much. Like to see Rosie how she is now, she's such a lovely little thing. I wouldn't give her to anyone (Anna).

It would be easy, at one level, to put forward as an explanation the fact that many working-class girls do not have a career or even job prospects, making young motherhood a realistic and rational choice of job. However we think that in fact the situation is more complex. In our sample at least, all but one of the young mothers had done well at school. All but one had achieved at least five GCSEs, grades A–C, and one had achieved four grade As. All but one had been set for A levels and some for university. They were, then, precisely those working-class girls who were faced with the possibility of transformation into the bourgeois subject/career woman. As we have indicated, such a step for these girls could be quite frightening because it signalled huge differences from the familiar. At one level, then, having a baby kept the girl at home with her family, and particularly with her father, preventing the loss of home and family. As Teresa said about her father's reaction to her pregnancy:

> I think he thought he was going to take over, you know, and then of course, when he realised I was going to leave the house and everything and that he couldn't look after me in a sense, then he got a bit sort of funny about the whole thing.

We could therefore view motherhood as a complex attempt to maintain present status in the face of overwhelming change and loss, and in so doing to deal with the contradictions of positioning. For example one of the working-class 21 year olds who had had a baby at sixteen wanted to avoid being seen as a slag. While it could be argued that having a baby could be seen as 'slaggish' (Lees, 1986), the very fact that she had not used a contraceptive showed that she had been unprepared for sex and therefore not a slag. The baby could therefore be understood as an embodied resolution to the painful contradictions she experienced. Yet her and her family's decision to continue the pregnancy and keep the baby is interesting in the light of the desperate desire of middle-class parents not to see their daughters' careers thwarted. For both middle-class parents and daughters the thought of the loss of career was more daunting than having a baby.

If we look at the difficulties the working-class girls and their parents had in contemplating abortion – for most it was not seen as an option, or definitely not a route they wanted to take – then separation comes up in various ways, such as not wanting to separate themselves from the baby they were carrying because they identified too strongly with it. Yet for the middle-class girls it would have been impossible to contemplate anything other than an abortion. To understand why keeping the baby appeared to be a better solution to the working-class girls and their families, we need to understand their embodiment as the fecund body as a psychically and socially safe place to be, which kept them away from the terrifying path to transformation. The issue then becomes – what kind of family dynamics, anxieties and fantasies come into play around this decision and how do these relate to the complex discursive positioning?

Young adults or daddy's girls?

Anna, Zoe, Teresa and Holly saw having a baby as a solution to the conflicting desires of wanting to be looked after and of being independent. If the girls had fantasies of independence, then the middle-class girls could actually make this happen through a carefully constructed and assiduously maintained set of social and class norms: they could go to university or go travelling and actually take their time moving out of the parental home. There was a constant leaving and returning for a number of years, so the more permanent transition from parental home to their own home was much more gradual than for the working-class girls. The physical separation of moving out of the parental home was much harder for the working-class girls. It was more dramatic in the sense that there was no gradual transition. Also they had to be able to earn enough to pay rent and so on. So for the working-class girls being in a partnership was more crucial as the financial burden of running a home would be easier if shared.

For all of the young mothers, their relationship with their fathers was a central issue. We were very interested to find that all of them were known as 'daddy's girls' and so we shall spend some time exploring the importance of that designation. This term was used by the girl and/or one of her parents. In all cases the father, although initially hostile, took a central role once the baby was born. The girls who had early pregnancies were all in some sense 'daddy's girls'.

Except for some biographical literature, feminist literature and theory concentrates on the mother–daughter relationship and tends to neglect the father–daughter dynamic, although there are some very interesting popular explorations of the subject (Maitland, 1988; Sharpe, 1994). So what does it mean to be a 'daddy's girl'? We shall use the psychosocial approach outlined in Chapter 4, which has been a feature of our attempt to understand our data. At first sight we have a set of 'face value' descriptions of the girl by her mother/father and/or herself as a 'daddy's girl,' or in the case of one girl Kerry, as always wanting to be a daddy's girl, but never quite making it. All of the young women discussed here had had a pregnancy, and had either miscarried, had a termination or had a child. There were six girls – five working class, one middle class – and the pregnancies had all occurred between the ages of 15 and 18. All the girls verbalised their initial concern about telling their fathers about their pregnancy.

The middle-class girl, Emily, said: 'last year I got pregnant and I thought "oh my god" and I wasn't worried about telling mum at all, and I thought "oh my god, dad is going to kill me". I just couldn't tell him, but when I did he was just brilliant and sorted everything out.' Emily's father, when describing his relationship with her, said he believed that 'a father's love should be disinterested', though Emily's fears certainly indicate that her feelings for him were far from the 'disinterested love' that he expressed.

If we explore the unconscious aspects of the father–daughter relationship in more detail, it could be that pregnancy is a way in which a daughter unconsciously expresses to her father a number of things, such as the fact that she is no longer a little girl – after all her sexual activity is visible to all – and she wants the transition to womanhood to be acknowledged. If the purpose of pregnancy is to end a chapter in the girl's life, if it is to end the 'daddy's girl' narrative – what does daddy do? It seems that he does a number of things: initially, he may reject the girl throughout her pregnancy, but once the child is born he becomes a doting grandfather; if the child's father is absent he takes on the role of father to the child. This creates a very complicated oedipal drama in which the biological father is usurped by the grandfather, and the daughter produces a baby for her father. We shall attempt to go below the surface of observations and statements and ask where is the 'daddy's girl' narrative coming from? Who is constructing it? What unconscious projections, introjections and transferences are at play in each family? Even if a young woman's father was absent during her childhood, this may not stop her believing she is or wanting to be a daddy's girl. The narrative can also be constructed by the absent father or by the mother as a way of keeping father and daughter connected even if he is absent. (An absent father doesn't have to be physically absent – he can be physically present but emotionally absent.) So at this level we are able to pick up on some of the unconscious projections.

The following example illustrates the complex nature of this very important relationship and the need to go beyond analysis of the 'face value' content of our research showing very clearly how the social and emotional are intricately linked: The following extract is taken from a discussion between the researcher and Kerry's mother about her daughter's pregnancy and termination:

Mother: We'd come back from France and she found out that she was
              pregnant and decided she was going to have a termination
              and she was really frightened to tell her dad. Because she
              thought he would go mad and throw her out. Because she's

got this thing in her head that, you know that's what he would do.

HL: Where do you think that comes from?

Mother: I think she's sort of made it up in her head because she wants him to be this daddy...she wants to be 'daddy's girl'. ... And she said please don't tell him, please don't tell him. And I said, I must. When I told him he was very understanding, he was there for her, he cuddled her.

Kerry was one of the working-class 21 year olds who became pregnant. If we go back to her earlier life, and in particular her school life, we can get an idea of how troubled she was in many ways, where that came from and the importance of her relationship with her father in all of this. We described Kerry's struggles at some length in Chapter 5. Kerry was having trouble at school and was only found to be dyslexic after expert help outside school was sought by her mother. Kerry was also bullied and attempted suicide at the age of 15. Kerry's father was largely absent from the picture Kerry and her mother painted of her growing up. He worked work long hours, but he was at home every night and at weekends. Even when he was there physically, she felt that he was emotionally absent. She talked about feeling unloved by him and he felt he was not demonstrative enough, that he didn't show his feelings. She was desperate to be daddy's special girl. She went to great lengths to be the 'angel' that she felt he wanted her to be – nothing seemed to work. Daddy was a fantasy figure, upon which to project all her fantasies and desires. Her pregnancy and then termination seemed like one final attempt to get closer to him. It was only at the point of the termination that he was able to show her that he cared, that he loved her and would help her through the ordeal. This proved to be a powerful turning point for Kerry: she started to stick up for herself more and began to prove herself in her career. Her father later talked about how he regretted not giving enough of himself emotionally. He was asked about what had happened over the last ten years. At first he found it difficult to answer. He said he didn't know what to do, that his mind went blank when asked a lot of questions or asked to describe things. The next thing he said was:

Hmm. One of the things that has happened is I, with me, I find it very difficult to have a relationship with Kerry. Um...a lot of it was due I think to when she was growing up. I spent a lot of...or too much time working....I was never here. So I was always the 'wait till your father gets home' figure.

Although he had been there physically, he acknowledged that this had not been enough and blamed himself for the difficulties Kerry had suffered later:

> You know, a lot of it I think is down to me. I didn't really have a relationship with either of them because I was... working.... Too busy working.... Personally, I have problems with showing things anyway as a person. I've never been able to, like, cuddle. Why can't I do anything about... this is what gets me... why can't I do what I want to do. Why am I held back? I don't know why I'm held back. Kerry is having a bit of a problem now. Really I should go up there and put my arms around her and say right, that's it, Kerry, you know, come on, come home... we'll sort things out. We'll... you know, I'll go and help you find another place to live. I know she doesn't want to come   home permanently.... I don't think that I was a rotten father or anything like that. I just think that I wasn't demonstrative in, like, an affectionate way.

Of the five young women who had pregnancies, one other besides Kerry attempted suicide. Both of these attempts took place before their pregnancies. There were many similarities as well as differences between these two girls. It is therefore of great interest that the connection between life and death was made by both the middle- and the working-class girls. For the middle-class girls, early pregnancy was equated with death, as in the 'it would kill my mother' type comments. For some of the working-class girls, pregnancy came after a suicide attempt, which seems to suggest how closely they were bound up together and attested to a painful desire to be both child and adult. Kerry was being bullied when she made the suicide attempt. When she became pregnant, her father actually managed to display the affection and protection she had so desperately wanted. In displaying herself as a fecund woman, therefore, she was conversely, able to be a child and receive a display of father-ly affection. In this scenario we would need to understand the father's positioning as masculine and the problems of feminisation we explored in Chapter 2, together with the particular complexity of sexuality and gender displayed in the relationship between fathers and daughters (always potential women, always little girls: Walkerdine, 1997).

Teresa, like Kerry, was a 'good' girl. They both had older sisters, who were seen as the rebellious, difficult ones, whilst Teresa and Kerry were seen as the 'good' girls', always trying to please, particularly their fathers. They both attempted suicide either just before or just after their GCSEs. Both were trying to shake off their carefully crafted 'good girl' image. For Kerry it was a time of liberation: she was suddenly able to stand up to the girl who had for so long made her life a misery, who had bullied her relentlessly throughout her secondary school life. Teresa made her suicide attempt after her exams. About a year before that she had become heavily involved in 'Goth' culture, much of which had symbols that were closely related to death, such as coffin earrings and heavy white make-up, producing a white, lifeless face. Psychoanalytically, suicide can be seen as a very aggressive act against one or both parents. It is a way of acting out deep anger and if successful it is the ultimate revenge. It is seen as an attack on the introjected object and is usually attempted when the person is depressed. Kerry had spent all her life being the 'good girl' whereas her sister was the rebel, the angry one; her father was also able to be angry when he needed to, but Kerry could not, she was the passive 'angel'. Years of repressed anger, particularly against her parents, were released in the violent act of attempted suicide. Like most people who attempt suicide, she was not conscious of the amount of anger she felt towards her parents:

> I used to get really angry because I never used to get my own space. I suppose in a small house... and that, but um... I can't really remember now because I used to just go off in massive tantrums and storm out of the house and I've always been the one that's not had a bad temper and... my sister was always like fiery and you know I was really quiet.

She added:

> Like I get really angry when people say that um... [suicide] it's a coward's way out. Oh, hundreds of time I've had arguments with people who've said... they haven't realised what I've done and they've said that and I've said but you just don't realise how much it takes to do that. No way is it a coward... I mean, do you know what I mean? Anybody that does that must really hate living so much that they can do that.

The few working class girls who went to university would do anything to avoid motherhood, and in fact connected much more closely with the aspirations of the middle-class young women than with those of their working-class peers who were not doing very well. It is interesting, therefore, that the working-class, high-achieving girls who got pregnant, in doing so accomplished something the others could not. They displayed their fecundity. Having a baby therefore acted as one response to that dilemma and it is not surprising that at least some of them still harboured an aspiration to study, an aspiration ironically more contemplatable now that they had established their womanhood.

Several of these young women expressed a desire to continue with their education. While we would certainly not expect this to be easy for them, nevertheless in each case we can see ways in which motherhood appears to have given them something of value – a source of strength and comfort.

Teresa (21), who had a young son, later tried to get the qualifications she had missed out on:

> I'm actually back at college. I'm doing A levels again. I started this September. ... I've changed my whole direction. ... What I would really really want to do would be some degree in criminology or psychology or something along those lines. But I would probably do Open University because of Gary. ... Cos, I want to work at the same time, and I've got such conflicting views on it all, as well as that there's child minding and stuff. Its so hard to, I mean where I'm going to college there's a crèche, but its very expensive and what I've had to do is to get the money from my Mum and Dad to actually pay for the crèche. ... I think if I went to university I'd have the same kind of problems.

Holly (21) had coped with tremendous difficulties and managed to study for an MA. She had two young children and a partner who, although he lived with her, was not supportive and did not help very much with the children: she was the only young women in the study who actually did manage to combine young motherhood with the reality of higher education. As we said in Chapter 6, she felt very supported by the discourses of powerful black womanhood, but it was motherhood that perhaps served as an anchor for the complexity of her mixed-race subjectivity and the complexities of her positioning in relation to her white mother.

Zoe had her baby at 16, but before she became pregnant her mother articulated clearly the deep ambivalence many working-class parents feel about success in education, especially about unhappiness and the pain of failure, as we set out in Chapter 5. It was within the context of the difficulties that surround educational success and failure that Zoe's mother spoke of teenage pregnancy:

JM: What are your hopes and aspirations for her?

Mother: I just want her to be happy and enjoy life and be able to make choices.

JM: What do you think is your biggest worry, you worry about her all the time, but what do you think is the biggest worry for her?

Mother: That she'll take the, it's all these choices again, that she'll choose to go in the wrong direction maybe and I think it's nowadays there's so much pressure on kids to do well, and have nothing at the end of it. You've either got to be really good, or that's the feeling, that you've got to be really good at something, or fail. I think it's really frightening. I think she's really frightened of that and I'm frightened that she'll make a conscious choice not to even bother and maybe, you know, go off with the first kid that comes along and have babies, because it sounds like a soft option. ... It's easier and not have to worry about looking after yourself and take responsibility for yourself. That's my biggest worry.

JM: But actually you end up taking responsibility for others ...

Mother: ...other people, but then you can't, that's something else you can't be told. It just looks like a soft option, doesn't it. When she sees her friend walking, her friend Mary was barely 15 when she got pregnant, well she was 15 when she had the baby and um, all she can see is that she's got her own flat and um ...it looks very cushy, you know, she's getting money from, to be looked after, it looks, she seems quite happy. Although she's told Zoe that she would do things differently, she wouldn't do that if she had the chance to do it, you know. But it sounds like a good option doesn't it really. When you've got all that in front of you, all that about succeeding and having to succeed. Because it doesn't matter what you say, the pressures are still out there.

So Zoe's mother places teenage pregnancy as a response to difficult and frightening pressures to grow up, succeed in school and enter the labour market. This is not so much the 'rational choice' of motherhood and a council flat for an educationally failing young woman, but a complex emotional response to the fear of failure, a response that stresses the other way of becoming a woman, not the career woman but the fecund body, as a defence against the fears that womanhood represents.

Nicky (21) and the other white working-class girls who went on to higher education were much more like the middle-class girls in their ambitions and aspirations than the working-class girls who were not successful at school. They all wanted to have successful careers before they embarked on motherhood:

Nicky: I like kids. I've always liked kids. I don't – I would like kids in the future. And I hope that I'd have some. But not yet – not for 10 years or so. It would be too soon. I mean I suppose I'm thinking more about them now – I suddenly realise I'm turning 21 and everyone I know is getting married or having kids, of my friends, of my age. One of my close cousins I'm closest to has just got herself married, and there's a year between us. So I suppose that makes you stop and look around and think – here what's going on.

HL: Is that another difference between other people in the family, you know that they're kind of in relationships and settling down and all that kind of thing and in fact you're only just, you know, jumping off the high board really.

Nicky: I think I can honestly say that most people by my age in my family were married or in a serious relationship.

HL: So how do they view your single status?

Nicky: Oh it's a source of great amusement to many of them.

HL: Right. Do they comment on it?

Nicky: I'm always getting asked about it, honestly, it's awful when you go home. Even up here they just, er, think it's quite amusing, but you get used to it I suppose.

HL: And what do you think they think – or are they just intrigued?

Nicky: I'd hate to think what they think [Laughs]...but I don't know, I think maybe they are just intrigued, that – but I've never had any great aspiration to settle down and live in a fancy cottage somewhere with 2.4 children or whatever. I don't know, that's never been there for me in the immediate future, I mean if you ask one of my cousins he swears blind I will never get married, honestly – had a huge conversation with him a few months ago, he would probably die of a heart attack – I think that seems to be the whole general opinion...

HL: What because you're all for your career?

Nicky: Yeah yeah, and he's never sort of seen me in a relationship with anyone so he just thinks it's highly amusing. And my parents would probably die of shock as well.

As the above extract illustrates, while Nicky's intentions might have been like those of the middle-class girls, that is, to have children later and not at 21, her experience of this ambition was lived quite differently from that of the middle-class young women. She was not following a path in which pregnancy was highly regulated. Quite the reverse: not having a family made her feel different from her friends and family, who would have been able to make more sense of her choices if she had had a baby at that age. For her, then, not to have a family, not to be the fecund body, represented a difficult struggle, and it puts the babies of the other young women who did well at school in a clearer light.

The pressures presented by the fecund female body of the young woman result in a problematic path through education and life, whatever the class position. Middle-class young women take up positions in which their fecundity is regulated in favour of education, while working-class girls find it difficult to escape being the embodiment of fecundity.

Sitting in judgement

In our last example we want to explore what happened to a working-class young woman who entertained an ambition to be a judge. This ambition was certainly a very modern one and one that was not likely to have been imagined by young women in her position even 20 years ago. However a celebratory discourse that applauds her ambition and hails it as evidence of a 'female future' fails to engage with the deeper aspects of ambivalence and contradiction that inhabit such an ambition.

Sharon, who we first met in Chapter 2, was positioned within her family as 'clever' although she had done very poorly at school. Within the family dynamic she was viewed as 'an Einstein compared with her brother'. Sharon had an ambition for a career in law, in fact to become a judge; an ambition acknowledged by her parents, but her own and her parents' understanding of what that meant, of the structural differentiation that existed in the law profession, was minimal and hazy, as was their knowledge of the normative routes to such a profession:

> I don't know really, it's something different. Because all my mates like, they want to be like hairdressers and nurses and things like that. It was something different. And ever since I was twelve I've always. My mum and dad think I can do it, but I don't think that my nan does, so I want to show the rest of the family that I'll be able to do it (Sharon).

I believe that Sharon's got the brain-power, will-power, common sense or common whatever they like to call it, to go a long way. And I don't know why she didn't do that well during the GCSEs. Not as well as I expected, or we expected... But she's still going to college, she wants to be a solicitor, barrister, a lawyer and a judge eventually. So she's got that – you know – I don't think – will they ever make women judges? (Sharon's father)

Well the career she wants to go into – law. I mean there's nothing else is there? She don't want to be a nurse. She's always said that she wanted to be a judge, even from the primary school she's always said that she wanted to be a judge. ... Perhaps she gonna hang her brother. ... She won't get to be a judge. She might get to be a barrister, but I doubt if she'll get to be a judge (Sharon's mother).

In fact Sharon had done poorly in her GCSEs and at the time of the first interview was about to be asked to withdraw from a BTEC in business administration.

No, I went to all the classes and that, but like most of my mates dropped out anyway, because they felt that they weren't learning enough anyway. But I was the first one to actually drop out, and they – most of my friends have gone now (Sharon).

Sharon began the same course again at another college, where she encountered a teacher who felt strongly that she had the ability and determination to do well and achieve her aim of going to university, although the teacher was aware of the possibility of personal issues getting in the way:

And I think she will do it, but there are things in her personal life, I don't really know what's going on but there are things in her personal life I think that affect her, I think that would be what stops her, not from her driving ambition (Sharon's teacher).

It is these 'things in her personal life' that may have been the unmaking of her ambition. Actually, none of the family displayed any conscious understanding of the incredible difficulties that would confront Sharon in pursuit of this career. Even to get a law degree place would present a serious hurdle. Yet at some level it is clear all of the family recognised that this ambition was both real and a fantasy. Sharon's story starkly reveals how complex and frightening the road to achievement can be for working-class girls. For while she displayed considerable determination and ability, she was also putting into place a set of unconscious barriers to the possibility of achieving her goals. In fact Sharon, who was 18 years old at the time, had embarked on a relationship with an older man she felt strongly about, but neither he nor she was willing to take any contraceptive precautions. The following excerpt from the interview shows how Sharon was unable to face the risks she was taking:

Sharon: It's the chance that you take though in't it? Really...

JM: Yeah sure, but...I mean you don't – if it happened it happened kind of thing, it doesn't cause you any anxiety...

Sharon: I, me and my mum said to me if it happens, it happens. Just cross that bridge when we come to it.

JM: Right. And you what – do you use contraceptives?

Sharon: No.

JM: You don't – not at all?

Sharon: No.

JM: So it's possible that you might get pregnant?

Sharon: Yeah.

JM: And are you hoping that you will?

Sharon: No not really. Hope in a couple of years I will but not yet.

JM: Right – so it's quite likely that you will, if you're not using any contraceptive.

Sharon: That's the chance innit.

JM: Right. Um.

Sharon: S'pose I'd be scared if I didn't have my mum and dad's backing.

JM: Right – so do you think you're trying to get pregnant?

Sharon: No.

JM: On some level?

Sharon: [Untranscribed]

JM: But if you're not using contraceptives then it's very likely that you will.

Sharon: Yeah it's likely that I will but I'm not like going out of my way to get pregnant or nothing like that.

JM: Right. But you're not avoiding it so – um, and is your boyfriend quite happy about that possibility?

Sharon: Oh he don't he don't, want me to get pregnant

JM: So what – he doesn't use any contraceptives?

Sharon: No.

It is clear that this exchange caused the interviewer, June, some anxiety, as she tried to push Sharon into admitting that she was likely to get pregnant. June noted in her fieldnotes:

I felt incredibly irritated with her. I wanted to tell her how bloody stupid she was. It was nothing to do with morality. I don't have any strong feelings about whether she gets pregnant or not. I felt she was being quite hostile towards me (or was I feeling hostile towards her?) and was very ambivalent about being interviewed. In fact I really don't think she wanted to be interviewed at all. It seemed that she would do anything rather than give me a straightforward answer and that she was hoping to give me as little information about herself as she could get away with. Possibly in the hope that I would not be able to build up an accurate picture of her.

In an interesting reflection of her ambitions for a legal career the interview took on an almost courtroom-like dynamic of questioning and denial. What is unsettling is that it is clear to the observer that at some level, indeed a level that seemed largely unconscious, Sharon was making sure that she would never be the lawyer of her dreams. Unlike the parents of the middle-class girls, Sharon's parents, according to her, were supportive of the idea of her getting pregnant ('if it happens, it happens. Just cross that bridge when we come to it'). The middle-class parents in the sample simply would not have tolerated the idea of anything, and certainly not pregnancy, getting in the way of educational success. This complicity between Sharon and her mother suggests that there was a great deal of ambivalence around, and not simply on the part of Sharon. It suggests that as much as both she and her parents were proud of her ambition, they were secretly terrified of it and what was at stake in its production. A baby was a much better known quantity and it would keep her on known territory and position her as a woman, a mother. Working-class families may find some comfort in things staying the same and therefore give a less disapproving message to their daughters about unplanned pregnancy. For if their daughters were successful, this would mean coping with enormous and far-reaching changes since their daughters would leave home and enter an entirely different world – one which the parents, and especially the fathers, may experience as a deep and frightening loss. (This intersects with changing constructions of working-class masculinity.) While middle-class children receive the message from birth that not only are they able and clever, but also their destiny is to go to university and become professionals, this is certainly not the destiny of working-class girls, nor is it presented as such. Is this why girls like Sharon, and those who had achieved examination success like Teresa, Nicky and Maura, faltered on the path to success, even when they had a sure footing on that path?

In this sense, then, the path to reinvention for Sharon was littered with obstacles. While Sharon may have wished at one level to become one of Wilkinson's (1994) 'new women', the very terror of that option for her manifested itself in the ambivalence of her ambition on the one hand and her contraceptive practices on the other. It was the fecund body that asserted itself as the rock in her pathway, the very thing that might thwart her ambition and place her in that much more familiar and safe territory of young motherhood. Not only does the case of Sharon reveal some of the problems of class and femininity, but it also demonstrates the difficulty of upward mobility, of the remaking of the working class-subject as the bourgeois one, and how it is impossible to understand the complexity of the social shifts that are taking place without a consideration of the psychosocial processes through which they take place. In this analysis the psychic is not separable from the social. Class emerges as a set of marks or ruptures in the smooth surface of the discourse of the woman as unitary rational subject, just as the fecund body comes also to haunt that possibility in a classed way.

Conclusion

We have sought in this chapter to explore the place of pregnancy and motherhood in the newly reinvented femininity and the regulation of femininity that has accompanied it. We can conclude that class is a central parameter of the regulation of the sexuality and fecundity of young women in Britain today. We can therefore argue that it does not make sense to view teenage motherhood in terms of a working-class pathology. The place of pregnancy and motherhood in the production and maintenance of the social and the subject needs to be understood. Indeed while teenage girls who have babies may now be seen as outside the norm, it is clearly not the case that theirs is a personal pathology. Indeed it is the relation between the production of subjectivity and social regulation that is of central importance to the production of sexuality for both groups today.

Both groups of young women – working class and middle class – present us with a class organisation that is different from that of their mothers' generation. Middle-class girls want to have a career first and motherhood later, while working-class girls want to integrate having a baby with a later career. Yet, discursively and in terms of fantasies and fictions of femininity, these two groups are poles apart. One group is positioned as the scrounging female underclass and the other the superwoman. In that sense they are each other's Other. Both are highly though differently regulated, producing different subject effects and different bodily inscriptions. Middle class girls are self-regulating, while the norms of regulation come down more heavily on working-class girls, who become the object of a more obvious surveillant gaze. Yet within that the regulation of these young women is accomplished in part through their active self-regulation by means of conscious and unconscious processes, the fantasies as well as the fictions, the bodily practices that write themselves so materially, so painfully upon the female body. In this sense, too, as we saw with the example of Sharon, self-invention for women turns out to be very slippery stuff. Holding together fecundity and intelligence is no mean feat for women of whatever class position, but it is starkly and differently organised for the two groups. Crossing over to the other side, whether to the masculine professions or to upward mobility, is psychically and socially extremely difficult and only achieved at great cost, even amidst its celebration.

Chapter 9

Conclusion

This book has been about girls growing up and entering womanhood in the very changed social and economic climate of the early twenty-first century. We have told a story in which class differences between young women figure as largely as they did 20 or 30 years ago, despite the face of class having changed considerably. We began the book by looking at the transformations in the Western and global economic landscape, characterised by a move away from manufacturing in industrialised societies towards the service, communications and financial sectors. This transformation has had a huge impact on women's as well as men's employment and has helped produce the argument that class is no longer a viable category because the traditional sources of male manual work, from which the working class was drawn, have largely disappeared. All this, plus the drastic weakening of the trade unions in the 1980s and 1990s, has prepared the way for the politics of the euphemistically named 'third way' (Giddens, 1998), in which self-management and self-invention are to be celebrated with the demise of the concept of 'jobs for life'.

It is this context that is so important to the celebratory tone of the Labour Party think-tank Demos's work on women in the British labour market with which we began the book. While Wilkinson *et al.* (1997) argue that 'women's importance in society is set to rise', we set that triumphalism against the fact that women's significance in the labour market is cross-cut by class, with middle-class women dominating the professional and managerial scene. Furthermore, as Adonis and Pollard (1998) have argued, the public professional sector has been transformed as a lower-status occupational choice because high-flying men from the middle classes are now moving into the international finance sector, with its huge salaries and million pound bonuses. By extrapolation, then, it becomes clear that women's participation in the professional labour market is not, in any simple sense, pushing aside the participation of middle-class men, as much of the furore about girls' performance at school might suggest (Epstein *et al.* 1998). This is because these men have actually moved from the public to the private sector, from professions to financial services. The issue then becomes not the academic performance and job suitability of middle-class boys but the working-class low achievers with no manual work to go to, and the group who are hardly ever mentioned, working-class girls with few or no qualifications. It is these uncredentialled young people who are most likely to enter and remain in the most vulnerable, insecure and poorly paid sectors of the labour market. Wilkinson *et al.* (1997) describe this group as 'Frustrated Frans', a playful typology maybe, but one which overlooks the fact that this group is entirely working class.

There is no doubt that the notion of self-invention and self-regulation offers a way to understand the social and psychological changes that have been central to an understanding of the changed times for young women and their families. It is the fragility of the present arrangements for all subjects that is highlighted, and this demands certain psychological strategies to defend against uncertainty and fragmentation. This challenges not only traditional psychoanalysis (Elliot and Spezzano, 1999), but also traditional divisions between psychology, sociology and cultural theory. We have attempted to demonstrate how young women live that uncertainty in the way in which they cope with the contradictory social demands placed upon them. Throughout the book we have highlighted the way in which the intransigence of class still insisted on its presence alongside the important transformations in the way in which subjectification and subjectivity were lived for all the young women and families in our study. We do not believe that class has been rendered unworkable as a category, but we do insist that how it is understood needs to shift dramatically. Classification operates in and through subjects: it is marked on bodies and minds, it ruptures the smooth surface of the discourses of classlessness, it can be 'spotted a mile off' in the way that it inscribes subjects. As we have explored, that subjectification works not only on complex conscious and rational processes but also on desires, wishes and anxieties, and creates defensive organisations through which participants live their inscription into the discursive practices that make up current sociality. Unlike accounts of class processes of old, we argue that regulative discourses and practices and unconscious processes are central to understanding how class functions and is lived today.

In Chapter 2 we addressed the transformations of class between the 1970s and the 1990s, looking at the way in which the lives of the young women and their families had changed. We focused on two families, the Greens and the Coles, who had moved out of London in the 1980s during the period of council house sales and house price boom. We showed that their upward mobility was at best shaky and partial and its successes vied with confrontation with the fact that it was not as easy as had been be imagined. From Erica's desire to be 'respected in Hampwick' to Sharon's unconsciously blocked ambition to become a judge, the path to a middle-class female future for these young women was shown to be strewn with difficulties. During this time the parents' work had changed too. Many of the parents saw their daughters face difficult employment situations that ran counter to the easy employment situation in their own youth. Yet during this period many working-class fathers had faced a difficult time and all of the mothers now went out to work, and some of the young women remarked that they did not want to end up struggling to juggle work and family as they had watched their mothers do.

Chapter 3 showed the complexity of women's position in the labour market in the 1990s, with a divide between highly paid professional work and low-paid service work with built-in periods of unemployment. In our study the young women's employment patterns mirrored the national trend. And, as we have said, they faced the probability, whatever their class, of having to combine work and family responsibilities for the whole of their working life.

In Chapter 4 we showed how important it was to work with emotions, and it has particular relevance to our demonstrating the effectivity of class. In particular, we looked at one middle-class family in which two sisters, Angela and Heather, were respectively positioned as clever and a slow learner. We explored how these very class-specific designations of ability were constituted within the family dynamic in a way that would allow us to understand the centrality of unconscious processes in the making of sociality. We also demonstrated that we cannot understand unconscious family dynamics without a clear understanding of the social practices and fictions within which such dynamics are produced. Angela's 'failure' was not only a fantasy constructed by the family participants, but was also evidence of the need for explanations that can cope with a complex psychosocial dynamic.

Referring back to earlier work with some of the young women when they were four, Chapter 5 looked at the classed work of socialisation accomplished by the two groups of mothers, and especially the way in which the middle-class mothers had prepared their daughters for the rationality that was to be the cornerstone of their academic success. The educational achievements of the two groups were very stark, with no working-class girl going on to higher education in any straightforward way, and only one middle-class girl opting out of the conveyer belt from school to university that middle-class life represented for these young women. In fact the educational trajectories of the two groups simply got farther and farther apart as they moved through the education system. It was these huge differences that prepared them for such very different places in the labour market.

We went on to explore the emotional costs of success and failure for both groups of girls, looking at the way in which happiness and distress were treated during the educational careers of Kerry and Naomi. In Kerry's case distress was read as lack of ability, while in Naomi's case it was not attended to because it would get in the way of her sparklingly successful path to Oxbridge. The place of happiness in the education of the working-class girls was also explored, especially in relation to the deeply ambivalent feelings of the many working-class parents whose experience of school failure had left painful scars.

Against all odds a small number of the working-class girls managed to succeed in education, and this was explored in Chapter 6. We argued that it is useless to compare working- and middle-class practices for the production of educational success because they operate in very different circumstances and with quite different dynamics. It is not by being like middle-class girls that working-class girls succeed, but rather a complex mixture of determination to live a different kind of life from that of their peers and an emotional support from parents that is not disrupted by the parents' distress at the difficulties their daughter has to face, bringing up, as it does, memories of their own failure. The route to upward mobility through higher education for women involves a difficult emotional trajectory and necessitates a transformation in classed subjectivity. This can be as painful and frightening as it is exciting. In this light, we can review the case studies discussed in Chapter 8, and note with interest how some of the working-class girls who were doing well at school had to deal with the reality of pregnancy just at the moment when they might otherwise have had to face a painful class transformation. The baby served to keep them bound within a community and social milieu that was known and familiar.

Chapter 7 looked at the making of the bourgeois subject as feminine in relation to the production of middle-class girls as the embodiment of the bourgeois rational subject. As we saw, this is achieved by taking excellent performance as the norm. If a middle-class girl is expected to achieve the best results, she is then not accorded the elaborate praise received by working-class girls for much more modest achievements. This leads to an endemic anxiety about performance, which serves an important function in the regulation of the feminine as rational. It is the feminine body, especially the fecund body, that has to be regulated at all costs, which is in stark opposition to the image of the single working-class mother as welfare scrounger that we encountered in Chapter 8. Here, for many young women and their families, pregnancy is a safer and more familiar state than career achievement and the two positions form an opposition: the superwoman, who cannot have a baby for fear of interrupting her career; and the scrounger, whose very fecundity ensures her 'career' as a welfare mother. What both these positions belie is the complex of fiction and fantasy, regulation and defences in which young women's bodies and minds are inscribed. Class is not something that is simply produced economically. It is performed, marked, written on bodies and minds. We can 'spot it a mile off' even in the midst of our wish for it no longer to be there. It is there in the discourses and practices through which difference is made. It is at once social and profoundly psychic, but not in the ways that previous syntheses of Marxism and psychoanalysis have suggested. It demands that we find a new way of working that crosses the boundaries between social science disciplines to find a theory and practice that does not dualistically divide psychology and sociology but goes beyond them to incorporate a social and discursive psyche, a cultural, specific and local account. One that takes note of the effects of the serious burdens of liberty, can cope with the discursive production of subjection as multiple and fragmented, but does not think that this should stop us from looking at the way in which people desire, fear, love and live.

Ever since the 1944 Education Act, which opened up state education in Britain and gave a larger number of children access to grammar school, and later the opening up of higher education, there have been debates about inequality in the take-up of academic education. From the 1950s onwards, sociologists and psychologists took to investigating the working class, the most popular thesis being about its demise through the affluence of the worker (Halsey *et al.*, 1980). We have written elsewhere (Walkerdine, 1997) of the double-bind in which this placed the working class: on the one hand the left saw them as becoming too bourgeois, getting into the infantile gratification of mass consumption; on the other hand the liberal state pushed against the power of mass movements towards an individualisation that fed on the hopes and aspirations of a people hurt and oppressed first by the depression and then by the war and its aftermath. It is instructive that, despite the death-knell of the working class having been sounded so vigorously and for so long, this volume attests to the fact that what we might describe as class differences are as insidious as ever. Indeed individualisation is being pushed as the only hope in a global market that no longer offers the basis for a mass socialist movement.

We have struggled in this book to tell a different story, one in which girls face the labour market of the future deeply regulated and bitterly divided by something that it is difficult to call by any other name than class. From the middle-class superwoman with the straight As and an Oxbridge degree to the working-class 16 year old single mother or the fast food restaurant manageress, the much hyped girl power and female future looks decidedly unsteady and, for most, extremely difficult. Even though the classes are still starkly separated by wealth and privilege, this does not mean that the middle-class women face an easy future – economically, socially or psychically. While 'girls just want to have fun', and many accounts have stressed the fun they do have, far fewer narratives speak of the complex hardships that the current sociality brings. If we have concentrated on these things it is because we feel that it is imperative for Britain to address the deep inequalities that divide a nation set on a course towards life-long self-invention. While the third way may be being debated just as it is being put into practice, little attention is being paid to the emotional and social costs of the remaking that the young women of Britain are having to face. The new situation involves complex losses just as it involves change. The psychic economy of the way those losses are played out in the social world are just as important to address as the financial economy of the country. It is far too easy to blame women for those losses and changes and to make them bear the emotional brunt of the terrible consequences of what is happening. We hope we have shown conclusively that women can hardly be seen as responsible for what is happening, and that, just like men, they too have to face the difficulty of what confronts us all. Women's position in the new economy is not comfortable. Young women watch their mothers struggle and do not want to have to combine work and family, but know very well that that is precisely the future they face. Indeed more than that, they may also have to cope with men who are feeling intensely the loss of previous modes of masculinity. In these circumstances it would be difficult to say that the female future is rosy.

Yet alongside all this, it is difficult not to be impressed with the incredible ability with which the young women of today face both present and future. From the single mother combining an MA with a young family to the young doctor with a desire to enter journalism, young women reveal a dynamism that, although produced by the exigencies of the times, is nevertheless breathtaking. As we embark on the twenty-first century we hope that our present polity will struggle to be worthy of what these young women have to offer. And we hope that our research might help to shed some light on a situation that demands our most urgent attention.

References

Abercrombie, N. and Urry, J. (1983) *Capital, Labour and the Middle Classes*, London, Allen and Unwin.

Adkins, L. (1995) *Gendered Work: Sexuality, Family and the Labour Market*, Buckingham, Open University Press.

Adkins, L. (2001) 'Cultural Feminisation: "Money, Sex and Power" for (Wo)men', *Signs*, vol. 26, No. 3, pp. 31–57.

Adler, P. A. and Adler, P. (1987) *Membership Roles in Field Research*, Beverley Hills, CA, Sage.

Adonis, A. and Pollard, S. (1997) *A Class Act: The Myth of Britain's Classless Society*, London, Penguin.

Ainley, P. (1993) *Class and Skill: Changing Divisions of Knowledge and Labour*, London, Cassell.

Aitken, S. C. (1998) *Family Fantasies and Community Space*, New Brunswick, N.J, Rutgers University Press.

Allatt, P. (1993) 'Becoming Privileged: the role of family processes', in Bates I. and Riseborough G. (eds) *Youth and Inequality*, Milton Keynes, Open University Press.

Althusser, L. (1969) *For Marx*, London, New Left Books.

Anthias, F. and Yuval-Davis, N. (1992) *Racialised Boundaries: Race, Nation, Gender, Colour and Class and the Anti-Racist struggle*, London, Routledge.

Argyle, M. (1996) *The Psychology of Interpersonal Behaviour*, Harmondsworth, Penguin.

Ashton, D. N., Maguire M. J. and Spilsbury M. (1990) *Restructuring the Labour Market: The Implications for Youth*, Basingstoke, Macmillan.

Back, L., Cohen, P., Keith, M. (1998) 'First Takes', *Finding the Way Home*, working paper, London, CNER, University of East London.

Bakker, I. (1988) 'Women's Employment in Comparative Perspective', in J. Jensen *et al.* (eds) *Feminization of the Labour Force*, Cambridge, Polity Press.

Barbelet, J. M. (1998) *Emotion, Social Theory and Social Structure: A Macrosociological Approach*, Cambridge, Cambridge University Press.

Bates, I. and Riseborough, G. (1993) (eds) *Youth and Inequality*, Buckingham, Open University Press.

Baudrillard, J. (1988) *Selected Writings*, M. Poster (ed.), Stanford, CA, Stanford University Press.

Bauman, Z. (1991) *Intimations of Postmodernity*, London, Routledge.

Beck, U. (1992) *Risk Society: Towards a New Modernity*, London, Sage.

Bernstein, B. (1977) *Class, Codes and Control*, vol. 3, London, Routledge and Kegan Paul.

Bertaux, D. and Thompson, P. (1993) (eds) *Between Generations: Family Models, Myths and Memories*, Oxford, Oxford University Press.

Bhabba, H. (1984) 'The Other Question: the Sterotype and Colonial Discourse', *Screen*, 24, 18–36.

Bhabha, H. (1990) 'The Third Space', in J. Rutherford (ed.) *Identity*, London, Lawrence and Wishart, pp. 207–21.

Biggart, A. and Furlong, A. (1996) 'Educating "discouraged workers". Cultural diversity in the upper secondary school', *British Journal of Sociology of Education*, 17: pp. 253–66.

Bion, W. (1962) *Learning from Experience*, London, Heinemann.

Blackman, L. (1996) 'The dangerous classes: retelling the psychiatric story', *Feminism and Psychology*, vol. 6, no. 3, pp. 361–79.

Blackman, L. (1998) 'Culture, technology and subjectivity' in J. Wood (ed.) *Virtual space and embodied knowledge*, London, Routledge.

Blackman, L. (1999) 'An extraordinary life: the legacy of an ambivalence', *New Formations*, no. 36, Special Issue on Diana and Democracy, pp. 111–24.

Bohannon, L. (1954) *Return to Laughter*, New York, Harper and Row.

Bourdieu, P. (1984) *Distinction: A Social Critique of the Judgement of Taste*, London, Routledge and Kegan Paul.

Bowlby, J. (1984) *Attachment and Loss*, vols 1–3, 2nd edn, Harmondsworth, Penguin.

Bradley, H. (1996) *Fractured Identities: Changing Patterns of Inequality*, Cambridge, Polity Press.

Bratlinger, E., Majd-Jabbari, M. and Guskin, S. L. (1996) 'Self-Interest and Liberal Educational Discourse: How Ideology Works for Middle-Class Mothers', *American Educational Research Journal*, 33(3): pp. 571–97.

Briggs, J. L. (1970) *Never in Anger: Portrait of an Eskimo Family*, Cambridge, MA, Harvard University Press.

Briggs, J. L. (1987) 'In Search of Emotional Meaning', *Ethos*, 15: pp. 8–16.

Britzman, D. (1995) 'The Question of Belief: writing post structural ethnography', *Qualitative Studies in Education*, vol. 8, no. 3, pp. 229–38.

Brown, C. (1992) 'Racial inequality in the British labour market', *Employment Institute Economic Report*, 5 (4).

Brown, L. M. and Gilligan, C. (1992) *Meeting at the Crossroads: Women's Psychology and Girl's Development*, Cambridge, MA, Harvard University Press.

Brown, P. (1997) 'Cultural Capital and Social Exclusion: some observations on recent trends in education, employment and the labour market', in A. H.

Halsey *et al.* (eds) *Education: Culture, Economy and Society*, Oxford, Oxford University Press.

Butler, J. (1990) 'Gender trouble: feminist theory and psychoanalytic discourse', in L. J. Nicholson (ed.) *Feminism/Postmodernism*, New York, Routledge, pp. 324–40.

Butler, T. and Savage, M. (1995) (eds) 'Gentrification and the urban middle classes', in T. Butler and M. Savage (eds) *Social Change and the Middle Classes*, London, UCL Press.

Callender, C. (1996), 'Women and Employment', in C. Hallett (ed.) *Women and Social Policy: An Introduction*, London, Harvester Wheatsheaf.

Cashmore, E. and Troyna, B. (1983) (eds) *Black Youth in Crisis*, London, George Allen and Unwin.

Child Poverty Action Group (1997) *Britain Divided*, London, CPAG.

Chisholm, L. (1993) 'Youth transitions in Britain on the threshold of a "New Europe"', *Journal of Education Policy*, vol. 8, no. 1, pp. 29–41.

Clark, E. (1989) *Young Single Mothers Today: a Qualitative Study of Housing and Support Needs*, London, National Council for One Parent Families.

Cockburn, C. (1991) *In the Way of Women*, Basingstoke, Macmillan.

Cohen, P. (1997) *Rethinking The Youth Question: Education, Labour and Cultural Studies*, Basingstoke, Macmillan.

Cohen, P. (1999) *Strange Encounters: Adolescent Geographies of Risk and the Urban Uncanny*, Centre for New Ethnicities Research, Finding the Way Home Working Papers no. 3, London, University of East London.

Cohen, P. and Ainley, P. (2000) 'In the Country of the Blind?: Youth studies and cultural studies in Britain', *Journal of Youth Studies*, vol. 3, no. 1, pp. 79–95.

Cohen, P., Keith, M., and Back, L. (1996) 'Issues of Theory and Method', working paper, *Centre for New Ethnicities Research*, London, University of East London.

Connell, R. (1977) *Ruling Class, Ruling Culture: Studies of Conflict, Power and Hegemony in Australian Life*, Cambridge, Cambridge University Press.

Courtenay, G. (1988) *England and Wales Youth Cohort Study. Report on Cohort 1, Sweep 1*, Sheffield, Manpower Services Commission.

Courtenay, G. and McAleese, I. (1993) *England and Wales Youth Cohort Study. Report on Cohort 5, Sweep 1*, Sheffield, Employment Department.

Cowie, E. (1997) *Representing the Woman: Cinema and Psychoanalysis*, London, Macmillan.

Craib, I. (1989) *Psychoanalysis and Social theory: the limits of sociology*, London, Harvester Wheatsheaf.

Craig, G. (1991) *Fit for Nothing? Young People, Benefits and Youth Training*, London, The Children's Society.

Crompton, R. (1993) *Class and Stratification: An Introduction to Current Debates*, Polity Press, Cambridge.

Crompton, R. (1996) 'Consumption and Class Analysis', in S. Edgell, K. Hetherington and A. Warde (eds) *Consumption Matters*, Oxford, Blackwell.

Crompton, R. and Sanderson, K. (1990) *Gendered Jobs and Social Change*, London, Unwin Hyman.

Crook, S., Pakulski, J. and Waters, M. (1992) *Postmodernization*, London, Sage.

Cross, M. and Keith, M. (1993) (eds) *Racism, the City and the State*, London, Routledge.

David, M. (1985) 'Motherhood and Social Policy: a matter of education?', *Critical Social Policy*, 12, pp. 28–44.

David, M. E. (1993) *Parents, Gender and Education Reform*, Cambridge, Polity Press.

David, M. E., Edwards, R., Hughes, M. and Ribbens, J. (1993) *Mothers and Education: Inside Out? Exploring Family-Education Policy and Experience*, Basingstoke, Macmillan.

David, M. E., West, A. and Ribbens, J. (1994) *Mother's Intuition: Choosing secondary schools*, London, Falmer Press.

Delamont, S. (1989) *Knowledgeable Women: Structuralism and the Reproduction of Elites*, London, Routledge.

Denzin, N. K. (1978) *Sociological Methods*, New York, McGraw-Hill.

Department for Education and Employment (1995) *Employment Gazette*, 103, London, HMSO.

Devine, F. and Savage, M. (2000) 'Conclusion: Renewing Class Analysis', in R. Crompton, F. Devine, M. Savage and J. Scott (eds) *Renewing Class Analysis*, Cambridge, Blackwells.

Donald, J. and Rattansi, A. (1992) (eds) *'Race', Culture and Difference*, London, Sage.

Donoghue, B. (1992) *The Time of Your Life? The Truth About Being Young in 90's Britain*, London, British Youth Council.

Douglas, J. D. (1976) *Investigative Social Research*, Beverly Hills, CA., Sage.

Douglas, J. D. and Johnson, J. M. (1977) (eds) *Existential Sociology*, Cambridge, MA, Cambridge University Press.

Drew, D. (1995) *'Race', Education and Work: The Statistics of Inequality*, Aldershot, Averbury Press.

Drew, D., Gray, J. and Sime, N. (1992) *Against the Odds: The Education and Labour Market Experiences of Black Young People*, Sheffield, Employment Department.

Eder, K. (1993) *The New Politics of Class: Social Movements and Cultural Dynamics in Advanced Societies*, London, Sage.

Ehrenreich, B. (1990) *Fear of Falling: The Inner Life of the Middle Class*, New York, Harper Perennial.

Elliot, A. and Spezzano, C. (1999) *Psychoanalysis at its Limits*, London, Free Association Books.

EOC (1996) *Prospects for Women*, Manchester, Equal Opportunities Commission.

EOC (1996) *'The Labour Market', Briefings on Women and Men in Britain*, Manchester, Equal Opportunities Commission.

Epstein, D., Elwood, J., Hey, V. and Maw, J. (1998) (eds) *Failing Boys? Issues in Gender and Achievement*, Centre for Research and Education on Gender, Institute of Education, Buckingham, England; Philadelphia, PA, Open University Press.

Erikson, E. H. (1959) *Identity and the Life Cycle*, New York, International Universities Press.

Essen, J. and Wedge, P. (1982) *Continuities in Childhood Disadvantage*, London, Heinemann Educational.

Eurostat (1998) *Facts through Figures: Eurostat Yearbook at a Glance*, Brussels, Statistical Office of the European Communities.

Evans, K. and Furlong, A. (1997) 'Metaphors of Youth Transitions. Niches, pathways, trajectories or navigations', in J. Bynner, L. Chisholm and A. Furlong (eds) *Youth, Citizenship and Social Change in a European Context*, Aldershot, Avebury.

Fanon, F. (1969) *Black Skin, White Mask*, Harmondsworth, Penguin.

Field, F. (1989) *Losing Out: Emergence of Britain's Underclass*, Oxford, Blackwell.

Finch, J. (1984) *Education as Social Policy*, London, Longmans.

Flanders, M. L. (1994) *Breakthrough: The Career Woman's Guide to Shattering the Glass Ceiling*, London, Paul Chapman Publishing.

Fonow, M. M. and Cook, J. A. (1991) *Beyond Methodology: Feminist Scholarship as Lived Research*, Bloomington and Indianapolis, Indiana University Press.

Foucault, M. (1972) *The Archaeology of Knowledge*, London, Tavistock.

Foucault, M. (1979) *Discipline and Punish*, Harmondsworth, Penguin.

Foucault, M. (1980) *Power/Knowledge: Selected Interviews and Other Writings 1972–1977*, C. Gordon (ed.), Brighton and New York, Harvester Wheatsheaf.

Foucault, M. (1987) *The History of Sexuality Vol. 2, The Use of Pleasure*, Harmondsworth, Penguin.

Foucault, M. (1988) *The History of Sexuality Vol. 3*, Harmondsworth, Penguin.

Frazer, E. (1988) 'Teenage Girls Talk about Class', *Sociology*, 22, 3, pp. 343–58.

Freud, S. (1905) 'Fragments of an Analysis of a Case of Hysteria', *Standard Edition of the Complete Psychological Works of S. Freud*, vol. 7, London, Hogarth Press.

Freud, S. (1933) *New Introductory Lectures on Psycho-Analysis, Standard Edition*, vol. 22, London, Hogarth Press.

Frosh, S. (1999) *Racism, Racialised Identities and the Psychoanalytic Other*, paper presented at the Millennium World Conference of Critical Psychology, Sydney, 1999.

Furlong, A. and Cartmel, F. (1997) *Young People and Social Change: Individualization and Risk in Late Modernity*, Buckingham, Open University Press.

Furstenberg, F. F. Jr. and Cherlin, A. J. (1992) *Divided Families: What Happens to Children When Parents Part*, Cambridge, MA, Harvard University Press.

Furstenberg, F., Lincoln, R. and Menken, J. (1987) *Teenage Sexuality, Pregnancy and Childbearing*, Philadelphia, PA, University of Pennsylvania Press.

Garcia-Ramon, M. D. and Monk, J. (1996) (ed.) *Women of the European Union: The Politics of Work and Daily Life*, London, Routledge.

Gee, J. P., Hull, G. and Lankshear, C. (1996) *The New Work Order: Behind the Language of the New Capitalism*, New South Wales, Allen and Unwin.

Gershuny, J. I. and Miles, I. D. (1983) *The New Service Economy: The Transformation of Employment in Industrial Societies*, London, Pinter.

Gewirtz, S., Ball, S. J. and Bowe, R. (1995) *Markets, Choice and Equity in Education*, Buckingham, Open University Press.

Giddens, A. (1990) *The Consequences of Modernity*, Oxford, Polity Press.

Giddens, A. (1991) *Modernity and Self Identity: Self and Society in the Late Modern Age*, Oxford, Polity Press.

Giddens, A. (1998) *The Third Way: The Renewal of Social Democracy*, Oxford, Blackwell.

Gillborn, D. and Gipps, C. (1996) *Recent Research on the Achievements of Ethnic Minority Pupils*, London, Office for Standards in Education.

Gilroy, P. (1987) *'There ain't no Black in the Union Jack': The Cultural Politics of Race and Nation*, London, Hutchinson.

Gilroy, P. (1993) *The Black Atlantic*, London, Verso.

Ginzburg, C. (1990) *Myths, Emblems, Clues*, London, Hutchinson.

Goldthorpe, J. H. (1980) *Social Mobility and Class Structure in Modern Britain*, in collaboration with C. Llewellyn and C. Payne, Oxford, Clarendon Press.

Goldthorpe, J. H. and Lockwood, D. (1968) *The Affluent Worker: Political Attitudes and Behaviour*, Cambridge, Cambridge University Press.

Goldthorpe, J. H., Lockwood, D., Bechofer, F. and Platt, J. (1968) *The Affluent Worker: Industrial Attitudes and Behaviour*, Cambridge, Cambridge University Press.

Goldthorpe, J. H. and Marshall, Gordon (1992) 'The promising future of class analysis: a response to recent critiques', *Sociology*, 26, 3, pp. 381–400.

Gorz, A. (1982) *Farewell to the Working Class*, London, Pluto.

Griffiths, M. and Troyna, B. (1995) (eds) *Anti-racism, Culture and Social Justice in Education*, Stoke-on-Trent, Trentham Books.

Guardian (1997a) 'Parents told to sign reading pledge', 29 July, p. 1.

Guardian (1997b) 'Up, up and away', 29 July, p. 18.

Guardian (1998) 'Girls on top form', 6 January, p. 6.

Hakim, C. (1996) *Key Issues in Women's Work*, London, Athlone Press Ltd.

Hall, S. (1992) 'The West and the Rest: Discourse and Power', in S. Hall and B. Gieben (eds) *Formation of Modernity*, Cambridge, Polity Press.

Hall, V. (1996) *Dancing on the Ceiling: A Study of Women Managers in Education*, London, Paul Chapman.

Halsey, A. H., Heath, A. F. and Ridge, J. M. (1980) *Origins and Destinations: Family, Class and Education in Modern Britain*, Oxford, Clarendon Press.

Hattersley, R. (1995) 'Tone of the Times', *Guardian*, 27 April, p. 8.

Henriques, J., Hollway, W., Urwin, C., Venn, C., and Walkerdine, V. (1998) *Changing the Subject: Psychology, Social Regulation and Subjectivity*, London, Routledge, 2nd ed.

Hey, V. (1997) *The Company She Keeps: An Ethnography of Girls' Friendships*, Buckingham, Open University Press.

Hey, V. (1997) 'Northern Accent and Southern Comfort: Subjectivity and Social Class', pp. 140–51, in P. Mahony and C. Zmroczek (eds) *Class Matters: Working Class Women's Perspectives on Social Class*, London, Taylor and Francis.

Hoggett, P. (1992) 'A Place for Experience: a psychoanalytic perspective on boundary identity and culture', *Environment and planning: Society and Space*, 10, pp. 345–56.

Holland, J. (1993) *Sexuality and Ethnicity*, London, Tufnell Press.

Holland, J., Ramazanoglu, C., Sharpe, S. and Thomson, R. (1998) *The Male in the Head: Young People, Heterosexuality and Power*, London, Tufnell Press.

Hollway, W. and Jefferson, T. (1997) 'Eliciting narrative through the in-depth interview', *Qualitative Enquiry*, 3(1), pp. 53–70.

Hollway, W. and Jefferson, T. (2000) *Doing Qualitative Research Differently: Free Associations, Narrative and the Interview Method*, London, Sage.

Holton, R. J. and Turner, B. S. (1989) *Max Weber on Economy and Society*, London, Routledge.

Hopkins, E. (1991) *The Rise and Decline of the English Working Classes 1918–1990*, London, Wiedenfeld and Nicholson.

Hothschild, A. (1983) *The Managed Heart*, Berkeley, University of California Press.

Hudson, A. (1983) 'The Welfare State and Adolescent Feminity', *Youth and Policy*, 2(1).

Hudson, F. and Ineichen, B. (1991) *Taking it Lying Down: Sexuality and Teenage Motherhood*, London, Macmillan.

Hughes, M., Wikeley, F. and Nash, T. (1994) *Parents and the Children's Schools*, Oxford, Blackwell.

Hugill, B. (1998) 'Estate kids are so alienated that even other children can't figure them out', *The Observer*, 12 July, p. 22.

Hunt, J. (1989) *Psychoanalytic Aspects of Fieldwork*, London, Sage.

Jameson, F. (1981) *The Political Unconscious: Narrative as a Socially Symbolic Act*, London, Methuen.

Jenson, J., Hagen, E. and Reddy, C. (1988) (eds) *Feminization of the Labour Force*, Cambridge, Polity Press.

Johnson, J. H., Salt, J. and Wood, P. (1974) *Housing and the Migration of Labour in England and Wales*, London, Saxon House.

Jordan, B., Redley, M. and Jones, S. (1994) *Putting the Family First: identities, decisions, citizenship*, London, UCL Press.

Joseph Rowntree Foundation (1995) *Inquiry into Income and Wealth*, York, Joseph Rowntree Foundation.

Kiernan, V. (1995) *Imperialism and its Contradictions*, London, Routledge

Klein, M. (1946) 'Notes on some schizoid mechanisms', *International Journal of Psycho-Analysis*, 27: pp. 99–110; republished (1952) in M. Klein, P. Heimann, S. Isaacs and J. Riviere, *Developments in Psychoanalysis*, London, Hogarth Press.

Klein, M. (1952) 'Some theoretical conclusions on the emotional life of the infant', in M. Klein, P. Heimann, S. Isaacs, J. Riviere (eds) *Developments in Psychoanalysis*, London, Hogarth Press.

Klein, M. (1959) 'Our Adult World and its Roots in Infancy', in M. Klein, *Envy and Gratitude and Other Works; 1946–1963*, London, Virago Press.

Krieger, J. (1986) *Reagan, Thatcher and the Politics of Decline*, Cambridge, Polity Press.

Kuhn, A. (1995) *Family Secrets: Acts of Memory and Imagination*, London, Verso.

Kvale, S. (1999) 'The Psychoanalytic Interview as Qualitative Research', *Qualitative Inquiry*, 5 (1) pp. 87–113.

Laplanche, J. and Pontalis, J. B. (1988) *The Language of Psychoanalysis*, London, Karnac.

Lareau, A. (1989) *Home Advantage: Social Class and Parental Intervention In Elementary Education*, London, Falmer.

Lash, S. and Urry, J. (1994) *Economics of Signs and Space*, London, Sage.

Lees, S. (1986) *Losing Out: Sexuality and Adolescent Girls*, London, Hutchinson.

Leidner, R. (1993) *Fast Food, Fast Talk*, Los Angeles, University of California Press.

Lincoln, Y. S. and Guba, E. G. (1985) *Naturalistic Inquiry*, California, Sage.

Littlejohn, P. (1992) *Teenage Pregnancy and Adolescent Motherhood in Australia*, research in progress.

Lockwood, D. (1995) 'Marking out the middle class(es)', in T. Butler and M. Savage (eds) *Social Change and the Middle Classes*, London, UCL Press.

Lucey, H. and Walkerdine, V. (1999) 'Boys' Underachievement: Social Class and Changing Masculinities', in T. Cox (ed.) *Combating Educational Disadvantage*, London, Falmer Press.

Mac an Ghaill, M. (1988) *Young, Gifted and Black: Student–Teacher Relations in the Schooling of Black Youth*, Milton Keynes, Open University Press.

Mahoney, P. and Zmroczek, C. (1997) (eds) *Class Matters: Working Class Women's Perspectives on Social Class*, London, Taylor and Francis.

Maitland, S. (1988) (ed.) *Very Heaven: Looking Back at the 1960s*, London, Virago.

Malinowski, B. (1967) *A Diary in the Strict Sense of the Word*, New York, Harcourt, Brace and World.

Marshall, G., Newby, H., Rose, D. and Vogler, C. (1988) *Social Class in Modern Britain*, London, Hutchinson.

Massey, D. (1995) *Spatial Divisions of Labour: Social Relations and the Geography of Production*, London, Macmillan

May, J. (1996) 'Globalization and the politics of place: place and identity in an inner London neighbourhood', *Transactions of the Institute of British Geographers*, 21, pp. 194–215.

Maybury-Lewis, D. (1965) *The Savage and the Innocent*, London, Evans.

McDowell, L. (1997) *Capital Culture: Gender at work in the City*, Oxford, Blackwell.

McNall, S. G., Levine, R. and Fantasia, R. (1991) *Bringing Class back in: Contemporary and Historical Perspectives*, Oxford, Westview Press.

McRae, S. (1991) *Maternity Rights in Britain: The Experience of Women and Employers*, London, Policy Studies Institute.

McRobbie, A. (1982) *'Jackie': An Ideology of Adolescent Femininity*, London, Macmillan.

Mercer, K. (1990) 'Welcome to the jungle: identity and diversity in postmodern politics', in J. Rutherford (ed.) *Identity*, London, Lawrence and Wishart.

Miles, S. (1996) 'Use and consumption in the construction of identities', paper presented to the conference on *British Youth Research: The New Agenda*, University of Glasgow, 26–8 January.

Miles, R. (1989) *Racism*, Milton Keynes, Open University Press.

Mirza, H. (1992) *Young, Female and Black*, London, Routledge.

Mizen, P. (1995) *The State, Young People and Youth Training: In and Against the Training State*, London, Mansell.

Moore, S. M. and Rosenthal, D. A. (1993) *Sexuality in Adolescence*, London, Routledge.

Morley, L. (1999) *Organising Feminisms: The Micropolitics of the Academy*, Basingstoke, Macmillan.

Morrison, D. (1985) *Adolescent Contraceptive Behaviour: A Review, Psychological Bulletin*, 98 (5) pp. 38–68.

Moylan, D. (1994) 'The dangers of contagion: Projective identification processes in institutions', in A. Obholzer and V. Z. Roberts (eds) *The Unconscious at Work: Individual and Organizational Stress In The Human Services*, London, Routledge.

Muller, W. and Karle, W. (1993) 'Social Selection in Education Systems', *European Sociological Review* 9(1), pp. 1–23.

Munt, S. R. (2000) (ed.) *Cultural Studies and the Working Class: subject to change*, London, Cassell.

National Council for One Parent Families (1994) *Key Facts*, London, National Council for One Parent Families.

Nava, M. (1997) (ed.) *Buy this Book: Studies in Advertising and Consumption*, London, Routledge.

Newby, H. (1977) *The Deferential Worker*, London, Allen Lane.

Newson, J. and Newson, E. (1976) *Seven Years Old in the Home Environment*, London, Allen and Unwin.

Oakley, A. (1974) *The Sociology of Housework*, London, Robertson.

Oakley, A. (1981) *From Here to Maternity: Becoming a Mother*, Harmondsworth, Penguin.

Observer (1998) 'Boys Performing Badly', 4 January, p. 6.

Observer Life Magazine (1997) 'M is for Market research', 4 May.

Offe, C. (1985) 'Work – a central sociological category?', in C. Offe (ed.) *Disorganized Capitalism*, Cambridge, Polity Press.

Office for National Statistics (1999) *Social Trends*, 29, London, The Stationery Office.

Office of Population, Census and Surveys (1995) *Birth Statistics Series FMI*, London, HMSO.

Pahl, R. E. (1989) 'Is the Emperer Naked? Some Comments on the Adequacy of Sociological Theory in Urban and Regional Research', *International Journal of Urban and Regional Research*, 13: pp. 709–20.

Pajaczkowska, C. and Young, L. (1992), 'Racism, representation, psychoanalysis', in James D. and Ali R. (eds) *'Race', culture and Difference*, London, Sage.

Pakulski, J. and Waters, M. (1996) 'The Reshaping and Dissolution of Social Class in Advanced Society', *Theory and Society*, 25: pp. 667–91.

Pheterson, G. (1993) 'Historical and Material Determinants of Psychodynamic Development', in Adleman, J. and Enguidanos, G. (eds) *Racism in the Lives of Women in New York*, New York, Haworth Press.

Phillips, M. (1998) 'Slums are not the problem – people are', *The Sunday Times*, 20 September, p. 15.

Phoenix, A. and Tizard, B. (1996), 'Thinking Through Class: The Place of Social Class in the Lives of Young Londoners', in *Feminism and Psychology*, 6 (3): pp. 427–42.

Phoenix, A. (1991) *Young Mothers?*, Cambridge, Polity Press.

Phoenix, A. (1996) 'Social constructions of lone motherhood: a case of competing discourses', in E. B. Silva (ed.) *Good Enough Mothering? Feminist Perspectives on Lone Motherhood*, London, Routledge.

Pile, S. (1996) *The Body in the City: Psychoanalysis Space and Subjectivity*, London, Routledge.

Pile, S. and Thrift, N. (1995) *Mapping the Subject: Geographies of Cultural Transformation*, London, Routledge.

Pilling, D. (1990) *Escape from Disadvantage*, London, Falmer Press.

Pilling, D. (1992) *Approaches to case management for people with disabilities*, London, J. Kingsley Rehabilitation Resource Centre, City University.

Pitt, A. (1998) 'Qualifying resistance: some comments on methodological dilemmas', *Qualitative Studies in Education*, 11(4): pp. 535–53.

Plummer, G. (1998) 'Forget gender, class is still the real divide', *Times Education Supplement*, 23 January, p. 21.

Plummer, G. (2000) *Failing Working-Class Girls*, Stoke-on-Trent, Trentham Books.

Polanyi, M. (1946) *Science, Faith and Society*, London, Oxford University Press.

Raphael Reed, L. (1995) 'Reconceptualising Equal Opportunities in the 1990's: a study of radical teacher culture in transition', in M. Griffiths and B. Troyna (eds) *Anti-racism, Culture and Social Justice in Education*, Stoke-on-Trent, Trentham Books.

Raphael Reed, L. (1999) 'Re-searching, re-finding, re-making: exploring the unconscious as a pedagogic research practice', paper presented at the *Gender and Education Conference*, Warwick University.

Reay, D. (1995) ' "They employ cleaners to do that": habitus in the primary classroom', in *British Journal of Sociology of Education*, 16(3): pp. 353–71.

Reay, D. (1996) 'Dealing with difficult differences: Reflexivity and social class in feminist research', *Feminism and Psychology*, 6(3): pp. 443–56.

Reay, D. (1997) 'The double bind of the Working Class Feminist Academic: The Success of Failure or the Failure of Success?', in P. Mahony and C. Zmroczek (eds) *Class Matters: Working-class Women's Perspectives on Social Class*, London, Taylor and Francis.

Reay, D. (1998a) *Class Work: Mother's Involvement in their Children's Primary Schooling*, London, UCL Press.

Reay, D. (1998b) 'Rethinking Social Class: qualitative perspectives on class and gender', *Sociology*, 32(2): pp. 259–75.

Reay, D., Davies, J., David, M. and Ball, S. J. (1999) 'Choices of degree and degrees of choice: a report from work in progress', paper presented at *BERA Annual Conference*, University of Sussex.

Reay, D. and Lucey, H. (2000) ' "I don't really like it here but I don't want to be anywhere else", Children and inner city council estates', *Antipode: A Journal of Radical Geography*, 32(4): pp. 410–28.

Redclift, N. and Sinclair, M. T. (1991) (eds) *Working Women: International Perspectives on Labour and Gender Ideology*, London, Routledge.

Reid, I. (1994) *Inequality, Society and Education*, Loughborough, Loughborough University of Technology.

Reynolds, T. (2000) 'Black women and social-class identities', in S. Munt (ed.) *Cultural Studies and the Working Class*, London, Cassell.

Reynolds, T. (1998) 'Class matters, "race" matters, gender matters', in P. Mahony and C. Zmroczek (eds) *Women and Social Class*, London, Taylor and Francis.

Ribbens, J. and Edwards, R. (1998) *Feminist Dilemmas in Qualitative Research*, London, Sage.

Riseborough, G. (1993) 'Learning a Living or Living a hearning?' in Riseborough, G. and Bates, I. (eds) *Youth and Inequality*, Buckingham, Open University Press.

Riviere, J. (1985) 'Femininity as Masquerade', in Donald J. and Kaplan C. (eds) *Formations of Fantasy*, London, Routledge.

Riviere, J. and Klein, M. (1937) *Love, Hate and Reparation*, London, Hogarth.

Roberts, H. (1993), 'Women and the Class Debate', in D. Morgan and L. Stanley (eds) *Debates in Sociology*, Manchester, Manchester University Press.

Roberts, K. (1984) *School Leavers and their Prospects*, Milton Keynes, Open University Press.

Roker, D. (1993) 'Gaining the Edge: Girls at a Private School', in I. Bates and G. Riseborough (eds) *Youth and Inequality*, Milton Keynes, Open University Press.

Rose, D. and O'Reilly, K. (1997) *Constructing Classes: Towards a New Social classification for the UK*, Swindon, Office for National Statistics and Economic and Social Research Council.

Rose, G. (1993) *Feminism and Geography: The Limits of Geographical Knowledge*, Cambridge, Polity Press.

Rose, N. (1991) *Governing the Soul: The Shaping of the Private Self*, London, Routledge.

Rose, N. (1996) *Governing the Soul*, 2nd edn, London, Free Association Books.

Rose, N. (1999) *The Powers of Freedom*, London, Routledge.

Rubery, J. and Fagan, C. (1994) 'Occupational Segregation: plus ca change...?', in R. Lindley (ed.) *Labour Market Structures and Prospects for Women*, Manchester, Equal Opportunities Commission.

Rubin, L. (1992) *Worlds of Pain: Life in the Working Class Family*, London, Basic Books.

Sammons, P. (1995) 'Gender, ethnic and socio-economic differences in attainment and progress: a longitudinal analysis of student achievement over nine years', *British Educational Research Journal*, 21(4): pp. 465–85.

Saunders, P. (1990) *A Nation of Home Owners*, London, Unwin Hyman.

Savage, M., Barlow, J., Dickens, P. and Fielding, T. (1992) *Property Bureaucracy and Culture, Middle-class Formation in Contemporary Britain*, London, Routledge.

Sayers, J. (1995) *The Man Who Never Was: Freudian Tales*, London, Chatto and Windus.

Sclater, S. D. (1997) 'Narrating Subjects in Culture: Methodology Matters', paper presented at the Culture and Psychology Symposium, 5th European Congress on Psychology, Dublin, July.

Scott, J. (1991) *Who Rules Britain?*, London, Polity Press.

Seabrook, J. (1978) *What Went Wrong? Working People and the Ideals of the Labour Movement*, London, Gollancz.

Seccombe, W. (1974) *The Housewife and Her Labour under Capitalism*, London, IMG Publications.

Sennett, R. (1998) *The Corrosion of Character: the personal consequences of work in the new capitalism*, New York, Norton.

Sennett, R. and Cobb, J. (1993) *Hidden Injuries of Class*, Cambridge, Polity Press.

Sewell, T. (1997) *Black Masculinities and Schooling: How Black Boys Survive Modern Schooling*, Stoke-on-Trent, Trentham Books.

Shavit, Y. and Blossfeld, H.-P. (1993) *Persistent Inequality: Changing Educational Achievement in Thirteen Countries*, Boulder, Co, Westview Press.

Shaw, J. (1995) *Education, Gender and Anxiety*, London, Taylor and Francis.

Sharpe, S. (1994) *Fathers and Daughters*, London, Routledge.

Sibley, D. (1995) *Geographies of Exclusion: Society and Difference in the West*, Routledge, London.

Silverman, D. (1993) *Interpreting Qualitative Data: Methods for Analysing Talk, Text and Interaction*, London, Sage.

Simms, M. and Smith, C. (1986) *Teenage Mothers and their Partners*, London, HMSO.

Sinclair, M. T. (1991) 'Women, Work and Skill', in N. Redclift and M. T. Sinclair (eds) *Working Women: International Perspectives on Labour and Gender Ideology*, London, Routledge.

Skeggs, B. (1996) *Becoming Respectable: An Ethnography of White Working-Class Women*, Cambridge, Polity Press.

Skeggs, B. (1997a) *Formations of Class and Gender*, London, Sage.

Skeggs, B. (1997b) 'Classifying Practices: Representations, Capitals and Recognitions', in P. Mahony and C. Zmroczek (eds) *Class Matters*, London, Taylor and Francis.

Smith, D. (1988) *The Everyday World as Problematic: A Feminist Sociology*, Milton Keynes, Open University Press.

Smith, D. (1989) 'Women's Work as Mothers: A New Look at the Relation of Class, Family and School Achievement', in J. A. Holstein and G. Miller (eds) *Perspectives on Social Problems: A Research Annual*, vol 1, Greenwich, JAI Press.

Smith, S. J. (1989) *The Politics of Race and Residence*, Cambridge, Polity Press.

Smith, S. J. (1993) 'Residential Segregation and the politics of racialization', in Malcolm Cross and Michael Keith (eds) *Racism, the City and the State*, London, Routledge.

Smith, T. (1993) 'The Influence of Socioeconomic Factors on Attaining Targets for Reducing Teenage Pregnancy', *British Medical Journal*, p. 306.

Smith, T. and Noble, M. (1995) (eds) *Education Divides: Poverty and Schooling in the 1990s*, London, CPAG.

Smithers, A. and Robinson, P. (1995) *Post-18 Education: Growth, Change, Prospect*, London, Council for Industry and Higher Education.

Social Exclusion Unit (1998) *Bringing Britain Together: A National Strategy for Neighbourhood Renewal*, London, Social Exclusion Unit.

Stanley, L. (1993) 'On Auto/Biography in Sociology', *Sociology* 27(1): pp. 41–52.

Stanley, L. and Wise, S. (1990) 'Method, methodology and epistemology in feminist research processes', in L. Stanley (ed.) *Feminist Praxis: Research, Theory and Epistemology in Feminist Sociology*, London, Routledge.

Statistical Office of the European Communities (1998) *Facts Through Figures: Eurostat Yearbook at a glance*, Brussels, Eurostat.

Steedman, C. (1986) *Landscape for a Good Woman: A Story of Two Lives*, London, Virago.

Strauss, A. L. and Corbin, J. (1990) *Basics of Qualitative Research: Grounded Theory Procedures and Techniques*, London, Sage.

Sudbury, J. (1998) *'Other Kinds of Dreams': Black Women's Organisations and the Politics of Transformation*, London, Routledge.

Summers, D. (1991) 'No Room for New Faces at the Top', *Financial Times*, 7 May.

Tattum, D. and Herbert, G. (1997) (eds) *Bullying: Home, School and Community*, London, David Fulton.

Thompson, P. and Ackroyd S., (1995) 'All quiet on the workplace front?', *Sociology*, 29(4): pp. 615–33.

Thompson, P. and Samuel, R. (1990) (eds) *Myths We Live By*, London, Routledge.

Thrift, N. (1997) ' "Us" and "Them": Re-imagining places, re-imagining identities', in H. Mackay (ed.) *Consumption and Everyday Life*, Milton Keynes, Open University Press.

Tizard, B. and Hughes, M. (1984) *Young Children Learning*, London, Fontana.

Tizard, B. and Phoenix, A. (1993) *Black, White and Mixed Race*, London, Routledge.

Tokarczyk, M. and Fay, E. (eds) (1995) *Working class women in the Academy: Labourers in the Knowledge factory*, Amberst, University of Massachusetts Press.

Tomlinson, S. (1999) 'Ethnic Minorities in Britain: New Disadvantages', in Theo Cox (ed.) *Combating Educational Disadvantage*, London, Falmer Press.

Toynbee, P. (1998) 'The estate they're in', *The Guardian*, 15 September.

Van Maanen, J. (1988) *Tales of the Field*, Chicago, University of Chicago Press.

Vincent, C. (1996) *Parents and Teachers: Power and Participation*, London, Falmer Press.

Vincent, C. and Warren, S. (1999) 'Becoming a "better" parent? Motherhood, Education and Transition', *British Journal of Sociology of Education*, 12(2).

Walby, S. (1997) *Gender Transformations*, London, Routledge.

Walden, R. and Walkerdine, V. (1985) 'Girls and Mathematics: from primary to secondary schooling', *Bedford Way Papers 24*, London, Heinemann.

Walford, G. (1984) (ed.) *British Public School: Policy and Practice*, London, Falmer Press.

Walford, G. (1986) *Life in Public Schools*, London, Methuen.

Walford, G. (1990) *Privatization and Privilege in Education*, London, Routledge.

Walkerdine, V. (1984) 'Dreams for an Ordinary Childhood', in E. Heron (ed.) *Truth, Dare or Promise*, London, Virago

Walkerdine, V. (1989) *Counting Girls Out*, London, Virago.

Walkerdine, V. (1991) *Schoolgirl Fictions*, London, Verso

Walkerdine, V. (1992) *Didn't She Do Well?*, London, Metro Pictures.

Walkerdine, V. (1997) *Daddy's Girl: Young Girls and Popular Culture*, London, Macmillan; Cambridge, M. A., Harvard University Press.

Walkerdine, V. (1998) 'Developmental Psychology and the Child Centred Pedagogy', in J. Henriques, W. Hollway, C. Urwin, C. Venn, and V. Walkerdine (eds) *Changing the Subject: Psychology, Social Regulation and Subjectivity*, London, Routledge, 2nd edn.

Walkerdine, V. and Lucey, H. (1989) *Democracy in the Kitchen: Regulating Mothers and Socialising Daughters*, London, Virago.

Whyte, W. S. (1957) *The Organisation Man*, New York, Touchstone.

Wilkinson, H. (1994) *No Turning Back: Generations and the Genderquake*, London, DEMOS.

Wilkinson, H. and Mulgan, G. (1995) *Freedom's Children: Work, Relationships and Politics for 18–34 year olds*, London, DEMOS.

Wilkinson, H. and Howard, M. with Gregory, S., Hayes, H. and Young, R. (1997) *Tomorrow's Women*, London, Demos.

Williams, R. (1961) *Culture and Society 1780–1950*, Harmondsworth, Penguin.

Willis, P. (1977) *Learning to Labour*, Farnborough, Saxon House.

Winnicott, D. W. (1957) *The Child and the Family: First Relationships*, London, Tavistock.

Wolf, D. L. (1996) (ed.) *Feminist Dilemmas in Fieldwork*, Oxford, Westview Press.

Worcester, R. M. (1991) *British Public Opinion: a guide to the history and techniques of political opinion polling*, Oxford, Basil Blackwell.

Wragg, T. (1997) 'Oh Boy', *Times Educational Supplement*, 16 May.

Wright, E. (1985) *Classes*, London, Verso.

Index